WITHDRAWN 16/04/24
RM.

MAKING IT HAPPEN

JOHN HARVEY-JONES

MAKING IT HAPPEN

Reflections on Leadership

COLLINS
8 Grafton Street, London W1
1988

William Collins Sons & Co. Ltd
London · Glasgow · Sydney · Auckland
Toronto · Johannesburg

BRITISH LIBRARY CATALOGUING IN PUBLICATION DATA

Harvey-Jones, John
Making it happen: reflections on
leadership.
1. Industrial management—Great Britain
2. Leadership
I. Title
658.4   HD70.G7

ISBN 0-00-217663-7

First published in 1988
Reprinted 1988
Second reprint 1988
Third reprint 1988
Copyright © John Harvey-Jones 1988

Set in Linotype Palatino by
Wyvern Typesetting Ltd, Bristol
Made and printed in Great Britain by
Butler & Tanner Ltd, Frome and London

Contents

1	Making it Happen	1
2	Setting the Direction	18
3	Switching On or Switching Off?	48
4	The How	72
5	All Change	94
6	Do We Want to be International?	117
7	Catalysts and Judo	130
8	Boardmanship	146
9	The Emperor's Clothes	167
10	The Top Job	184
11	Board Work	205
12	The 'U' Factor	225
13	And So to Tomorrow	246
	Index	263

1

Making it Happen

It would be very difficult for anybody who experienced the winter of 1946/7 to forget it. It was the year the North Sea froze. The year when Europe was still heavily rationed, and short of almost all the basic commodities of life. The year when most of us were far from our homes. And the year when the industrial base of Germany was being systematically dismantled and shipped to the victors. Little did those of us who were involved in that exercise know that we were laying the foundations for the industrial resurgence of Germany.

Little for that matter did I believe that this experience was to be the start of a whole new direction in my life, the lessons of which I have attempted to set out in this book. I have grown very tired of the 'in one mighty bound Jack was free' sort of management book: the instant prescription, which if followed will solve every ill from bankruptcy to athlete's foot. The life that I have led has never been like that! There has never been an instant solution, indeed in some cases there has been no solution at all. What there has been is a steady process of learning that management and business is a pragmatic matter depending entirely on people and how they react. Everything I have learnt teaches me that it is only when you work with rather than against people that achievement and lasting success is possible. It is this belief that I am trying to express, for it is an art which is applicable to any enterprise of any size in any area of life's activities. It is as applicable to the running of the parish council as it is to the leadership of IBM and I hope that you find in this book something, even if only one thing, that you can apply and that will help you gain the results you seek.

I arrived perplexed, cold and totally ill-prepared as a young naval officer at Wilhelmshaven that winter. My task, after having been subjected to a six months' course to learn Russian,

was to supervise the packing up of the Wilhelmshaven dockyard, and arrange its shipment back to the Soviet Union as part
reparation for the enormous damage that had been done to that
country by Nazi Germany. I was twenty-two years old, and had
never had any industrial experience of any sort. I was a serving
naval officer, whose experience had been almost entirely in
small ships and submarines, where I had learnt some of the
problems of leadership of compact teams, for whom the aim
was painfully apparent: sink, or be sunk. I was now faced with
the administration of a problem of almost mind-boggling
complexity. The Germans, defeated, suffering every form of
deprivation, were not and could hardly be expected to be
enthusiastic about dismantling the only source of their liveli-
hood and handing it over to the hated Russians. The Russian
team of twelve, who were my primary responsibility, disliked,
or, more accurately, hated the Germans. They believed that
anything could be obtained by force and were determined to
exact the last drop of blood.

The Wilhelmshaven dockyard had been, in its day, the largest
naval yard in Europe, and is likely to go down as the largest
purely naval yard in history. The Russians were determined to
remove every last item of its inventory, down to the lavatory
brushes and the steel tracks on which the dockyard trains ran:
indeed it was a miracle to me that they did not demand the
cobblestones as well. They were deeply suspicious. Although,
as I soon found out, the Russians themselves were models of
inefficiency and poor organization, they nevertheless believed
that anything that went wrong was a deliberate act of sabotage
rather than the normal sort of mistake which occurs in every
large organization. In the middle of all this there was a small
team of British, a number of whom were regulars, who found
the task they were being given something they had neither
expected, nor been trained for. The majority were individuals
doing their national service, who had little enthusiasm for that,
let alone for a task of this type in this perishingly cold country.
They found themselves sandwiched between the unhappy and
unwilling Germans, and the aggressive, intolerant and uncomprehending Russians. There was no communication of any sort
between the Russians and the Germans, not only in the linguistic sense, but in every other sense as well. They had suffered

too much at each other's hands to be able to communicate now.

This rather unpromising background was my first introduction to the complexities of industrial problems and industrial leadership. Although I hated every moment of it, and found the task unbelievably difficult, in retrospect it was a marvellous learning ground. There was, after all, no doubt as to the aim and objective of the exercise, which was to transport the yard, in working order, to Russia. What happened after that was no business of ours. We had unlimited German labour available, and also at our command their talent for organization, which is rightly seen as a German national characteristic. We had the potent, theoretical motivator of vast unemployment in the area, and those who were working for us were considered to be the fortunate. Moreover, in a country where all supplies of food were quite inadequate, the food provided for our workers was less inadequate than that of others. In theory the task should have been simplicity itself. In practice we proceeded at absolute snail's pace, and every step that we took was hindered by constant misunderstanding, suspicion and argument. Nothing went smoothly, even when it appeared that the most minute details had been described with no further room for misunderstanding. It was only by being constantly on the scene, as a neutral, that we seemed to me to move at all. I was particularly fortunate to have my neutrality reinforced by the sort of understanding which derives from speaking both languages. I had learnt German at Dartmouth where I had specialized in my last year in what would now be known as arts subjects: languages, English and history. I learnt Russian by a more accidental process, really motivated by a wish to attend a university in any sort of role I could achieve. I had spent six months at the Admiralty's expense at Cambridge acquiring an interpretership in Russian. Despite this great advantage I don't think that I have ever, before or since, worked in such frustrating conditions. Indeed when the time came to leave Germany I made a mental decision never to return. I'm glad to say that in the Navy such luxuries were not a part of our conditions of service, and when I was ordered back to Germany in 1949 I had no option but to return. I thus started a relationship with that country that has been constantly rewarding for the rest of my life, and indeed I now regard it almost as my second homeland.

It was apparent to me, even then as a young officer, that what was missing in this sorry scene was any commitment to the task on the part of those who had to execute it. Moreover, when I actually stopped to think about the problem I became uncomfortably aware that it was very unlikely that I would be able to obtain such commitment. Why, after all, should the Germans derive any satisfaction from the task of giving to the victors that which they themselves had worked so hard to build up? The only occasions on which we got fleeting moments of commitment were ones where I or my British colleagues were present and involved. We could, for short periods of time, motivate our work force to achieve the objective which was our responsibility, but as soon as we left, things invariably fell to pieces again. It was a vital lesson. Plainly, in any large enterprise the boss cannot be directly involved in everything, and some means has to be found to transfer his belief and commitment to others.

It was the custom, in those days, on leaving a command or a ship in the Royal Navy, to receive a handwritten report known as a 'flimsy'. Unlikely though it may seem, as I wandered miserably in the snow in a duffle coat, puffing my pipe, around the cobblestones and concrete of Wilhelmshaven, I was still, in naval terms, serving aboard a ship, HMS *Royal Rupert* to be precise. The Commanding Officer of Wilhelmshaven at that time was Captain Eric Condor, a legendary man in postwar Germany, and a man who carried out his difficult tasks with exemplary fairness. He had a degree of concern for the vanquished Germans, and respect for them as individuals, which taught me another valuable lesson, and which still makes his name in Wilhelmshaven one which is honoured rather than reviled. When I left he handed me my 'flimsy', which was meant to be a summation and extract of the very full personal report that was submitted secretly to the Admiralty, and on which one's future chances of promotion very greatly depended. The words on my 'flimsy' were 'Lieutenant Harvey-Jones is an able officer, who knows how to make things happen, albeit tactfully.' I have been trying to learn how to make things happen ever since.

Some years later, when it was apparent that my daughter would not recover from her poliomyelitis, I felt that it would no longer be possible to continue serving in the Royal Navy, which entailed long periods of separation from my home. It became necessary to look for other employment. I needed a job which would enable me to work at home, and be with my family every evening. At that time I believed that the United Kingdom would be facing severe economic problems in the future, and I decided that I wanted to work somewhere where I could serve the community, and make a contribution to the resolution of those problems. I wanted to find a job which was basic rather than peripheral. I wanted to find a job which I believed would be secure, since my primary responsibility was, and remains to this day, the support of my family. Perhaps I was not at first sight the most employable of people. I was merely a naval officer, with some years' experience in intelligence, and two languages. But I thought about my experience at Wilhelmshaven, and the fascination of the task there, despite the appalling environment. That had at least prepared me, in ways that no other part of my experience could have done, for the chaos and complexity of industrial life. And I knew that I had shown some ability to fight my corner. I knew that I could achieve results despite the difficulties, and I knew that I had been able to demonstrate the ability to work with people of other countries.

I had been deeply impressed by a number of experiences in my life. My time in submarines had brought me closer to people of a totally different background and I had learnt a great deal from my sailors about their home circumstances before the war. I still number some of them as personal friends all these years later, but at the time what struck me was their unbelievable competence and sheer quality compared with the wretchedly small scope they had been given in prewar Britain. My experience of working with other nationalities both at Wilhelmshaven and later, when with David Wheeler I had set up the German Fishery Protection Service in the Baltic, also taught me some fundamental lessons. This tiny group of former German naval people, never more than forty in all, produced a disproportionate share of the leaders of the postwar German Navy. We ran the ship, an ex E-boat modernized and stripped of its armament, as a German ship. The officers messed with the men, and in the narrow confines of this tiny craft got to know each other very well indeed. Here again I learnt to admire and like these people, with whom I had been so recently at war, and to see clearly both the differences and the similarities between people of different nationalities and the fantastic ability of people to respond to leadership tuned to their needs. I liked and respected people, but here I learnt to listen to and rely on others.

At that time one of those coincidences, which so often appear in life, cropped up. My brother-in-law was working for ICI and liked the company. In addition, two colleagues in naval intelligence had recently been taken on by ICI to be trained as work study officers, and spoke enthusiastically to me of how they were treated by the company. I applied for an interview, and shortly afterwards found that I had a new job. I did not expect another career, since I felt that I had already had one, but in the event I found not only that, but a fascinating path through life that my original naval calling could not possibly have produced. I have had constant new experiences, and I have never stopped learning. The job itself changes, the conditions are never static.

It is these experiences which have prompted me to set down in this book some of the lessons I have learnt over the years. I am no longer the chairman of ICI, having retired at the beginning of April 1987. Even though I use many examples and experiences from my years with that company, the views expressed are mine and if my recollections or impressions vary from others' that is to my account, and not ICI's.

My choice of industry might seem surprising, in view of my wish to make some sort of contribution to the world's well-being. Industry is widely misunderstood in the world today. A smaller and smaller part of the population is directly involved in industrial manufacture. Most people's historical picture of industry consists of the concept of the ancient production line, the dark satanic mills and so on. There is little understanding of the tasks and challenges of the present day. The purpose of industry is to create wealth. It is not, despite belief to the contrary, to create jobs. The jobs are created from the wealth that industry produces. There are not many of us left who, in the economists' phrase, 'add value' – we toil on in manufacturing industry, in the extractive industries, and in agriculture. There is of course, now, a growing ability to add value in other ways, particularly in the knowledge industries. But without manufacturing, mining, and agriculture the world cannot – in the present state of science – survive. It is these primary industries which will decide our economic success. I don't want to suggest that social problems can be cured by the application of wealth. But without wealth they cannot be tackled at all. The provision of more, and better, education, the provision of more, and better, health care, the building of roads and housing, all these depend on the creation of wealth. It is for these reasons that I felt then, as I do now, that in pursuing an industrial career I was performing a social service, of no less significance than my service in the armed forces. So what is the world of industry really like, and why do I find it so interesting? First, and perhaps most importantly, it is a world of change. The task of industry is continuously, year on year, to make more and better things, using less of the world's resources. Management in particular is not about the preservation of the status quo, it is about maintaining the highest rate of change that the organization and the people within it can stand. The pressures for change in industry come from three main areas. First of all, of course, there are the changes in people, and in their aspirations – both the people within and outside the company.

One doesn't have to be a reader of Shakespeare to know that there are many enduring human characteristics, but when it comes to work, and the part it plays in individuals' lives, what they bring to it, and their expectations of it, one sees an enormous rate of change. To give some small examples within my own experience, ICI, in the past, expected its managers to be prepared to move, and work, anywhere. Indeed it was a condition of service with the company, and still is. My company is an outstandingly tolerant one, and has great respect for the individual. Nevertheless, we seldom considered, in my early years with the company, the effect on a wife's career if we asked a manager of promise to move to another part of the country. We of course understood if he could not move on personal grounds, but those grounds could be related to health, or elderly parents, or children's schooling – never his wife's career. Now only some fifteen or twenty years later we would know that both partners in a marriage are likely to have important careers, and may well have decided that neither one of the two should be the 'lead operation'. Companies, in the past, have tended to expect that their employees should conform to the wishes of the company. This is becoming less and less practicable as a philosophy of operation, and I believe absolutely that in the future it will be the company that conforms to the individual that attracts and motivates the best people. Companies will have to be more flexible in their demands, to accommodate more and more the individuals' different hopes, wishes and ambitions. To do this is not easy, for it means in turn abandoning many of the systems of personnel management, and taking far more responsibility for encouraging and supporting difference. In all large companies there is a lot of comfort derived from administrative systems that purport to be 'fair' but in reality remove from individual managers the responsibility of trying to reward and administer people's careers while allowing for differences which are immeasurable in quantitative terms. The problem only becomes worse where the end results – the rate of pay, or the hours worked, or the promotion achieved – are easily quantified and compared. It is this conflict which leads increasingly to the urge to treat people as groups rather than as individuals – but it is an abnegation of responsibility on the part of the leaders and for the future it will not do. All over the world individuals are asserting themselves and refusing to be codified, or grouped or collectivized. Unless companies change they simply won't attract the best, and so they will die.

Important though changes in people's expectations are, the most obvious force for change in industry is technical advance. It is technical advance which makes it possible to create the world's goods with the labour of fewer and fewer people. It is technical advance also which is increasingly removing the natural advantages of countries with low labour costs. There is no reason why a British robot shouldn't be just as productive as a Japanese one. Technical progress, as well as affecting the means of production in ways which are making industry a matter for brains and creative thinking rather than brawn, is in addition creating, almost daily, possibilities for new products. Working as I do for a technically based industry, I hope I may be forgiven for believing that almost anything can be achieved through technology, if we are clear enough about what is needed. Technology however does not replace the role and contribution of the individual. The craftsmen, and we shall always need them, combine through the use of the whole range of human skills such extra elements as proportion, difference, originality, and the ability to work with the grain or the particular unique characteristics of the materials they work with. There is indeed a skill of craftsmanship in applying technology; knowing just how far to go in programming the machine and what to do by hand; selecting from the materials and technologies and applying them in different ways; deciding exactly what one should attempt to achieve through technology. All of these things demand the application of human gifts and call for the experience, skill and taste which categorize the craftsman.

This brings me, of course, to the last driving force for change in industry, which is the force of competition. Competition is what keeps industry moving, and indeed those of us who have had the experience know that almost the most difficult industrial task is to run a near monopoly. The fact that it is very difficult to do doesn't prevent a lot of people wishing to achieve it, but it is very seldom that, in the industrial world, anybody has achieved and held continuously a pre-eminent position over a very long period of time. Industrial organizations are amongst the most fragile in the world. When so much attention is paid to the vast power of multinational companies, it is perhaps wise to think of the numbers of international names that have disappeared from the scene, even during our own lifetime. Even though we may think that in Britain we have had more than our share of industrial decay and change, the catalogue of proud names that were in the vanguard of German or American industrial might at the turn of the last century is very different from the list of those who are in front today. Let me give a few examples of vanished empires which at the time seemed invincible. It is of course true that the work they carried out may or may not be done by a small part of some other organization but this in itself is a startling example of fragility. In 1905 the most powerful companies in the United Kingdom would have included J. & P. Coats, The Calico Printers' Association, The Bleachers' Association, Sir W. G. Armstrong Whitworth & Co., Bolckow Vaughan and many others who have either closed down or been absorbed into other more powerful groups. Interestingly enough I looked into the same situation in America and Germany and in all three mighty industrial countries six out of the top ten firms had gone. So over half the

strongest firms have fallen in these eighty years. Little wonder
then that the battle for sheer survival is so important a part of the
task.

There is an intrinsic impermanence in industry, and indeed
the management task is to recreate the company in a new form
every year. Industry is a bit like the human body. The cells are
continuously dying and unless new cells are created, sooner or
later the whole thing will collapse and disappear. These three
potent forces – people, technology and competition – mean that
industry cannot afford to become institutionalized. We have to
be more adaptable, and quicker on our feet than many of the
other great national institutions which create the external conditions under which we operate. I would imagine that industry
confronts and copes with more forms of change than any other
branch of our life.

The second characteristic of my industrial world is that it is
incredibly international. In a multinational company people of
every colour, creed and race work together for the achievement
of a common end. It is one of the very few institutions where the
shared goals overcome nationalist or racial considerations. No
industrialist can think in terms of a single market. If he does, he
is signing his death warrant. My own company operates in
more than seventy countries, and we employ more people in
other parts of the world than we do in our homeland, the United
Kingdom. There is never a month that I am not overseas, and
hasn't been for many years – long before I achieved my present
position. My telephone calls, my business colleagues, my competitors, my own ambitions for my company, are all international in nature. I am perhaps fortunate in having lived in a
number of other countries. In addition to having worked in
Germany and the USSR, and lived for some time before the war
in France, I was brought up for the first five years of my life in
India in a native state where I was the only white child. All my
friends and playmates were Indian and, since my father's job
was to act as guardian to a Maharajah some five years older than
me, I looked upon Bahadur as an older brother. This experience
has left me with a love of the East and an ability to feel at home
there which has been an immense help in my business life. I was
fortunate to have had these advantages; it is quite impossible to
operate at any level in industry without being aware of the

world forces which are pressing upon us.

My colleagues and I spend far more time discussing world developments than we do national ones, as indeed we should, since nearly eighty per cent of our business occurs in the rest of the world. Cartoonists may portray the international business-man flitting from five-star hotel to five-star hotel, and waking up to wonder if he is in New York or Tokyo. But although we must operate throughout the world, we cannot ignore the national differences in the marketplace. National characteristics come to the fore continuously, and I am always interested to see how widely differing they are. I believe it is true to say that my company has hardly sold a single product in Japan (and we sell many) without having to respond to some particular specifi-cation, different to that pertaining in other parts of the world. This is not, as it is sometimes believed to be, a matter of crude protectionism; it is a measure of Japanese difference, and has to be recognized as such. It is not the slightest use my pointing out that my product is good enough to sell in America, or Italy. If it is to sell in Japan it has to be in the form, and of the character-istics, that the Japanese wish and require.

Another feature of the international nature of our competition is that within our own home market, the United Kingdom, we meet every one of our international competitors who maintains a UK subsidiary company. There is thus a British branch of the Dow, Dupont, Hoechst, Badische, Bayer and Ciba Geigy com-panies in my home market in exactly the same way as there is an ICI company competing in America, Germany or Switzerland. None of us has our own patch to ourselves, and we meet, fight and compete in nearly every country in the world. It is vital for the industrialist to have a degree of sensitivity and understand-ing of national differences. It is surprising how easy it is for businessmen to assume that other nationalities will react in exactly the same way as they themselves do. I remember a graphic example of this when I was working for a blessedly short period as a Russian interpreter in Berlin in 1946. Leaving alone the fact that I and many of the other interpreters were singularly ill-equipped for the task, the room for misunder-standing far exceeded the chance of agreement and harmony. The quadripartite Allied government sought to agree on how to control, in the most detailed way, every facet of the running and

administration of Germany, a country where, at that time, there
had been a complete collapse of the economy, the agricultural
system and everything else without our 'help and interpretation'. In those days the interpreters were allocated on a first-
come, first-served basis, irrespective of relevance of experience
or choice. Fate decreed therefore that my very first exposure to
this unlikely world was as interpreter for the British representative (a pleasant dairy farmer used to having a hundred cows he
knew by name) at the milk pasteurization subcommittee of the
Central Agricultural Control. The United States representative,
as I recall, had a background in a state university, the Russian
had run a vast collective farm and the qualifications of the
French representative did not emerge during my short acquaintance with this example of Allied teamwork. The interpreting
was sequential and formal. We were obliged to interpret from
our native tongue into the language concerned and everything
was repeated in English, Russian and French. I was struck with
terror, since my Russian vocabulary, while exemplary on
maritime matters, extended little further than 'cow', 'milk' and
'bull' which I didn't feel was quite adequate for the occasion. I
need not have worried. The meeting opened in fine form with
the American Chairman outlining a bewildering series of stat-
istics about some abstract point of milk production. This was
interpreted impeccably (since the American interpreters had the
advantage of speaking all three languages fluently). The
Russian replied. Russians are robust and tend to avoid circumlocution; he therefore said the figures were wrong and the
American was a liar. I waited with bated breath for this statement to be interpreted in some tactful way, such as, 'Could you
please check your figures since mine are at variance with yours?'
But no. The interpreter stood stolidly there and interpreted
verbatim. Uproar, the end of the meeting, and a day off for
Harvey-Jones, but a quite unnecessary break in what was really
a rather uninspiring task in any event. It may seem trite to
observe that Eskimos are not, at heart, British public schoolboys
who choose, for greater comfort, to live in igloos and wear fur
clothes. Although few of us would expect an Eskimo to react or
think in the same way as we do, we are nevertheless continually
guilty of the same foolish assumption in regard to nationalities
closer to home. Perhaps the biggest area of misunderstanding

here is in our approach to our American customers and competitors, where we are lulled into complacency by our similar language.

Working within this international world it is, of course, a great help if one speaks several languages, but my own experience has been that it is not the ability to speak another language, rare though this essential tool of international business is amongst British people, but the experience of having lived and worked with people in another country which is the decisive factor. One of the many things which has changed out of all recognition during my lifetime is our ability to teach languages to mature students. Sadly, teaching of languages in schools has not kept pace with the relevant technological advances, but we find now that it is almost never necessary to recruit an individual specifically for linguistic skills. The use of modern language laboratories and deep immersion techniques can teach practically any individual, either manager or shop-floor worker, enough to work in another country after some two to three months' experience. I recently visited a plant in Mexico where two employees of my company, a Canadian and an Englishman, were operating happily in Spanish, with an entirely Mexican management and labour force. In fact their total experience of Spanish had been a two-and-a-half-month deep immersion course, which they had both undergone only three months before my visit. It was an impressive demonstration of what can now be done. The point that I am trying to make is that the experience that they are gaining, by working and living with their people, day in and day out, will give them a depth of understanding which, sadly, no amount of university training would give. It is an interesting fact that countries can be divided by their ability to adapt to other cultures. Perhaps because of our seafaring and imperial history, British people rate very high in this international league table, second only after the Dutch, who possibly derive their skills and abilities from the same type of background. Not only are British managers outstandingly good at adapting to foreign countries, but they tend to leave an equally indelible imprint when they have gone.

Because we are international, and operate across the world, we have to be keenly aware of economic change and budgeting policies world wide. At any moment the fortunes of ICI are more likely to be affected by the trend in exchange rates, or oil prices, or the budgetary policies of the United States of America, or the attitude to international trade of the Japanese, than by things which are more directly within our own control. This forces upon us a breadth of interest and concern which readily prevents us from becoming too absorbed in the affairs of our own small island.

The last characteristic of the industrial world that I would like to mention is the whole area of achievement. Industry is, in some ways, rather like war; there can be no doubt whether one is winning or losing. Unless a company is progressing the whole time, it is, in fact, moving backwards. It is quite impossible to maintain the status quo, or a steady-state position in the international marketplace. One has only to think of the British motorcycle industry and its once-prime position to see the folly of believing you can sustain a world leading position without constant innovation. While such world-famous names as BSA and Triumph were modestly adjusting and 'tarting up' models which in their day had been in front, the Japanese and particularly Honda looked at the situation through new eyes. They did not accept the limitations and constraints the British world position had led us to assume. They reasoned, correctly, that a substantial increase in the revolutions per minute of the engine would increase the power to weight ratio and permit a whole range of new developments. This they did and we all know what happened. Interestingly, when Honda's pre-eminence was threatened by other Japanese companies and they began to lose market share, their instant reaction was to increase the rate of innovation. In one year they launched more new models than their leading competitors put together. It shows yet again that good habits persist as do bad ones. Provided you are honest about the causes of success you can revive them again. Moreover, the forces of international competition deal very harshly with failure, and failure cannot be concealed. The profit and loss statement, and the viability of one's company, are the clearest possible indication of the success of one's efforts. It is not a fair world. But then what world is? The international businessman is battered and buffeted by so many external forces that even if he is operating skilfully within his own limitations he may not always win. But at least it is a world where one is in no doubt whether one is winning or losing, and where the prizes of success are substantial ones, not only for oneself, but for all one's friends and colleagues within the organization. There is a certain sadness in the harshness of this environment, since few, if any, marks are awarded for effort, and indeed some of the most difficult industrial situations involve tremendous effort in trying to retrieve a position which has already been lost. The irony is that all too often one needs the very best people to deal with the very worst industrial situations, which are seldom of their own making. Not all industrial situations are retrievable, or winnable. Once a certain amount of market position has been lost, retrieval is very difficult indeed, and usually is only possible through some outstanding technical or production achievement. Running down, or, as the current euphemism has it, rationalizing a business, while keeping the enthusiasm, loyalty and commitment of one's people, and fighting back in the marketplace, is one of the most difficult of industrial situations, and certainly separates the sheep from the goats in a management sense. All too often it is this harsh environment which actually develops some of the best management, and it is noteworthy within our own company, how many of the leaders of the company have come from businesses which have had more than their fair share of struggle and adversity. I am, however, not totally convinced that those who have learnt their craft in such 'bad weather' conditions make, necessarily, the best aggressive 'fair weather sailors'. This is because the qualities required for contracting a business are not always those required for aggressive expansion, although some are common. Both tasks require courage of a high order, imagination, and the ability to lead people, but the last is very much easier when plainly you are advancing, and your organization is on a winning streak, than when you are trying to hold the team together while struggling against what at times appear to be nearly impossible odds. This last characteristic of achievement is one which either one likes, or which one finds extremely difficult to endure. I personally have always liked the one-hundred-per-cent aspect of life; I have always enjoyed life at the extremes. People either like the risk of absolute success or failure (and the one rarely comes without the other) or prefer a more modulated and less risky environment. A friend of mine once asked me why I always sought to heighten experiences, and could not be satisfied with the middle ground. I do not know the answer, but I do know that I'd rather win or lose. After all, if you do lose it is usually all too obvious what you must do about it!

Looking back on the elements I have enumerated – of change, internationalism and achievement – I do not find it so surprising that I chose an industrial career, although I knew nothing of all this when I joined I C I. While the characteristics of the industrial world do not lead to comfort they certainly lead to stimulation, and I found I continually had to adapt and learn. There is singularly little chance in industry to put your feet up, and become self-satisfied, or set in your ways, for the tide will just sweep you away. This is the world that I enjoy, and that I have spent the second half of my life so far in exploring and learning about. The rest of this book seeks to outline some of the lessons that I have learnt in my service in this world. My comments are not meant to seek to prescribe to others how they should go about things, nor are they written in the belief that the ways that I have so painfully worked upon are necessarily the best, or the only ways of doing things. But, and it is a big but, I learnt the hard way and have been proven in practice.

I find myself intolerant of management books that seek to prescribe exactly 'how it should be done'. My own experience shows that there are many different ways of achieving one's aims and many different ways of leading an industrial company. I have worked with leaders whose style is so totally different to my own that I have found it incomprehensible that they achieve results, but nevertheless they do. Each one of us has to develop our own style, and our own approach, using such skills and personal qualities as we have inherited. The chapters that follow seek to outline the ways in which I have pursued and developed my own management skills, and the lessons that I have learnt on the way. My own experience of trying to teach and train managers is that it is extremely difficult to teach grown-up people anything. It is, however, relatively easy to create conditions under which people will teach themselves. Indeed most people wish to improve their own performance and are eager to do so. That is why there are so many books on management published and that is why I have read practically all of them. As I said earlier, too many make impossible promises and claims for no one can manage or lead in someone else's clothes. What each of us does over a long period of trial and error is to acquire a set of tools with which we are comfortable and which we can apply in different ways to the myriad problems which we need to solve. I hope that this book will stimulate you to look at problems in another way and try some approaches which are different from those you normally use. If you do and they work you will keep them, or adapt them until you feel comfortable with your 'tool kit'.

Management and industrial leadership is an art, not a science. Each of us approaches the problem from a different background, and each of us is dealing with a different situation, and a different culture, and from a different starting point. There are, of course, common points and common factors which apply to us all, but prescribed systems of management are seldom transferable. There seems to me to have been a growing wish to find this 'philosopher's stone', a universal system which can be applied to everything, everywhere. Just as it is almost impossible to apply what is now called the 'Japanese' system of management to other parts of the world, because of the differences of culture and background of the people who are working in industry, so it is equally unlikely that the particular, precise ways that I have found so useful will have the same application to others. Nevertheless, since I have spent so much of my life developing these ideas it may be that some of my experience will hit a chord of recognition or cause others to reflect or contemplate. Management is an absorbing interest. Industrial management, perhaps above all, has depths of fascination which few other callings can enjoy. I have found over the years that it is immensely helpful to take time out and try to think things through, and I would imagine that most other managers do the same, even though all of us are heavily action-orientated. One of the lessons I have learnt in life is that a bit more time thinking and planning will immeasurably increase the effectiveness of one's input: if these comments help any of my friends and colleagues in this way it will be, for me, as great a reward as I C I's success today is a satisfaction and recognition of our predecessors.

2

Setting the Direction

Although I am convinced that the prime management problem is 'making it happen', one has to accept that in life there is always at least an evens chance that one is going the wrong way. Not only is it extremely easy to go the wrong way, and indeed many businesses have foundered on the basis of one, usually inadvertent, mistaken direction, but all of us are aware that a lot of businesses aren't going anywhere at all. This is indeed the most dangerous situation of all. It is deceptively easy to keep busy maintaining the status quo, and belief in this function of management has been the source of the relative decline of many proud companies. You may be improving your productivity every year. You may be maintaining your profits more or less in line with inflation, and hence giving a spurious impression of growth. You may be laboriously producing marginal improvements on your primary product. But you can be absolutely sure that, if that is the position of your business, somebody else somewhere has got your card marked as an easy number and is about to take you by surprise.

Many of these points characterized ICI's position during the 1970s. In 1980 a series of events occurred which forced us to look at ourselves in a new and harsh light. The trigger was a rapidly strengthening pound which quickly pushed our exports into loss. At that time they accounted for nearly two thirds of our production. But worse was to follow. Our UK customers first began to look shaky and soon afterwards began to shut down at an alarming rate. Before the worst was over and the pound began to depreciate again, some twenty per cent of them had gone for ever, and a further ten per cent were so weakened that they too shut down in the next two years. In the first quarter of 1980 the ICI group was making profits at a rate of six hundred million pounds a year and in the third quarter we posted a loss for only the second time in our history. This was a mind concentrator of the first order and forced us to examine every facet of our business and the way we did things.

When the full force of competition hits, it is desperately hard to recover your company, set the new tempo that is required, and seize the initiative back from the competition, for remember, at that stage he will be hitting you not only with his carefully laid plan for the first phase of his attack, but also, without any doubt whatsoever, he will have his reinforcements grouping for a second and third attack. The business that is not being purposefully led in a clear direction which is understood by its people is not going to survive, and all of history shows that that is the case.

One of the fascinations of the industrial world is that there are no limitations of any sort on what a company can achieve if it wants to. At the end of the day a company is no more (but even more importantly, no less) than the sum of the people and the skills that comprise it. The physical embodiments of the company, the balance sheet and the money, the ironmongery, are to a considerable degree wasting assets unless purposefully managed and constantly changed. Almost by definition the manufacturing assets of the company are out of date the moment they are put up, because of the march of technology (the purpose of management is, after all, continually to improve things). You have to start with the assumption that each plant that you have built, however good of its kind or however modern, is already on the road to obsolescence. It is the job of those responsible for managing that plant and that technology to be thinking furiously what the next step is, and what changes and improvements they can see, because if you are not doing this your competitors will. During the 1970s my colleague Bob Malpas, who was responsible in ICI for technology, coined the phrase 'designing the plant after next'. It was a potent stimulator for our technical people, not just for the marginal improvements from our operating experience which would be built into the next plant, but to look for the major change in thinking which alone would put us ahead of the competition.

Even if your company's main task is, for example, to carry on business in the chemical industry, this can probably be changed, if you wish to, merely by going to the annual general

meeting. There are many examples of companies which have
developed right away from their original business and yet still
remain proud names. Singer no longer make sewing machines.
Thyssen doesn't make steel. They are unfortunately exceeded
in number by the famous names of the past who clung to what
they knew best without being prepared to adapt or change, and
slowly but inexorably saw their business disappearing beneath
them. Far too many leaderships, far too many industrial
managers, fail because of the acceptance of self-imposed constraints. Indeed one of my personal invariable rules is that when
I have mentally decided that something cannot be done, for
what appears to be a very good reason, I test that apparent
constraint, hopefully to destruction.

For example the most usual constraint we impose on ourselves is to believe that it is incumbent on us to carry out all the
steps of a manufacturing process ourselves. At some time or
other the twin siren songs of forward and backward integration
have led most large companies to do everything for themselves
from manufacturing their own plant and spares, sometimes
even as far as owning their own retail outlets. Once such a chain
is established, even if you are aware of the weak links, you are
accustomed to believe the whole lot is interdependent. But in
reality you can always break the chain at a number of points by
buying in. It is only when you test the possibility of buying, the
price and delivery, and the actual consequences, that you
realize that you have constrained your thinking unnecessarily.

Many companies today have changed their image dramati-
cally. One can think of tobacco companies who decided that
their future lay in financial services, like BAT, or in foods, like
the Imperial Group. One can think of companies like Hanson
Trust which, though still present in transport, its original roots,
is now a mighty conglomerate in two continents, or companies
like W. R. Grace, far away from shipping now, or Allied in the
States where chemical activities are now only a small part of the
whole. There are no practical limits to the changes that can be
made, but the process of change in leaving one's own skill base
is an extremely risky one – much, much riskier than trying to
develop and adapt your existing business, which you know and
understand, to the changing conditions of tomorrow's world.

Probably more management books have been written on the

problems of planning, or strategic direction, or strategic analysis, or competitive advantage and how to assess it, than on any other subject. There is no lack of advice, much of it very useful, on how to analyse your situation, and of course there is no point in deciding where your business is going until you have actually decided with great clarity where you are now. Like practically everything in business this is easier said than done, as the plethora of books, theories, advice and consultants testify. Just as the most difficult task of the manager is ruthless intellectual honesty about his own skills, weaknesses and motives, so it is notoriously difficult to be as near as possible totally objective about the strengths and weaknesses of your company, particularly because in many cases a perceived weakness can actually be utilized as a source of strength.

For example, for many years we in I C I considered that we were too thinly spread and too diverse both in technological and in geographical terms. This astonishing diversity manifested itself in great complexity of relationships and in our lacking dominance almost everywhere. It had one advantage of which we were aware. In former days the economical cycle hit different parts of the world at different times and the spread gave us a degree of stability. But as the world became increasingly interdependent this ceased to be the case and we became more concerned at our apparent weakness. When, however, we took time out and discussed it, we realized that the fact that we were more diverse offered us a strength against our competitors if we could only capitalize on it. From this came the concept of linking the market needs of the world to the diversity of our science base, and a number of organizational and behavioural changes which would enable this to happen.

Establishing with clarity the starting point of a business is rather like playing three-dimensional chess. You have first of all to establish where you are, or where the business stands relative to where it has come from, because that indeed will produce the current direction and speed of movement which unless changed will tell you pretty inexorably where you are likely to end up. In this part of the analysis optimism tends to reign. I've never known any business that does not claim to follow the 'hockey stick' pattern of earnings and every one of us must be familiar with it. This invariably shows some modest dip in earnings in the immediate future to be followed by continual improvement stretching to infinity. Each year the 'hockey stick' moves on a year, or sometimes two years, and the only certainty is the constant conviction that five years out everything is going to be all right. Anybody who has operated in business for more than five years knows that invariably in five years the business is not all right unless something has been done about it. When you analyse the 'hockey sticks' you usually find the claim that, despite all practical experience to the contrary, a simultaneous combination of your own increasing volume with increased prices will work the miracle. This is an even more beguiling picture since the forecasted increase in demand will bring the existing plants up to capacity and necessitate the building of a new one, of course on much the same technological base as exists today.

This optimistic picture of forward growth of earnings and constant expansion lay behind the overexpansion of ICI's Agricultural division ammonia capacity in the late 1960s, and the heavy overexpansion of our Vinyl Chloride Monomer capacity in the 1970s. In the first case a combination of inflation and world growth ultimately saved us (as it did so many other sixties' optimists), and subsequently ammonia and fertilizers became one of our most successful businesses. In the latter case, only a decade later, the world had changed, inflation was being controlled and growth had slowed, so that recovery from the overexpansion could only be achieved by retrenchment. For another industry that followed the same path one has to look no further than the world's steel industry. Vast amounts of capital and capacity were installed all over the world in expectation of continuing rising demand and no technological change. Not only was the demand not to materialize but the revolution in distribution costs introduced by containerization, changes in marine technology and handling methods at docks opened up the world from what had been a series of regional markets to a single one. Then the pendulum swung again and the concept of the low capital cost mini mill was introduced in the USA. Such mistakes in the future are likely to have an even more serious result, because of the changes in expectations of inflation, the reduction of growth, and a new factor, the shift of many of these basic businesses to lesser developed countries.

If establishing where you are relative to your own past and predicting your future trajectory is difficult, assessing your position in relation to your competitors' strengths, weaknesses, position and strategies is even more so. For an international business like ICI this is particularly the case. We may tend to assume that other companies and cultures operate with the same sorts of motivations and criteria of success as we do, despite the fact that Japanese companies, for instance, turn in a very low rate of profit compared to those in the United Kingdom, and indeed do not need to do so because of the low interest charges and ready availability of capital in their country. Equally well one's German competitors tend to be financed by banks, rather than by equity, and their approach to the handling of their shareholders is very different from our own.

My American competitors operate against yet a different set of expectations and criteria of success. Their stock market and their investors are particularly ruthless on short-term performance and I always admire the ability and determination of American companies to operate long-term policies of research and development in the face of such intense short-term pressures. For example, despite horrendous pressures for short-term earnings after the acquisition of Conoco, the Dupont company never wavered in its support of its superb research department even though many of the targets and pay offs lay far in the future. Ultimately it is the development that your competitors will make that will give you the opportunity – or the problem. These comments may seem to apply only to the large international manufacturing corporation, but nowadays there is no business so small that it is immune to the effects of international competition, and many service businesses are only just beginning to feel these effects. The small town café which finds Kentucky Fried Chicken or McDonalds producing crippling competition in its own area, is just as much a victim of these trends as ICI, Shell or Unilever.

Not only do you have to work out where your competitors stand at present, but you also have to try and project their future course in the same way you have projected your own and look at how this will affect your own policies in future. It is quite obvious that if all of you are going for the same niche in the marketplace, as is happening increasingly at present, then it will be a highly competitive situation where you will have to rely even more than usual on the superiority of your own skills or technology to bring you through.

Interestingly enough, more and more information is now available on a world basis about competitive strengths. There is a mass of well-informed financial analysis of companies and the directions in which they are going. A study of the patenting profiles of competitors reveals with great clarity the direction of their technical thrust. We have studied this, and other features of our competitors, for many years. As a generalization, competitors are more open with each other than they have been in the past and there is much more information available. It is a poor leader who does not know his opposite numbers, and while I do not go to the extent of General Montgomery in the desert with a picture of my primary competitors hanging on the wall of my office, I know them all, and have a healthy respect for them. I am continually reappraising in my own mind their strengths while looking for their weaknesses (although there are depressingly few of these visible). I try to put myself in their shoes, because it cannot be emphasized often enough that business is very much like war, despite the optimistic view that there is enough scope and space for everybody to be successful. The war analogy is not too far-fetched since for every winner in industrial competition there is bound to be a loser. Moreover, just as war involves every branch of a country, every citizen and every skill, so does industrial success. Many of the statements on strategy and thinking of Clausewitz or the earlier Chinese military authors are as applicable to competition in the business world as they are in military matters. Furthermore, industrial success or failure on a grand scale can have as much, albeit slower, effect as military defeat on the lives and well-being of a country's citizens. The difference is of course that we fight for economic superiority, but many wars have derived from the same aim. Even though companies' actions are the result of a substantial contribution of views from many people it is surprising how often one can predict the competitive gambits from knowledge of the characteristics and prejudices of the leader. We know, in ICI, which of our competitors' leaders look on loss of market share as a personal affront and will react accordingly, and we know which will always seek technical excellence regardless of commercial application. We know who likes to 'do the deal' himself and who delegates such matters. We know who, because of his background and upbringing in a particular business, will stick with it through thick and thin despite losses. The leader still has the same weaknesses and strengths as any other man and it is as well to study and know them. Nowhere is this more obvious than when looking at the competitive reactions to the acquisition of other companies. No one likes to be outsmarted, and the man who loses out once will be that much more aggressive and determined the next time, although others may react by refusing to deal with those that they don't know and trust.

The aim of the business leader must be to be the best, for only the best command their own destiny and achieve the sort of rewards that are sought for themselves and their people. In a cycle of reinforcement, the best people wish to join the best companies. The best companies are able more readily to make alliances or purchase technology or be welcomed into countries other than their own, or obtain financial consideration from banks or shareholders, or escape some of the more scathing criticisms which can be so damaging to a company if produced in the public arena. But remember that the best is a relative not an absolute measure. The standards of the best are set by the competition and one's aim is always to exceed them. However, as in many other aspects of business management the best, if sought in absolute terms, is the enemy of the good.

Perhaps because the company in which I have spent most of my industrial life is scientifically based, we have a passion for perfection. We have all heard the phrase 'paralysis by analysis', and it is depressingly easy to analyse to greater and greater degrees of minutiae, becoming ever more dissatisfied with the conclusions that you are forming, until eventually you decide that there is not sufficient data to take any action at all. But be sure that others will not be so inhibited, and too much hesitation will lose the competitive race. The greatest help in setting a strategy is a hefty slice of cynicism and the openness of mind to re-examine cherished beliefs.

When this operation has been done according to the conventional wisdom you then decide whether you like where you are apparently going to end up. Then, if you don't, you must decide

what else you will do. It is at this stage that suddenly the chorus
of advice dies away and the armies of theoreticians depart. This
is the decision that shows the true quality of industrial leadership. It is in this area that the majority of people expect the chief
executive to have a personal vision of where the company
should be going. I believe, on the contrary, that in deciding
where you would like to be, as opposed to where you are
probably going to end up, you need a great deal of discussion
and a great deal of development of new thinking and new
processes. The idea of doing this through the planning department, or through a paper on strategy presented to the board,
seems to me to be quite inadequate. This process involves large
amounts of time and constant discussion with those involved
lower down the line who will actually execute the strategies on
which the whole picture relies. This sort of circular debate,
frequently widening out to involve others within and without
the company, goes on until all are satisfied that the result is as
good as they are going to get. The whole exercise may be held
up while consultants are asked for a view on a particular market,
technological advance or commercial strengths, and with that
new input the whole cycle will start again.

I start with the view that the final responsibility for the future
of the company depends upon the board as a whole, and
therefore the direction in which the company is to be led is the
unique responsibility of that board. We have a peculiarity in
Britain, inasmuch as the clear responsibility for the company
rests with each member of the board in a collegiate sense. No
one can remove that personal responsibility from you, and if
you do not discharge it (through fear of a powerful chairman, or
personal ambition, or even seeking an easy life), you should not
have accepted the job in the first place. It is a sad commentary
that in many cases and places, board members have failed to
observe their responsibilities, and powerful chief executives
have, to a large extent, hijacked their boards. There remains
however the subtle difference that in this case no board member
can be hijacked unless he or she is a willing and compliant co-
conspirator. If you think that this cannot happen, read Lee
Iacocca's book on his years in the Ford Motor Company.

In deciding where the company ideally would like to be, I
believe that businesses should operate both from a bottom-up

and a top-down view. Very frequently people closer to today's marketplace than to the board are more realistic about the possibilities for their business than those at the top. It took an enormous amount of discussion to persuade me that we had enough intrinsic skills to mount a successful oil operation, but those closer to the competition and the marketplace knew better than I their own relative abilities. An industrial manager at any level should endeavour to have a clear view of the future, and the role that he would like his business to play in that future. After all, if he doesn't like the future he has the personal possibility – and responsibility – of moving to another outfit whose potential he thinks is greater. At the very least one owes it to one's family to do this, as well as to oneself and even one's current employer. Most people ensure that they spend their lives working for something which they think has a future, and which will provide the sort of life and opportunity that they wish for themselves and their dependants. Be they industrialists or Buddhist monks it is necessary to tap into those views of the future which the young people have, for they see a different perspective, and often greater opportunities, than the board does. Given their commitment and dedication, very often they will prove themselves right, as our Fibres people showed us when they decided to change from a bulk to a speciality business, in the face of our scepticism. After all, our record of innovation into the marketplace, of the sort of fashion-sensitive effects wanted and needed in the garment business, did not seem a good one. We had a long record of significant invention and development of such items as polyester fabric (Terylene and Crimplene) but were we really capable of producing to order, so to speak, a constant family of new variations on a theme? Even if we could, could we do it quickly enough? Even given that all the changes worked, would such a new strategy pay? Every new development costs money and every new product into the market has a launch cost. Was it really possible to command such a premium price that one could recover the extra investment? We doubted that it was technically possible, or that there would be a niche for such a business, but they proved us to be wrong and that was the beginning of the launch of Tactel, our highly successful family of fibres for leisurewear, the I C I record campaign, and so many more besides.

One reason why you should try to develop the direction in which you think the company should go from both ends of the company at once is that in the process you gain the commitment of those who will have to follow the direction – and 'make it happen' – and in a free society you are unlikely to get this commitment without a high degree of involvement and understanding of both where the ultimate goal is, and the process by which the decisions regarding that goal have been reached. Ultimately the responsibility lies with the board, as the most experienced businessmen in the company and also, particularly, as those who look at the corporation as a whole. A high degree of constructive conflict is almost essential in this process and I should perhaps quote the comments of a wise manager I worked for at one time, who pointed out that in industry the optimum level of conflict is not zero; just as no friction or one hundred per cent friction immobilizes movement in a mechanical sense, so total absence of conflict or one hundred per cent conflict will immobilize movement in a company. The seeking of business success is far too difficult and serious a matter to be done in a cosy way. Of course one wants to avoid situations where the conflict reaches excessive levels and actually gets in the way of running the business, but if the right decisions are to be taken it is essential that conflicting views are heard and thrashed out. The fact that you are up at the top of a business hierarchy does not confer all-seeing wisdom. It also increasingly removes one from the contemporary marketplace, and makes it even more difficult to foresee the future. In my own case by the time I became chairman of ICI, I had not actively sold in the marketplace for nine years, although, of course, as a director of a large international company I was involved from time to time in negotiations of one sort or another. Even more importantly, I completely lacked business experience in certain vital parts of the world. Although I knew most of these countries from my naval days, the perspective one gains visiting the coasts of a country as a sailor is very different from the view of the businessman. I had not conducted business in Latin America or in Africa at all, and visits to both countries soon after I was appointed revealed how extraordinarily difficult it was to get an accurate view of both their problems and opportunities merely from reading, no matter how assiduously.

Most of us do not find it easy to imagine our futures and it is extremely rare to meet an individual capable of projecting himself mentally more than about five years ahead. If we are already working from an out-of-date database (because we have moved up the hierarchy) it is very likely our vision of tomorrow's world is much closer to today's, while others in the organization, whose database is perhaps more up-to-date, may well be able to see beyond us.

The directions in which the company and the business should head seem to me to be best developed by iterative processes, both within the board, including the non-executive directors, and between the board and those responsible for running the businesses at a wide range of levels. Probably the longest-playing show in town in this area has been the, at times, seemingly endless debate about the future of our colours business, the manufacture of synthetic dyestuffs – now securely on dry land and once more full of confidence and bounce. Throughout all our travails we have always known we wished to stay in the business which is the repository of our Organic Chemical skills and has been the parent of many of our best operations. This aim has never changed. The interesting thing has been that each time we have revised the strategy we have been partially right, but it has only been as a result of a whole series of revisits, reorganizations and reassessments, as well as changing people, perspectives and systems, that we seem to have got enough right to be able to fight our corner. We started many years ago by believing that innovation and uniqueness would provide the revenue to give us a good return, and for a time it did. We then realized that our costs were too high so we narrowed the range and cut the costs. We then realized that we had gone too far and lacked the critical mass to support the heavy selling effort involved, so we bought another company to fill out the range again. We had a terrible time administering the company, which we had bought very cheaply and which was in disarray. We continued to cut costs and still lost money. We then re-examined our whole hand, studied in more detail than before the costs and revenues from individual products and found, hey presto! that we had a mixed bag between the good profit earners and a few large loss leaders and so on and so on. Maybe we should have solved our problems more quickly (of course in a perfect world everyone always should), but better by far to have gone on and on, testing, probing, questioning and changing, until we finally had a solution which worked and could take us where we wanted to be. In our case this iteration has gone on at great lengths and I and my colleagues have had to struggle to ensure that we have allocated enough time to deciding the direction in which the company should be going, and the changes that have to be carried out in order to get it there. The overwhelming temptation and the external pressures will inevitably lead the other way; to take a quick decision and move on. The demands of running the company today always seem paramount, and have the added advantage that one is working from one's direct experience and not having to indulge in the extremely difficult and risky business of projecting into the future.

Even when you have decided a broad direction, and I should emphasize that it is only possible to set ambitions in a broad sense and only helpful so to do, there will inevitably come times when external events show that one has made a false assessment of one's starting point, or the ability of one's competitors, known or unsuspected, to seize the initiative. If it appears that the original decisions were taken on the basis of assumptions which have not stood the test of time it is as well to re-run the exercise. It is far better to recognize that external circumstances have changed, or simply that one made a mistaken series of assumptions about one's own relative strengths, rather than to plough on in a situation where plainly the goal you have set yourself is unattainable.

A good example from my own experience of this problem is the constant re-examination of our oil strategy in ICI. The strategy was originally conceived as far back as the late 1960s when it appeared to many of us that unless we obtained a greater command over our raw materials we would be exposed to a fatal squeeze from the oil companies, who were increasingly entering our own field of business. It was with this in mind that when oil was first discovered in the North Sea, ICI set about joining a number of exploration consortia. This initiative, in the event, paid off handsomely, both in terms of profit and in terms of giving us an illusion of independence when one of our consortia, which we shared with the Burma Oil company, discovered oil in what is now the Ninian field. By a stroke of good fortune Ninian was earning at its maximum rate when much of the rest of ICI was suffering severe competitive pressures from exchange rate movements. However it speedily became apparent that for us, oil was a totally different sort of business, requiring a different sort of perspective. The money we put into oil exploration, if we were lucky, would find us a new field which would have a limited life only. Government incentives, both in the North Sea and in most other parts of the world, are designed to ensure continuous ploughing back into exploration, because after all, that is the basis for the future prosperity of the country, taking, as most countries do, so large a part of the ultimate revenue. One therefore gets trapped into a situation where it appears much easier to carry on in the business than to divest, or move out. At the same time the oil business is very demanding of cash, and at the development stage enormously greedy for investment capital. Not altogether surprisingly, if you put a lot of capital in and the business succeeds, you get a lot of capital out. We have agonized over and over again about our relatively small oil business. We are, after all, a large chemical company, and a very small oil company. It has always seemed to us better to face our competition on the basis of our chemical abilities, where we are undoubtedly strong. The situation has recently become a great deal clearer, with the break in oil prices, which to some extent forces us to make up our minds.

When it is apparent that external circumstances have changed, you have to decide whether to cry chicken and run too early, or continue to reinforce and spend time, money and ever increasing numbers of your best people, who are invariably sucked into the most difficult areas of the battle, trying to fight a war which you cannot win. There is quite a lot of evidence in industry, and my own experience, that sheer determination can very often overcome structural weaknesses or difficulties which theoretically should scupper the entire effort. As always, however, these are nicely balanced by examples of people who have gone 'a bridge too far', stuck with totally unobtainable ambitions and allowed the whole company to be pushed into the pursuit, usually, of a product dream which the market has quite clearly rejected and which cannot be made to fly. It is very,

very seldom that adjustment of a product, once it has been rejected by the marketplace, will re-establish it.

A good example of dogged determination to try to force into the marketplace an extremely ingenious invention which had been rejected by the consumer, was our pursuit of merulite packings for soft drinks. These were a new form of packaging involving a collapsible polyester tube, coated to withstand carbonation, which was presented to the customer in a cardboard sleeve. The advantages were plain to see. There was no problem in moving empties to the bottling plant or destroying the empties after use. One was not moving either weight or air around the countryside. The sleeves themselves replaced bottles, which were difficult to dispose of, and the re-cycling of which was expensive. Plainly, merulite tubes removed one of the favourite weapons of attack at football matches, and since the containers were easily disposed of by burning, without any pollution effects, appeared to us to have strong advantages from an environmental point of view. The cost of the entire operation was competitive with glass bottles and, moreover, the package and contents could be dropped without damage or loss and therefore should have been an attractive proposition to supermarkets and bottling plants alike. Despite all these obvious advantages, which lured us to follow the extremely expensive development of the project, the product had only one snag. Consumers did not like it! Consumers liked being able to lift a bottle to their lips, and were not so hung up about the problems of disposing of bottles. We doggedly persevered in our pursuit of consumer acceptance, so convinced were we of the superiority of our product, but, as always, ultimately the customer is king, and our product was rejected and has joined the ranks of many other good ideas whose time may come one day, but certainly is not with us now.

If one has to take a view of the balance between the reinforce-and-stick-with-it, or the cut-your-loss schools, I think I tend to favour the cut-your-loss brigade. There are already, within any company, enough people with egg on their faces who will argue that one more mighty heave will get us there, but it takes, I think, more courage to be prepared to acknowledge that we were wrong in the first place. Plainly you cannot apply that view to everything or the whole of your business is in a continuous state of stop/go, or like the good old Duke of York's troops, marching up and down the same hill with monotonous regularity. In considering the issues of where you are, or where you would like to be, there is also a great tendency to think that the grass is always greener somewhere else. This is why it is so important that one's initial analysis of the strengths of the company be done in a very clear-minded and thorough way.

The whole of business is about taking an acceptable risk. Companies that take no risk disappear. Companies that take unacceptable risk plainly also disappear. The problem is therefore invariably to minimize the risk that can be minimized, while taking quite high levels of risk in areas which cannot. One of the areas where risk can well be minimized is avoiding the temptation of a total step out from your existing field of business. A great deal of work has been done in academic and business schools on the track record of success of those who have diversified totally outside their own fields of experience. While of course the whole business game involves doing better than most of your competitors, the attempt to diversify away from one's basic business, which so much experience elsewhere has shown to be an extremely difficult operation, is a risk that I have always tried to avoid. All companies have the need to adjust, or correct the faults of the existing portfolio of businesses, such as slow growth, or inadequate room for innovation, or environmental hazards, or product substitution from some other area of business. I have always tried, in these cases, to ensure that any diversification we seek is found in an area which is contiguous to our own skill base. Indeed ideally it will employ more than one of the skills which one has recognized as being competitive strengths.

For example, we have found that we can make good businesses by selling services that we developed for use in our own company. These are businesses which have grown naturally because of a need that we have recognized and it is reasonable to suppose that if we have done the job right, and tested the external market to see if such services are not available to our satisfaction elsewhere, we should start with some sort of competitive edge. It would also be surprising if the problems for which we have developed such services, be they, in our case, radio isotope testing, or information retrieval software, or com-

puter systems for stock or other control, were not equally
recognized by competitors and people in other fields of business. These can provide the basis of a new business opportunity
with relatively little risk. Equally we have found some success in
moving into areas where, for example, we bring either a
customer base, or a skill or research base which can be applied to
another business. I have always been, however, and I believe
with some justification, unconvinced of the virtues of taking a
punt totally outside my own business. I have to observe that
there are some business leaders who have apparently succeeded in doing this, very frequently by forming conglomer-
ates; but I have never believed very much in the conglomerate.
It seems to me that unless you can convince yourself that a
grouping of companies adds more than the sum of its parts,
there is no *raison d'être* for the company at all. My colleagues and
I spent many hours discussing this issue, when we first sat
down to decide how we were going to approach the running of
our company. Unless we were adding value to the constituent
parts of the group it seemed to us that our plain duty would be
to break the group into smaller constituent parts and hand them
back to the shareholders. After all, unless we can show that we
are able to do better with the totality of the sums, and the totality
of the business, why should any shareholder believe that we
know better how to deal with his money if we are to invest in
areas outside our particular expertise, than he can by individual
investments?

It is far more important that the owners of the company, the
shareholders, be given the choice of whether they want to
invest in, let us say, a bank, an agricultural business, a food
business, or a retail chain, than that we should build our
business in different fields, unless we can demonstrate a high
degree of mutual reinforcement from such an exercise. In other
words we have to be able to demonstrate that we can do better
by some sort of synergy in the group; if we can't do that then the
group is better broken up and the individual parts allowed to fly
free and attract their own shareholding. This is, I think, a
difficult message for industrial enterprises to take, but it may be
one which is even more necessary than in the past. There have
not been many examples of large companies breaking themselves up voluntarily. But there is little doubt in my mind that

the future will only go to the large company if that large
company is really able to release the energies and the synergies
that ought to be a part of the grand design and make more than
the sum of the parts. The large company is by definition more
difficult to run than the small one. I and others are devoted to
the idea of obtaining simultaneously the massive resources of
the large together with the speed of movement, closeness to the
market and greater personal satisfaction of the small. Nevertheless the onus of proof is in my view on demonstrating that the
large is able to do things the small cannot, as well as not
hampering the smaller units. The necessity therefore to ensure
that size does not become an aim in itself is overriding. That is
after all the task of the board and leadership of a company.

When deciding where the company should be going for the
future it is extremely important that one should not lose sight of
the need for synergy since adventuring outside one's own field
contains high added risk which the shareholders will very
quickly appreciate. On past experience it seldom brings high
added reward unless the benefits of synergy are there.

When considering the future direction of the company it is as
well to remember the advantages of not following whatever
current fashion is sweeping through one's competitors. There is
at present in my business a great dislike of the bulk chemical
businesses, and a great wish on the part of most people to shift
out of them. Like all generalizations, this is too simple. Our own
bulk chemical businesses vary between some which are very
good, because most of the competition has abandoned the field,
and some which are very bad, because they are in areas which
are attracting new entrants the whole time, and moreover, new
entrants who are seeking to compete in either a slow-growing or
non-growing market. One thing is absolutely clear: no bulk
chemical business can afford the elaborate overheads, the heavy
research and development, or the expensive sales force that a
fast-growing high-margin business can. Bulk businesses have
to survive on the basis of their costs.

An outstanding example of this occurs in the whole field of
petrochemicals. The Middle East in particular, with very low oil
costs and large amounts of entrained gas, starts with an almost
unbeatable comparative advantage in terms of its raw material
costs, which in the petrochemical business typically are over

half of the total cost picture. However, it is important when you
see an advantage in one area not to minimize the advantages
you may have in others. The capital cost of building plants in the
Middle East is very high. The operability in the past has tended
to be low. Although manpower costs in petrochemicals are
extremely low by comparative business standards, averaging
around six to seven per cent, nevertheless in that area costs of
effectively trained manpower are much higher in the Middle
East than they are in Europe.

You can imagine the trauma of facing up to the realities of our
competition. Polythene was perhaps the most significant invention ever to come from our research labs. Not only was it an
important factor in winning the Second World War, for its
specific electrical insulating properties were a key to the
development of radar, but it is one of those rare inventions
which create an entirely new industrial development. Although
we think of it now as a packaging material and the ubiquitous
polythene bag appears to be a major support of modern life, its
primary contribution was in the impetus it gave to the plastic
moulding industry and the first development of plastic buckets,
sink bowls and so on. Probably, in terms of company drive, this
product was the sacred cow of all sacred cows and yet the
economic tide was flowing against us. Not only was the material
advantage of the Middle East one which would ultimately prove
critical, but also we had, through our own fault, lost the
technical leadership. Union Carbide as well as others, including
ourselves, had developed a new product – linear low-density
polythene. This offered cost advantages in production which
we had judged insufficient to warrant its development.
However, others saw in it greater advantages than we had and
were keen to invest. All in all, with new investment in an
oversupplied market and loss of economical competitiveness at
the raw material end, it looked like a blood bath for us. We
therefore laid our plans and moved out in good order over a
long period of time. Although the first fruits of this decision
took place in 1982, the writing had been on the wall, and read by
us many years before that, and it took a period of some years to
find a way of moving out of polythene, which was not only
ICI's own proud invention, but an area where we had been
acknowledged world leaders for many years.

On the other hand, in certain other areas of our bulk chemicals we have been very successful in maintaining a good margin business over a long period of time. The mere fact that something is sold as a bulk product to a specification need not, in itself, decide that one should move out of it. It seems, for example, very unlikely that world agriculture will be able to do without fertilizers for a number of years to come, although one can dream of a technological situation in the next century where direct nitrogen fixation will have been genetically engineered into plants and the whole nature of the fertilizer business will have changed. The problem in considering the future of fertilizers is rather to consider the changes which will occur in world agriculture, and it is already apparent that they will be many. One cannot really believe that the whole of the world is going to go on maximizing production of agricultural produce, when so much is already destined to end up as mountains of grain, or butter, or meat – or lakes of wine or olive oil. Nevertheless the world will continue to require food, and efficient food production – until the era of nitrogen fixation – will require fertilizers.

For us the fertilizer business has been a good business, in many parts of the world over many years, and even its downturns have been of fairly limited duration. The business problem in that area has always been to ensure that we provide the maximum amount of service with our products, and that our production costs are as low as anybody else's.

There may well be cases where staying in a business in which others are getting out ultimately will bring its own substantial reward, at minimum in terms of having a good, sound, cash-generating business and one which is relatively unbuffeted by competition. But this will only occur if the style of running the business, the skills applied to the business and above all the cost base of the business, have been attacked ruthlessly in the interim period. This is a matter of having set an early direction against a clear vision of the future.

So far in this chapter I have tried to spell out how important it is to be clear where one starts from, where present trends are taking one to, and to be ruthlessly honest about the trends from the competition and from the external environment. I then advocated the creation of the vision of where the company should be going by means of an iterative process combining both bottom-up and top-down planning. I'm uncomfortably aware that this doesn't actually tell anybody exactly what they should do next. I'm also uncomfortably aware that nobody has yet, to my satisfaction, demonstrated the superiority of one way of attacking this problem over another. Let me with some humility, therefore, describe the manner in which I and my colleagues have sought to try and create our own dream of where our company might fit into tomorrow's world, and how this process of marrying the vision from the top with the visions from below has been carried out within ICI. It is far too early to say whether this produces the right result; only time and history will show. All one can say at present is that though the process is difficult, time-consuming, and at times very unsatisfying, it is at least an improvement over those processes we have followed in the past. I have seen many other companies working the same sort of processes, and I have yet to find one which seems to have the final solution. There is plenty of room for experimentation in this area. To a large extent the way in which the problems are tackled depends on the balance of technical skills, imaginative skills and the way in which the board is accustomed to working together.

Our own approach to this derives from our ethos and our history. Our forebears have given our company a tradition of open speaking and respect for differences of opinion which in my view is the most precious single inheritance that we have. There is no way in which a vision of the future can be developed among a group of people unless those people have a very high degree of mutuality of respect, tolerance, and above all humour. It is of course a great advantage if the organization starts, so to speak, with this in place and in our case I believe our scientific heritage and background lead naturally to a wish to hear, dissect and learn from others' views. However, plain speaking and tolerance are tender flowers which have to be nurtured and helped to grow. One 'hangover ridden' shortness of response, or a snappy turn-off to views you don't like, causes infinite harm. These understandable human reactions have to be channelled against the waffler, and the apple polisher: the man or woman who by verbal skill seeks to evade taking a position, or even in some cases actually saying anything at all. In corporate terms it has to be made more dangerous to acquiesce than to dissent and this is not an easy trick to turn. It has to be possible to dream and speak the unthinkable, for the only thing that we do know is that we shall not know what tomorrow's world will be like. It will have changed more than even the most out-rageous thinking is likely to encompass.

We invariably start our process by trying, together with the help of younger people, to look at what the present trends of the world are likely to lead to. Is the trend towards growth of technological leadership in the Far East likely to continue? Is the share of the world's manufacturing likely to move increasingly to the Far East? Is manufacturing as a part of gross national product likely to continue to decline in Europe and the USA? Is the European market likely to become a genuine market which operates in the same way as the USA, and therefore give Europe the basic strengths of a vast internal demand? Or is it more likely to be so affected by nationalism and the historical preferences of its peoples that it will remain a heterogeneous collection of individual markets linked together in a loose customs union?

What new commercial freedoms does the advent of the microchip give us? One can already see many examples where skilful use of information technology has given imaginative and creative business people enormous commercial advantages. Are such approaches applicable to our business?

How real are the present trends in India and China? For the first time for many hundreds of years both countries are able to feed themselves. One has seen within the vast population of India the emergence of a substantial middle class with purchas-ing power equal to any European nation. India looks as though it can be self-sufficient in energy within the next few years. Do these changes mean (since all of us who have had the privilege of working with Indians know the tremendous intellectual power of that nation) that India will begin to play the role in the world which many of us have expected and foreseen?

These and many hundreds of other questions, views and theories are debated endlessly by us as a group until we reach a view which satisfies us that, at least on the basis of the know-ledge and data we have at the moment, we have some sort of cohesiveness. We do not seek for all to be totally convinced. But we need to have a degree of common ownership of at least the broad parameters of what the world may look like, and we then seek the whole time to simplify down and down and down. Above everything, the view and the aim has to be looking outward rather than inward. There is a trap here into which many people fall. The actions which have to be taken are by definition inward ones – things we can do ourselves. After all, only Canute believed that he could alter external forces without actually doing anything, and we all know what happened to him! But the inward and internal actions are to respond to, and hopefully influence, external circumstances, and unless you are clear on this nothing will happen. The industrial equivalent of fiddling while Rome burns is to spend hours of internal management time arguing about the allocation of costs between departments or divisions, when the real problem is that the whole cost of the operation is too high. No amount of reallocation makes the total reduce and yet the first reaction to bad numbers is almost always a rush to blame someone else on one's own side! We need at the end to have simplified to a stage where one sentence, almost a slogan, will describe what we believe, and what we can accept and work to. This process of simplifying down involves attacking the 'weasel words'. We aim to make the simplifying process one of distillation and concentration, rather than trying to make 'umbrella' statements which are unobjectionable. We haggle and argue over single words. But we know when we have 'got it', and when we have got it we believe it and can work to it.

For example, we believe as a group that we can only survive in our chosen business of the chemical industry if we serve the customers who are at the leading edge of development, wherever they may be. We know from years of experience that we are not capable of reading other people's problems as well as they are. We also know that the time scale of development in our business is longer than in many other areas because, after all, in the chemical business we are, so to speak, molecular engineers: our skills consist of rearranging the chemistry of the world which has been created so that we can produce the new products. We therefore have to be in a position to share the dreams and the understandings of those people who we believe are making the running for tomorrow, wherever they may be.

Since we see, in many cases, that technical leadership and development is being exercised from, for example, Japan in some areas, or the USA in others, it follows that those businesses have to be established in those countries. Or at the least very strong links have to be created with those customers.

Another consideration which plays largely in our minds when thinking of tomorrow's world is the knowledge that all businesses go through cycles of growth and then reach maturity. In our sort of high-technology business, the high profits tend to be made over a fairly limited time, which in many cases appears to be getting shorter. It takes great patience to build up a new technological business. In the past, typically, businesses have remained cash-negative for up to twenty years. In many cases they have gone long periods before they have even made a profit. However, in the past, these businesses have been compensated for by very high profits when the business reaches take-off point.

An outstanding example of this sort of pattern in our own field is the synthetic fibre business which, historically, could be considered to have started in the days of rayon at the turn of the century. It took years before the business really took off with the addition of more and more synthetics, starting with the discovery of nylon and followed up by the discovery of acrylics and polyester. Enormous growth in this business occurred through the substitution phase and for a period of some years the business was extremely profitable. It is true to say, however, that since the business has become mature, the period of readjustment has been extremely painful and very few fibre companies have made much money over the last decade. The world is full of similar examples. There was a period during which lighting, which for many years had been provided by gas mantles, was starting to be provided by electricity. The demand for electric light bulbs quickly became phenomenal and continued at a very high rate for many years. This growth in demand was accompanied by more and more technical developments from the original flickering wire to the high-intensity lighting we see today. Even today we are still seeing developments in the electric light bulb, but the basic growth in the demand for them is over. There is never a situation in which there is simultaneously a demand from a marketplace which requires replacement sales of a commodity that it already has, as well as the basic growth which occurred as household after household abandoned gas and moved into the new form of lighting. Only if there is a totally new technical invention can one get substitution growth, which is probably the fastest natural growth in demand that the businessman can see. Invention, for example, of a completely new recording medium like the compact disc may grow very fast because all of us have become addicted to recorded music. The fact that there is something quite new and of a different quality means that we will rapidly discard the old and move into the new, just as colour television sets were substituted for black and white, and created a very high growth rate over a period of years. It is necessary to look continuously at the portfolio of one's businesses. If one possesses some which are at or near the high earning period one must plan in the realization that the high earning period is not likely to continue indefinitely.

For a dynamic company which is growing through its own efforts it is important that we should have other and new businesses of a similar nature coming along. This means seeing the opportunity years in advance. In the past, many of these businesses have arisen almost 'naturally' as contiguous to our existing areas of skills. But increasingly we are finding that they are developing across the interstices of the organizational and technical skills which have served us so well in the past. We and others have therefore introduced a sort of helicopter scanning of technological progress throughout the world from which we have sought to see where the enabling inventions may lie. This process of trying to take a broad overview of the whole field of technical progress, and understanding what will be the key development, calls for great knowledge coupled with an understanding of technical history, and imagination. Frequently the key to advance is in better ways of measuring or quantifying technical processes, or material advances which in themselves remove one of the constraints on development. Very often despite more and more sophisticated ways of manipulating data, the actual measuring sensor is still an old-fashioned thermocouple or flow measurement device. The modern control room fools us into thinking that we have more accurate and basic control, while the basics of actual quantification of change have not altered, merely the presentation of inaccurate data in more sophisticated ways. It is the same as the clinical mercury thermometer which one reads directly, or which can now present its reading electronically. The actual accuracy of the measurement has not changed, merely its presentation.

I recently read a paper by an industrialist I greatly admire, Sir Arnold Hall, in which he pointed out the enormous changes that have occurred in such mature manufacturing businesses as diesel engines, electrical transformers, and small electrical motors. In almost every one of the analyses that he showed, the primary enabling inventions that led to such advances lay in the materials field. It is our judgement at ICI that the world contains enormous further opportunities for those who are able to marshal the skills and have the imagination to direct the development of such products. One needs therefore deliberately to seek the setting up of some new high-growth businesses (in our case based technologically), which will replace those which are so successful at present, such as pharmaceuticals and agricultural chemicals.

In our dreaming we need also to think of the problems of style. Increasingly as the world becomes more and more competitive and as the skills of manufacture become more easily replicated, the selling of a defined product against a formula becomes, from a competitive point of view, a matter of cost and ability to command a market position. But there is already much evidence that the market is prepared to pay for services in a way quite different from that in which it pays for products. It could be, and indeed it is my belief, that the chemical industry of twenty years hence will be more of a service industry and less of a manufacturing industry. One can already see trends in this direction. Such successful companies as Nalco, in the USA, and some of the companies that ICI has bought recently from the Beatrice group, in the speciality field, discovered this secret many years ago. They have developed an ability to provide a chemical service to customers, rather than selling products in a bag. This involves turning a conventional chemical company almost upside down. The effort put into marketing and customer service far exceeds the effort in production and in research. The production task becomes one of very speedy reaction to customer need, and the research targets become ones of basic understanding of the products and processes, so that continual development of new effects can be created 'on the run'. But these are different ways of utilizing existing chemical skills in a new amalgam.

If we believe the nature of our industry is likely to change, then it behoves us to experiment, and set up different ways of running things to see whether such approaches are more successful than the traditional ways of doing business. An important part of the dreaming relates to balance. It is obvious that for any group of companies to grow, a good balance is required between those which continually need cash injections to stay in business (the capital-intensive type of enterprise which is typical of much of the chemical industry) and those which can generate very high profits and throw off cash when things are going well. It is impossible quickly to reposition a capital-intensive business – flexibility is seldom one of its features. Research-intensive businesses are also, of course, very high risk, but at least the cash input is more quickly controllable.

Geographical balance is important. My own company has for many years had the ambition to have our business spread in rough proportion to the pattern of chemical demand in the world market. Even though there are signs that the world's economies are beginning to operate closer together in time terms, nevertheless in the past it has been seldom that every part of the world has been simultaneously in total depression. Moreover the ideal geographical balance gives one almost automatically the best chance of picking up tomorrow's trends early.

In all of the dreaming for tomorrow, the question of balance is essential. I remember being shocked at one time when I heard one of my predecessors say that his objective as chairman was to retain our position as a private company operating on a world basis in the chemical sector. But the more I have thought about those comments, the wiser I think he was. Although the responsibilities of leadership certainly entail ensuring that the company is going somewhere, and can maintain its relative position, an even greater responsibility is to ensure that the company continues to survive. This is where the question of balance comes very much to the fore. Although one may from time to time admire people who hazard their entire company on one major throw, it has to be a risk that for most of us would be, hopefully, both an unnecessary one and certainly an undesirable one. Probably to the British the most stark example of this was when Rolls-Royce went bankrupt. It really was as though the Bank of England had shut its doors. The pride of British engineering going bust in the same way as an 'under the arches' car body firm. This modern disaster occurred because the whole company was bet on the development of one main aircraft engine and the ability to sell it profitably. As history showed, despite the engineering skill deployed and the excellence of the final product, the sums didn't work out and the whole company fell.

In addition to these sort of dreams of tomorrow's world, we also need to have dreams of tomorrow's social conditions: the needs and requirements of the young people who are making their way in industry today, as opposed to those of us who joined many years ago. We need to have technical vision, and technical imagination, and financial dreams. For example, if we are to see a major confluence of the world's financial markets, we need to have prepared our financial structure and planning in good time to take advantage of such changes.

The sharing of all these things can only be accomplished by hours and hours of talk. We have found that this sort of discussion requires a certain amount of structure, but a great deal of flexibility, and is best carried out in environments other than our normal working environment. We seek to make such discussions as different as possible from the normal way in which we work. We wear sweaters and jeans, we do not keep minutes of what individuals say, we do tremendous amounts of work on flip charts, we form a lot of our conclusions 'on the run'. The outcome of perhaps three days' work is often no more than ten points on a flip chart, and we would consider that a good rate of striking. The discussions are always, as indeed are practically all our discussions, highly informal and we encourage each other to produce ideas, no matter how fanciful. We normally continue working over drinks, over dinner, and frequently after dinner as well. We find the process simultaneously tiring, frustrating and rewarding when, at the end of tussling with some problems, we reach a shared view and a commitment to that view, which is usually of a different order to that which we can achieve by any other means. The essential is to keep on distilling down, and following ruthlessly the consequences of the dreams.

So far this has been the approach we have made to our top-down dreaming. It is paralleled by a sharing of what I have called the bottom-up dreams of the businesses themselves. We have to start with some broad-cut view of the areas of the company which we believe should be encouraged to go ahead, the areas of the company which we believe have got to be held back or even disposed of, those which are to perform the function of cash cows, and those we wish to encourage to develop in more aggressive and adventurous ways than they have hitherto.

When we have what one might call this coarse-cut overview, we then have tended to approach the businesses and ask them to produce a variety of scenarios ranging from what they would like to do in a totally free world with access to unlimited money, to the extremes of divestiture at the other end. We invariably ask the custodians of the business to exemplify what they would see as their preferred way ahead. We also seek to give some indication of the overall role we would expect the business to play in our picture of the future of the company, and ask them to develop plans which fit in with that role. We then all sit down together and discuss these various options over and over again until the board has reached a position of understanding of where in broad terms we think the strategy of the individual business should fit.

This is a process which may take a number of reruns to achieve what we would consider to be a satisfactory outcome. But when we have got such a satisfactory outcome, unless subsequent events show that we have got it wrong, or that we have wrongly read the environment or some other major change, we would aim to stick with it for some years. It is in this process of iteration that the commitment of the businesses themselves to their role in the future of the company is achieved. It is an essential part of the whole process as we work it.

I have tried to describe the process of setting the direction for our constituent businesses and the company as a whole, which I and my colleagues have been evolving over the past few years. While I believe that some parts of this routine are absolutely essential, I am only too well aware that the ideas still have to stand the test of time.

To summarize, the start of everything is to locate, as honestly as one can, the position of one's company and where the current trends will take one. That in itself is bound to reveal a number of outcomes consequent on pursuing present policies which are very different from those one would like. A considerable amount of scanning of the outside world, both the competitors in an individual business sense and the external environment in a broader sense, is then necessary. Then the development of broad-scale corporate dreams must be carried out by the board. These have to be married with the individual dreams of each business who, in addition to achieving the best they can ask for their business, have to perform and deliver what the board has asked of them for the company as a whole.

Lastly, although it would be nice to feel that everybody charts the forward direction absolutely correctly, the reality of life is that this is an almost impossible ambition. It is far more important to be moving forward in broadly the right directions than to be stuck still without the businesses going anywhere. The process of deciding where you are taking your business is the opportunity to get the involvement and commitment of others, which actually forms the motive power that at the end of the day will make it happen. While one cannot assert unequivocally that determination will win, in the balance of life you can alter direction more easily on the move than you can if you are static, and if you have set the direction in this way it will almost alter itself.

3

Switching On
or Switching Off?

Supposing we have decided, broadly, where we want to go, the problem then becomes how to get there, how to make it happen. This is of course where many good business ideas fail. Part of the secret, as I tried to demonstrate in the last chapter, is the way in which we discuss again and again our ideas and proposals up and down the company, continuously adjusting, altering and probing our positions until, at last, we reach a conclusion which we can all accept and work to. In deciding where we should go we have to transfer 'ownership' of the direction by involving everyone in the decision. Making it happen means involving the hearts and minds of those who have to execute and deliver. It cannot be said often enough that these are not the people at the top of the organization, but those at the bottom.

With the best will in the world, and the best board in the world, and the best strategic direction in the world, nothing will happen unless everyone down the line understands what they are trying to achieve and gives of their best to achieve it. In so many cases their best is so much more than they themselves think is possible. This is the reward of industrial leadership: to see people, who do not believe they have the capability of being a winning team, gaining confidence and effectiveness and morale, and the respect not only of their peers but also of their competitors and the world outside. When that has happened, an organization is difficult to beat, and even if the directions that were set are slightly wrong, a team with those characteristics is very nearly unstoppable. Very often such a team will achieve the unachievable and will overcome even the problems of what, in hindsight, might appear to be the wrong strategic direction. A good example of this would be our Fibres operation. Having led the world into polyester fibre and been highly profitable for many years, we lost the lead position due to a combination of circumstances. We failed to lead the race for new products and we contributed to and suffered from heavy overcapacity. By the time I was involved the business had chalked up losses for many years and was in deep trouble. The chairman of the division and I discussed endlessly what our strategy should be. We had a good nylon business which we judged, wrongly, was incapable of radical change although it needed re-equipment. We also had a polyester business where we had to both change the technology and the products if we were to win. At the same time we had to cut our costs and reduce the numbers to at least ameliorate the losses. I put a paper to the board saying I was not sure we could overcome all the difficulties and we might in the event have to quit the business altogether. The people in the business had lost confidence in themselves and all in all it was a dismal picture. My first meeting with the senior management did not go well. The chairman and I demanded what needed to be done and how we hoped to fund the re-equipment of polyester, when we had invested what was necessary from the nylon cash flow. We were greeted with disbelief and they finally said, 'You know nothing of this business, you come to us with a facile and futile plan. Surely you realize that if we could have done this we would have done. It's impossible and a waste of time.' I remember saying there was no choice. We did this or we shut down and if they wanted the latter we should shut down our plants immediately. In the event the strategy we laid out was wrong. Polyester was too far gone, starting from where we were, and with the limited resources we could put in. But, with a research department reduced by over a half and with the strategic use of a cash cow, the nylon business produced innovation after innovation. Today the business holds its head high and is a world leader in its specialized fields. This was achieved by resolve, leadership and teamwork, coupled with a fierce determination not to be beaten. Battles are won tactically; they are not won by strategy. But equally well, of course, you may have a brilliant tactical win and through a failure to appreciate the strategic significance of what is going on, throw away the game.

Since in the last resort everything has to be achieved by

people, the first thing we have to consider is the sort of
environment in which people can give of their best. The curious
thing about industry is that if we think for ten minutes and draw
a picture of the kind of organization we would least like to work
in, and hence the one where we are least likely to be effective,
we often look about and see just such an environment around
us. In part this occurs, I believe, because large organizations
have a curious and almost inevitable tendency to centralize.
Large groups of people become so fascinated with the internal
workings of their own organization that they are continually
tinkering with it. Far from seeing the main enemy without, they
increasingly become absorbed with blaming failures on
organizational, rather than behavioural omissions. You then
enter what I have termed the cycle of increasing authoritarian-
ism, or the cycle of increasing centralization. A business mistake
is made, and it is assumed that the mistake would have been
avoided if somebody at a higher position in the organization
had known about it, or had intervened. The assumption itself
may patently be wrong, but nevertheless it is difficult for people
in superior positions to realize that they are just as fallible as
those below. A power that had been delegated previously is
therefore removed, usually in quite a small way, by an instruction that in such and such a case the matter is to be referred
upwards. Of course exactly that case never occurs, or if it does it
occurs in such a way that it is not recognized as being a repeat
run of the previous bitter experience. You therefore get an
increasing tangle of bureaucratic instructions which seek to
legislate for an endless series of unlikely events which have
occurred at some time in the organization's past. Unless there is
a really determined effort to 'burn the books', and reduce this
tangle of bureaucracy, the people at the bottom of the organization on whom everything depends feel an increasing lack of
responsibility for the achievement of the objective. Success in
the organization becomes a matter of following the rules, and it
is much easier to obtain advancement and favour by avoiding
mistakes, than it is by actually achieving the goals so vital for
business success. Such organizations have many other characteristics which anybody who has worked in them for any length
of time will recognize. In the pages that follow I will characterize
some of the more obvious signs of a badly organized and

motivated operation. I would hasten to say that I have never yet had the misfortune to operate anywhere which possessed all these undesirable features, but every one of us has seen some of them, or combinations of them in different circumstances, and everyone knows, from their own personal experience, how demotivating these characteristics are.

Many of the observations that follow apply particularly to British people, and companies. It is perhaps inevitable that I think in these terms, since I have more direct experience of leading the British than any other nationality, and I am deeply conscious of our national foibles. Almost all the characteristics that I enumerate apply to other nations in one way or another. In a later chapter I address some of these differences in behaviour, values and approach, but the principles of 'switching on' apply everywhere. Some countries are more easily 'switched off' by one characteristic rather than another, and all nations have different approaches and traditions. No one would accuse the Americans of being frightened of the new, or the Indians of refusing to show emotion, or of inability to communicate, but all need to work in an environment which encourages them to give of their best, and encourages them to look outwards rather than inwards. As much attention needs to be given to the 'switch offs' in other countries, as in our own, and as much conscious effort has to be applied.

I suppose the organization which fails to make it happen is best characterized by a lack of truthfulness and openness. Truthfulness and openness without fear of the consequences is a most difficult trick to turn within a large group of people. It is not that large outfits inevitably seek to recruit liars. It is a tribute I suppose to the English language that there are so many forms of circumlocution that it is remarkably easy to persuade yourself that you have made a bold statement, or conveyed the bad news, whilst in reality there is no conceivable possibility that the recipient has actually understood what you are talking about. Truthfulness in these circumstances really does mean ensuring that the point that you are trying to get across has been received. Bad news in organizations is seldom received with much enthusiasm. The reality of life is of course that it is the bad news man who should be the most prized. It is all too easy to get people who will tell you the nice things, and after all there is not a lot that you can do about that, but those who will stand up without fear or favour and tell you, hopefully tactfully, that things are not really the way that everybody else thinks they are are pearls beyond price. I believe that 'political management' in large organizations stems primarily from this lack of absolute openness. After all, if you are discussing the realities of the situation it is quite difficult to trim, to conceal, or to mislead. People, however, are ill at ease with bluntness and, curiously, are almost as uncomfortable at stating things bluntly as they are at hearing blunt statements. Frankness is not an admired characteristic amongst British people, and in some cases is actually considered to be slightly uncouth. Truthfulness and openness are particularly difficult aims to have in a British organization where so much of our education and background has been devoted to concealing feelings and to suffering heroically without protest. As far as I am aware, no other country, certainly none in which my company operates, so prizes the stiff upper lip, rigid control of emotions, and 'politeness' which conceals rather than reveals, than the British.

There are many other characteristics of bad organizations, ones in fact which are designed to switch off their people rather than to switch them on. Let us start with the objectives. In bad organizations the objectives are decided unilaterally, very often as a result of a political trading-off process at the board and at other levels, and are perceived by those below to be quite unrealistic and impossible of achievement. Not only are they perceived to be such, but they are. The most unhelpful position that a board of directors can take when a business is performing badly is to respond by saying that such a performance is unacceptable. It may be an absolutely true statement, but it does nothing whatsoever to give any guidance as to the ways in which performance may be improved and merely passes a message down the line that those at the top do not want to know the bad news and would like to dissociate themselves from it.

In a good organization the objectives that have to be achieved are decided with considerable interaction between those who are going to carry them out, and those who ultimately have the responsibility for the leadership of the enterprise. This does not mean that the objectives have to be liked. No organization likes being told that it has got to hold back its expansion or abandon some pet project. But, first, they have to understand why such an instruction is given, even when it appears to be against their interests, and secondly they have to have been involved in the decision and to understand and accept the consequences of such a strategic direction. They have to believe that there will be an advantage commensurate with or greater than the sacrifice that they are going to make. In a well-led and well-motivated military force it has always been possible to form a rearguard who will fight tenaciously on behalf of their colleagues. Some in industry have to carry out the same operation.

The next characteristic of a switching-off organization is that there are far too many people and far too many layers so that each employee feels that he has little or no headroom. In such an organization you feel hemmed in by people who can refuse you permission to do something or who are only waiting to jump all over you if you appear to be taking the initiative, or achieving something which even they may recognize as being highly desirable, in 'the wrong way'. A feature of such organizations is that the means are all-important and the ends are of relatively secondary importance. It is far more important to be at one's office desk on time in the morning, to leave late at night, to process the endless paperwork which characterizes such organizations, to attend the endless meetings, and never to complain if they appear to achieve little, than it is actually to achieve the business objective of making more profit. In fact it is the preservation of the 'form' of company behaviour which becomes the aim of the actor on the scene rather than the actual business achievement. I worked at one time for a man who was incredibly able at doing his job, apparently effortlessly. So effortlessly in fact that he would often go off during working hours with his gun to bag a pheasant or a hare rash enough to have entered our grounds. He was universally considered to be no good, lazy and a bad manager. He was, in fact, a superb achiever and should have been recognized as such, and loaded with so much extra work and responsibilities that the pheasants would have been left in peace.

Organizations which set great store by behavioural conformity often develop patterns of operation which can appear ridiculous in their manifestations. At an earlier stage in my career I was transferred from one division of ICI to a new one. My previous employers were keen on understatement rather than fireworks. They liked calm achievement, and placed much emphasis on apparent control and not being taken by surprise. There was a strong sense of form. Manners and the preservation of an image of the manager as being all-seeing and ahead of the game, were very important. Everything was meant to have been thought out and planned, and woe betide any signs of undue excitement or stress. Imagine my amazement when, on my first day in the new set-up, I found that everyone fought for attention by dramatizing every event. Not, in that division, the belief that achievement would find its own reward. The form was to rush to the boss, roll on the carpet, explain excitedly the catastrophe one was faced with, and rush out again. Some hours later one returned and claimed, modestly, that one's own efforts alone had won the day, and the crisis had been averted. The whole performance was an almost total waste of time, and was accompanied by a belief that it was necessary to demonstrate that one was working long hours in the evenings, and preferably all weekends as well. Both patterns of behaviour occurred inside a single company, and within five miles of each other. Each had taken their cue, at some time or other, from the behaviours that were believed to be appropriate, and had developed to the point where they were thoroughly dysfunctional. Such organizations look inward rather than outward. Customers, or suppliers, or competitors, or even what is going on in the outside world, seem of far less importance than the endless struggle to achieve and operate the perfect bureaucracy.

As well as little headroom, there is even less support for the individual manager either laterally or vertically. In such an organization one's boss is forever seeking to cover himself and to avoid taking responsibility. The most headroom you will get from him is a wink and a nudge. Seldom if ever will he invite you to carry on, and assure you that if things go wrong he will bear the burden of guilt. Laterally things are even worse. The aim of your colleagues in the research department, or production, or sales, is to satisfy the written and unwritten codes of behaviour for their own functions rather than to sacrifice some part of the perfection in order to achieve some more profit for the enterprise as a whole.

To achieve anything in an organization such as I have described requires an endless study and understanding of the politics of what is going on, even if you yourself are not politically inclined. It would be foolish to believe that any group of people can interact without a political undercurrent. As long as individuals are different and have personal aims, ambitions and needs they will seek to achieve those for themselves. But there is a big difference between the organization where an individual's requirements are in the open, and those where, although evident, they are never tacitly acknowledged and therefore tend to dominate almost every decision and action. All too often the highly political organization derives from lack of clarity in the leadership as to what is expected, and lack of consensus about the common aim. Politics tends to develop and generate within all large groups of people, but in the bad organizations which I have described politics dominates everything. It all becomes a matter of working out how to get something done in the company, and this in itself is a matter of finding the right lever to pull, since all the concentration is on political in-fighting, and only the bare minimum on the actual achievement of a competitive advantage in the real world outside. Because of this there is little or no possibility that somebody somewhere else will recognize the merits of the actions you are taking, or the opportunity that you have uncovered, and of their own free will line up and help you. This is not the way this kind of organization works. Make no mistake, organizations like this exist in every trade and every setting, be it *Yes, Minister* or *The Corridors of Power*, be it in retailing, finance or manufacturing. Equally sadly the development of a company in this way can occur with a very strong autocratic leader or a weak one. The only breeding ground which is infertile is one running at high stress for achievement, tightly mapped and with the maximum openness. Unless there are political brownie points from on high it is most unlikely you will receive assistance.

The political process in such an organization is made even more difficult by the fact that there is little communication. Since the objectives themselves are unreal and unclear, and since there are so many people at every level, multiple messages come down the line the whole time. A characteristic of such an organization is often that it has a very large board. The board processes themselves often do not work, so one often hears the remark: the company policy is X, but of course I am not personally in support of this, I believe we should be doing Y. Since industrial success depends totally on getting the concentration of effort of widely differing groups of people with different skills to be applied at optimum effect to the achievement of the common goal, it is not difficult to see why such disparate messages strike at one's heart and give one a more than usual dose of despair. After all it is bad enough when you think you know what ought to be done, and instead it is decided to do something quite different. But it is infinitely worse if you are so divided that it is apparent you cannot take any action at all. This leads very quickly to the 'hoping something turns up' syndrome which is anathema to most managers.

The messages which start differently through each of the functions, and become even more disparate when relayed (because of the lack of commitment at board level), go through an endless chain of levels. They go through at least twice as many levels as they would in faster, more effective organizations. No man is complete without his deputy or deputies. More recently management theory has poured scorn on organizations which feature 'one on one' systems. They tend to favour a minimum of two or three reporting to one man at a level above them. This has led inevitably to situations where everyone has two or three deputies instead of none at all.

The endless levels might appear, superficially, to hold great promise of promotion for an ambitious man. In such an organization there is a constant movement of people through the outfit because of this plethora of layers. The achievement of such movement becomes an aim in itself. Unfortunately, as we know all too often, the players in the game of musical chairs are only a small part of the total group. The company rapidly becomes divided into two companies, one of which comprises the hewers of wood and carriers of water who are toiling away and actually achieving the relatively little that the company can achieve; while the others, a separate band, although quite possibly a band of high potential in actual business terms, are playing the game of political musical chairs. The constant movement is, of course, extremely bad in terms of the effectiveness of the company externally. The managers, in each area, have seldom had as much experience as their competitors. A lot of time is spent 'getting to know the new man', and the new man's characteristics. In my own case, from 1957 when I joined ICI until 1973 when I was appointed to the board, I had no fewer than nine jobs. Nine jobs in sixteen years gave me an average of almost two years in each job. I was therefore always just working in and becoming established with my boss, my staff, my customers and my competitors when I moved on. In my opinion it is very doubtful whether all this disruption to so many people was justified by the experience I gained.

Your boss, or your boss's deputy boss, changes every two to three years. Each change introduces other variants of how to do the job, seldom if ever a total change of direction, although even that has been known to happen. Enough disruption to ensure that the place is in a continual ferment of reorganization which in other companies may well be a good thing to have. Reorganization and change are a feature of the switched-on company, but the reorganizations and changes come from recognized broad strategic needs and are explicable. They do not arise from the continuous political efforts of managers who, hoping they will have a short tenure of office, try to make their mark by some evident organizational change.

Another feature of such a company is the 'bums and heroes' syndrome. Organizations like this are not good at remembering the things you have done well and if, as most of us are, you are at the bottom of the pile, you will find that you are considered to be alternately either the best thing since sliced bread, or a liability to the organization. As each new incumbent arrives in the levels above you he will have a different idea from his predecessor as to how things should be done. Inevitably, if you pleased the predecessor you will displease the new man.

In the bad organization the remuneration system is manifestly unfair. The remuneration system depends first of all, to some degree, on 'Buggins' turn', and the discretionary element which is a feature of most remuneration systems these days is entirely based on pleasing your boss of the moment. The golden boys, those who never give the bad news, who make sure that when the plant breaks down they are not available to inform anybody, and have made absolutely certain they weren't around during the run-up to such a disaster, are rewarded. The individuals who are recognized by their peers as those who actually keep the thing going, are not only unrewarded, but actually held back. Not for them promotion. They are 'too valuable' in the job which they are doing.

An interesting fact of large industrial organizations is that there is always a nearly unanimous clarity amongst those involved at the lower levels on who it is who is actually keeping the thing going, because in every organization somebody is. In far too many companies this is viewed as being somebody well down the line, very frequently a section manager, who is 'the only one you can get a decision out of', or 'the only one who actually knows'. The hierarchy which actually exists bears little resemblance to the way in which the thing actually works. Since ultimately everybody has to achieve something, enormous amounts of time are spent round the formal organization in order to achieve the little that is achieved. The informal organization is well recognized by everybody except those above it. It is well recognized because unless you have managed to work out how things actually happen you have no chance of achieving anything at all.

The sad thing about all the comments I have made so far is that in even the best organizations you can recognize one or more of these undesirable characteristics. What we don't see so often, however, is an attempt (when the characteristic is recognized by management and leadership) to correct it, or to understand why it exists and to try to set in train processes and plans to change these undesirable attributes. It is really quite extraordinary that this doesn't happen. In even the worst-run factory, faults on the production line are speedily recognized: even if there is not enough money to effect the ideal repair, something is done almost immediately. In even the worst-run sales department, the danger that you are going to lose a key sale is recognized and every effort is made, within the limited headroom that you have, to try and retain it.

Why is it that there is such total myopia in business about the things that lead to the release of human energy and talent? Why is it that we can look at organizations which we ourselves have worked in for most of our lives, where we have complained bitterly, where over drinks with our colleagues or at the Christmas pantomime or some other time we have given vent to our

irritation at these bad organizational and behavioural characteristics; and yet when we reach high positions in companies we
consider them to be something which is beyond our capability
to influence? It is almost as though bad organizations are self-
created Frankenstein monsters beyond the control or influence
of leaders.

I think part of the reason for this collective blindness or, more
accurately perhaps, this collective lack of action, is that we lack
conviction that many of these problems are solvable, and we
lack understanding of what actually can be and needs to be done
to correct them. It is true that the corrective measures that can be
taken do not usually have an immediate response, and that in
many cases they appear to be quite small actions, relative to the
size of the problem with which you are grappling. Nevertheless, nothing ever changes unless a conscious effort is made to
change it and no organization will make it happen unless its
people at all levels are switched on.

Let us go through some of the main features we discussed
earlier and consider some of the actions that can be taken to
correct them. First, the objective. In the last chapter I described
some of the iterative processes we carry out to try to ensure that
the objective is clear, understood, and has been achieved with a
large amount of involvement throughout the whole organization. Even when a clear objective has been achieved (and by a
clear objective I really mean a single sentence which everybody
can carry in their minds and which everybody can understand),
it is necessary to ensure that this is known, understood and
accepted at every level of the organization.

The achievement of such simplicity and clarity is not easy. It
means shaving away constantly at the sort of multiple objectives
which we normally like to set ourselves, until one reaches an
absolutely clear message of a mission and role. It could be, for
example, 'Achieve technical leadership in your field'. It could
be, 'Operate to maximize cash flow into the parent company'. It
could be, 'Operate within X and Y financial parameters and
develop the Chinese market'. Whatever it is, it needs to have
been thrashed out endlessly with the top leadership of the
business and to be able to be expressed in a single, understandable, clear and unambiguous sentence. The ideal organization
and the one which has the best chance of success is one where, if

you ask anybody from the chairman down to the newest recruit on the shop floor what that business is trying to do, you'd get the same answer. The answer need not have exactly the same words as your prize sentence, but the answer must indicate clarity at every level.

Clarity, ownership of the objective, and widespread knowledge of it only come from endless repetition and endless iteration and endless checking that the objective is still possible, and relevant. Your people will be switched off the moment the objective that you have set appears to be unobtainable. They will strive and fight for an end, even if they think there is only a small chance of success. But the stage at which they come to believe there is no way in which they can achieve the aim is the stage at which you need to re-examine the objective that the business has been set. You need, first of all, to have a sufficiently open system to know that this change has occurred, and secondly to be willing to acknowledge the change, and go through the whole exercise again. In such an open system individuals will feel secure enough to question directly with everyone concerned whether the objective is realistic. In closed systems the fear of being considered faint-hearted, or uninvolved, or unsupportive prevents such doubts being voiced at all. The good leader has his ear to the ground and will know the stage at which real doubts are growing. He can raise the issue by voicing his own increasing doubts about the achievability of the goal and can check very quickly whether he is trampled underfoot in the rush to agree, or scoffed at for his lack of understanding.

The second area to turn attention to after the objective, is this whole area of stretch. The demands made on people need always to be heavy. They need to be understood and to be considered and honest. One of our major industrial problems is that we usually do not ask enough of our people. People at all levels of the organization can accomplish very much more than they are asked to under contemporary conventions. You have only got to see what your people can achieve when you are in an enormous period of expansion. Some of us have only got to look back to what was achieved by people during the last war. I was at sea as an officer in the Navy by my seventeenth birthday. I was the second in command of a submarine before I was twenty-one. My captain at that time was aged twenty-four. One has seen people from the shop floor sent to help start up plants overseas, and seen them rapidly take responsibilities far beyond those which they had been given in their home organization. When occasions have occurred, as they do in all organizations, where it is necessary to take a 'big' risk on a young man whose experience and background we think inadequate for the task, nine times out of ten not only does he rise to the occasion but he does even better than we would expect.

Looking back I am constantly amazed and grateful for the high risks that others took by giving me responsibility in my early years in ICI. Indeed I have often chided myself with the realization that I have not lived up to the standards that they set. I remember, for example, being sent for just after I joined the Heavy Organic Chemicals division, and asked by the then chairman of the division, Tom Clarke, to take charge of a company mission to investigate the price of naphtha. Naphtha at that time represented half of our total costs, and was bought by central purchasing in London. The division, which prided itself on its knowledge of the oil companies and the oil world, believed (as it subsequently proved, with some justification) that we were paying more for our naphtha than we strictly needed to do. There had been an immense row inside ICI, and it had been agreed that a mission should be sent round the world to investigate the actuality of the situation. I had been in the division only about three months, and barely knew what naphtha was. It had not been my direct responsibility to purchase it and I was operating in a field where everyone else – the companies from which I might buy, those from which we now bought, and the management of the division – was an expert. Nevertheless, with all my lack of experience, the chairman of the division unhesitatingly gave me the responsibility for leading the mission, and it proved to be a turning point in my career. Perhaps because I was unaware of the enormity of the task I had been set, I went at it with tremendous dash and verve, and together with my two colleagues, nominated from other parts of the company, visited no less than twenty companies in eight countries in three weeks. The results formed a report which was out within a month, and which led to far-reaching changes in our company's approach to the problem. I learnt an enormous amount during this process, and I am sure that the company benefited from the results of the mission. All the same, I doubt very much that when I was in a comparable situation I would have had the same faith and determination that Tom did.

The reality is that we are conservative in our appreciation of others' abilities and we are reticent and uncertain about our own. Not only is it necessary organizationally to stretch others, but it is also necessary that we should stretch ourselves. How many times have you told yourself you could not do something but when you ultimately faced up and had a go, to your amazement you succeeded. The art of 'growing people' lies to a great degree in this stretching process. First, everybody in a well-run organization should feel himself under some pressure. Nothing is worse for young people when they start work, particularly if they join large companies, than to spend a year or so sitting with Nelly before they are trusted to do anything. A characteristic I look for is that young people coming just out of university should be frightened by the responsibility they are given, rather than bored by the lack of demand that is made on them. People's self-confidence grows when they achieve more. Each time they achieve more, an even more ambitious or difficult target needs to be set. I am firmly of the belief that most people in this world achieve only a fraction of what they are capable. Indeed one of the great worries that I have about life in general is the lack of growth which so many of our admirable people, particularly those who have not achieved educational qualifications, actually manage during their working lives. One sees again and again that such people grow in outside interests. Some time ago I commented in an article that too many people sought their main interests outside their work. This was not actually what I meant but it was reported as a sort of 'leadership whinge' and general complaint.

If we do not stretch people enough at work it is inevitable that they will do more outside. It is the responsibility of the leadership and the management to give opportunities and put demands on people which enable them to grow as human beings in their work environment. Many people have such potential energy and ability that even the most demanding work environment cannot stop them achieving recognition and expertise in other areas. I, for one, certainly would not wish to put people under so much pressure that they never have time to read a non-work book or attend a concert, or pursue a hobby, or do worthwhile work in the environment or the community. These are features of life that are needed for a balance. It is because there is so much potential in individuals that even the largest degree of stretch that we can put on them still leaves plenty more capacity, provided it is applied gradually, like stretching elastic; and I believe this is a prime feature of an organization which utilizes the skills of its people.

The next area is headroom. The headroom that is available is partly a feature of the number of layers, but also a feature of the tolerance and openness of the environment in which we operate, an element which we seek to encourage. It is important, because controls in large organizations are cumulative, that quite regularly one should examine the control systems in force, and clear out as many as possible. In my own company we recently made a bonfire of our control systems. The board now seek control on only the parameters of profit, cash and broad strategic direction. We seek to influence in many other ways. But in terms of actual control, we have forsworn many other areas where hitherto we sought to control by centralized edict. In the past we sought to monitor and control all the major variables in a business. We sought, irrespective of the relevance to the particular concern, to measure improvements in the use of energy, the productivity of capital, the numbers employed and improvement in productivity and so on. The point is that many of these specific areas of functional excellence are not independent of each other and improvements in one area may be at the cost of worsening in another. What matters is the ultimate profit, and if it can be increased by employing some more salesmen so be it, even if the numbers go in the wrong way. Such judgements, however, are best made as close to the action as possible rather than on a theoretical basis a long way away.

Paradoxically, my own company has always given plenty of headroom, but not everyone perceived it thus. In my early days, I had merely assumed, since I knew so little of industry, that I was employed to achieve certain ends. As I now recognize, I trampled happily across many unwritten preserves of others and must have sorely tested both my superiors and my peers. However, I was lucky enough to have joined a tolerant company that believed in giving people a chance. At no time can I remember ever being stopped from pursuing an objective which was of ultimate potential gain to the company. In our case I believe this stems both from the traditions of our company and also from the fact that we are a technical and scientifically based company: we therefore have the respect for the individual and the respect for novel ideas emanating from others that is a feature of the scientific method. I know of many other companies and organizations which do not, however, operate in this way.

Despite the openness and tolerance of our company, the possession of too many layers in the organization inevitably reduces the perception of the headroom that exists, and means that people put more effort into internal argument than external achievement. One of the early steps that I and my colleagues took was to encourage the removal of intermediate layers, and to try to apply the theory of 'added value' to hierarchical organization. This means that we should only add another layer of management if there was a unique extra job which would increase the value of the whole. Such job descriptions as 'supervise', 'advise' and 'coordinate' do not add value to that while the people can do so on their own. We started, and indeed I started, by removing all deputies in the organization, and then trying to persuade others to ensure that another hierarchical layer in the tree only occurred when there was a quite measurably different job to be done from the layer below it. Any job description which started off by describing the job as being 'supervision of others' was ruthlessly destroyed. Unless we could discern some clear difference between the task to be performed between the levels, including that of the board, we sought to get it eliminated. Not only did this operation result in vastly increased headroom, but it also, interestingly enough, led to vastly improved communications. I remember asking on the shop floor of a division, the board of which had been reduced from fifteen to four, what the major difference was felt to be down the line, and was told, to my surprise, that the biggest difference was that they now knew what was going on. This was not because the fifteen previous board members had sought to prevent communication, but in fact was purely because the news was always the same and there was much more identity of message coming from the top. This identity of message was recognized down the line, and had the effect that one would have expected.

The point of headroom is that those above should act as a support rather than as a control. The control and supervision must be done discreetly and quietly and hopefully even without the awareness of those who are being supervised. It is essential in a well-run company that in addition to the feeling of plenty of headroom and space to create and carry out one's job, there should be absolute confidence that those above will support one and that one can always look to them as a resource or as a help. If the burden becomes too much and the responsibilities too great, one must always feel that one can turn to somebody who is more knowledgeable, or has broader shoulders and who will share the burden.

The burden should be shared but the burden should not be taken away. If it is taken away one will never grow. If it is shared then trust and confidence will grow between the manager and his subordinate. Equally, support should come not only from one's immediate boss, who should be seen as a resource, rather than as a boss. I hope that as chairman of ICI the contribution that I can make is to be looked upon by people on all levels as someone whose experience they can call on at any time. Indeed I am always immensely flattered when somebody a long way down our hierarchy rings me up and asks me to do something which they believe I am in a particularly good position to do. It may be they know that I am meeting somebody they are trying to affect through his hierarchy; or it may be they need to find out something which they think I am in a better position to find out than they are. That is an admirable use of my time and a tribute to the openness of the system.

The support should also be available in a lateral sense. This support will become more readily available from parallel functions such as accounts, or selling or marketing or production or research, if all of you are crystal clear what the objective is. The support from one's functional colleagues requires first of all a high degree of mutuality of respect for each other's expertise and a shared acceptance of the objective that you are trying to achieve.

But even that is not quite enough. There is a need for

receptiveness to new ideas as opposed to the instantaneous rejection which is our normal British heritage. It is only in the United Kingdom that the word 'new' is not an instant recipe for making a sale. The word 'new' tends to mean untried, risky, scatterbrained, probably unworkable. The word 'new' actually means opportunity, the possibility of the removal of a constraint, the possibility of achieving competitive advantage, the possibility of moving faster in the direction which we have set.

But receptivity to new ideas is best achieved in organizations which have mutuality of trust where it is known that you will not be too harshly blamed for mistakes. Tolerance of mistakes cannot be infinite, and mistakes vary a lot in kind. But mistakes which are made in an attempt to change things, to introduce the new, to progress faster, deserve and should receive high degrees of tolerance and sometimes even praise. For many years I had the somewhat perverse view that instead of rewarding the salesman who always got the business, we should reward the one who lost it. This derived from my own sad experience when I was selling. Those who have not tried to sell – and particularly sell in a highly competitive market where there are very large contracts, the possession or loss of which can have a fatal effect on one's whole business – do not know how testing it is of courage and nerve.

I remember on one occasion having strained my own courage to the absolute limit on a contract worth £10 million, which at that time was very large indeed, in order to obtain another £200,000. I spent a week on the rack, far away from home, constantly trying to achieve this extra margin which, I hardly need to point out, would have gone straight down to the bottom line and would have been shown as profit. As the week went on I got more and more anguished telegrams from home telling me to conclude the deal and come home. But I was still convinced that we could get the extra £200,000. On the fifty-ninth minute of the twenty-third hour, as I was leaving the country, I finally achieved the contract. I felt exhausted, worn out, but very triumphant. When I got back to base, instead of being welcomed as the returning hero I thought myself to be, I was asked what had taken me so long. When I replied that I had been fighting for the extra £200,000 I had managed to achieve, I was remonstrated with for having put the business at risk.

If we wish to encourage risk taking, we have to be prepared to accept and recognize that people will fail. Particularly in the area of sales, the salesman who always gets the sale is almost certainly selling too soft. The task of the salesman is both to establish an ongoing relationship with his customer, and also to charge as close as possible to what the market will bear. Such a calculation is not a perfect one, and there is bound to be a failure from time to time if you are really trying to achieve that objective.

The next prerequisite with a switched-on organization is perhaps the most difficult of all to achieve in a British environment, and this is openness of communication. I touched earlier on some of the reasons why we find open behaviour in this country so difficult and I believe it is partly to do with emotion. Communication without emotion is almost impossible. Yet of all people the British seem to take the greatest pride in suppression of emotion. From one's earliest years one is taught that the showing of emotion publicly is 'bad form'. I do not mean by this that I expect managers to cry, or to clasp one another like footballers after a goal has been won. But I do expect to have a lot of laughter, I do expect to have a relaxed and open atmosphere. I do expect occasionally to have temper, because it is only when we are discussing the right subjects that temper will arise: if people lose their tempers it is because they are emotionally involved in the problem, and we are probably talking on a subject which needs to be aired. Somehow or other one has to make flattery, or play-acting at agreement, more dangerous than argument. Argument will only grow in a large organization if it is actually encouraged, and if the example is given from the top with courteous listening and praise for differences of view. It is even more essential, when for some reason the opposite view that is being expressed is not being accepted, to take extreme care to make it known how much you appreciate the views being expressed by the individual.

We have to have a far greater tolerance of difference and a far greater respect for differences of view. I have said many times I do not wish to hire yes-men. Yes-men come cheap. There is no need to pay high salaries to people who will continually agree. What we are looking for is what I call constructive no-men. My own personal rule for very many years has been that anybody is free to criticize me, to criticize the company, to question or argue

against anything that we are trying to do – provided they will
satisfy the one criterion that they will tell us what I or the
company should do differently. I have no time for bitching.
Continual moaning and criticism of others gets you nowhere.
But the sort of criticism that says 'if we want to achieve X, I
believe we are going the wrong way about it, what we ought to
be doing is Y', seems to me to be exactly the approach that is
needed. It should be possible for anybody in the organization at
any level to make such a suggestion. Even if the suggestion that
is made is not feasible, it should be listened to with courtesy and
responded to with the respect that such an offer demands. It is
not easy in a country as hierarchically inclined as ours to
continually question authority in a constructive way. It requires
a lot of faith to believe that such questioning will actually be
recognized, liked and rewarded.

The cultivation of openness in a large organization needs a lot
of things. Above everything it needs an example from the top
and a readiness to be critical of polite praise and to insist
continuously on the bad news. It needs the development of
shared values, and above everything, of mutuality of respect. It
needs the recognition that the enemy is without our organization, and not within it. I spend enormous amounts of time
trying to develop this characteristic in my company. I try to set
an example, and I am more than willing to accept any degree of
personal criticism and, indeed, get a lot of it – some of it rather
hurtful. But the prize is so infinitely rewarding and so badly
needed that a little hurt surely should be acceptable on the way.

The next area is the rewards system. I am personally very
interested in sociology, and sociological work. Although this
appears to be a field of management studies that is going out of
fashion, nevertheless I think one disregards the work of sociologists at one's peril. Certainly my own personal experience
tends to confirm Herzberg's theory that monetary reward is not
of itself an incentive, but poor or unfair reward is a major
disincentive. There is a growing belief that payment by results
schemes or reward linked to achievement of goals is an unleash-
ing factor and it certainly appears at the present time to be
working that way. But I do not believe that financial rewards are
themselves enough or are important except in the Herzberg
terms. Rewards which are perceived to be unfairly distributed

are a major switch-off. Relative rewards within the organization, unless demonstrably fairly apportioned, have the same
effect. Fortunately in real life this is not always as difficult as it
might appear. There is almost always total consensus in an
organization on the best and the worst performance, although
there is rarely any agreement at all about the ranking of the
group in between.

In the reward area, I believe public recognition is almost as
important as financial reward. Public praise is very seldom
given in the industrial world. Very seldom is enthusiasm
shown, or thanks given. We are quick enough to admonish and
complain and rebuke, but all too seldom do we actually give
praise when either an outstanding achievement has been made,
or even more rarely, when an outstanding effort has been made
but has not succeeded. Yet the effect of these things is totally
disproportionate. We have in my company a system of good
work bonuses which are totally unsystematized. They involve
quite substantial amounts of money at any time for a task which
we consider has been especially well done, usually, in fairness,
further than we would expect just for the execution of the job.
The receipt of such a bonus has an effect far outside the regular
annual rise, which again in the case of ICI is a matter of such
Byzantine complexity that it is often difficult to know whether
one is getting a good or a bad one! The importance of the good
work bonus, or the public recognition, is in its very
unexpectedness.

I make a habit of sending a certain number of cases of wine
each year to individuals at any level of the company who have
done something which I have come across which seems to be
particularly meritorious. I send it to the individual's home and I
include a personal note from me thanking him for his achievement. This kind of recognition seems to me to be as important in
its own way as the lavish rewards which American companies
give on complicated criteria.

I am not against linking rewards to achievement: rather the
reverse. But one must recognize that whatever system one puts
in has only got a limited life before it becomes irrelevant, and if
the payment is for achievement it must do just that. Lack of
achievement must result in reduction of reward. On the other
hand, I believe that in the area of remuneration it is the

avoidance of unfairness which is the most important single
factor, and the ability to reward and publicly acknowledge outstanding effort in ways which are cost effective seems to me to
be another important feature. Because in the United Kingdom
companies have not been influenced sufficiently, I believe, by
the problem of rewarding their shareholders and therefore have
tended not to pay enough attention to their stock prices, I am
very much in favour of share option schemes. Apart from
anything else, this gives the individual manager the best chance
of building some capital, and the problem of a large organization as opposed to the self-employed lies in the area of capital
accumulation. Capital accumulation is a relatively easy matter
for the self-employed but is almost impossible for the professional manager to achieve out of income. Unless we can get
professional managers who are as good entrepreneurially as
those who set up for themselves we shall have major problems
ahead.

What most of the foregoing amounts to is that in the organization that switches its people on, the individual is king. He feels
that he is trusted, respected as an individual, treated as one and
rewarded as one, and that it is his individuality that is needed:
his individual contribution, rather than conformity to some sort
of ideal 'company man'. I had the privilege of being interviewed
for *Desert Island Discs* some time ago, by the late Roy Plomley,
and his opening remark switched me off a treat. He introduced
me by saying in that courteous and gentle way of his: 'Our guest
this week is an industrialist, a company man.' I immediately
froze. I froze not because I am not proud to have worked for my
company, and indeed consider myself fortunate to have done
so – and not because I do not admire my company and put
everything that I can into serving it. Indeed my wife believes
that if when I die I am cut in half, the letters I C I will be found
stamped through me from top to bottom, like Blackpool rock.
What I reacted against, and what others will also react against, is
the implication that one's contribution is important only insofar
as it conforms to a company picture, and that it is not the
individual's unique and personal contribution that matters. I
pride myself on the efforts I have made to retain my individual
values while working for my company. I honour my company
for its willingness to accept me and my idiosyncrasies. It takes a

pretty tolerant company to put up with my taste in ties, for example.

It is this that one is seeking to transmit and show, and it is this which is the key to the wholehearted and free contribution of the individual. We must always remember that there is nothing that compels anybody to work for an individual company even in an era of high unemployment. You owe it to yourself and to your family to move on elsewhere if you are not satisfied that the objectives are worthwhile or if the prospects are insufficiently good. We therefore have to make the company one in which the individual feels wanted, needed and respected. Fortunately it is in the company's interests so to do, because it is only by such means that the free, wholehearted collaboration of free men can be enlisted.

There is one other characteristic that I would like to mention. It helps enormously if the external regard for your organization is high. It needs particularly to be so in the communities in which you operate. Again, in our case it is an absolute requirement that we should have the support of the localities in which we place our factories. Not everybody wishes to live near a chemical factory. We have to recognize that it is our responsibility to ensure that the natural fears and concerns that people have are allayed. We require also to recruit and motivate the best people and this in turn requires a good reputation, not only for the goods we make and the worthiness of our contribution to society, but also the way in which we do these things, the sort of people we employ and the contributions we make in the area, and whether we are good citizens or not. As with so many things in the industrial life, many of these aims are self-reinforcing. The best people are recognized as readily outside the company as within it. The best people involve themselves in their communities and you will find them playing a role disproportionate to their total numbers in such fields as education, the arts, local government and so on.

These are all parts of the switch-on mechanism because the switch-on mechanism depends upon a decent organization employing decent people and treating them as we individually would wish to be treated. That is the difference between switching on and switching off, and switching on is an absolutely essential ingredient to the art of making it happen.

4

The How

In my philosophy of management it follows that if the strategic objective has been worked out together and agreed, and the right conditions have been created in which people can be switched on, the 'how' of what is to be achieved is a matter for delegation. After all the whole purpose of agreeing the strategic objective has been to transfer the ownership to those who must achieve it. I tried to show in the last chapter that an essential part of the switching-on mechanism is headroom and the ability to do things in your own way without endless restraint by those above you. All of these things are self-reinforcing and form a sort of virtuous circle. The agreement of the strategic objective with a lot of interaction and discussion has the key effect of switching on people, and the full delegation of the 'how' both derives from switched-on people, and also reinforces it. It also, in turn, makes the agreement of the strategic objective much easier.

In the 'how', which one might describe as the 'tactics' of business, there are many more ways of achieving the objective than in either of the other two areas that we have discussed so far. Almost by definition, no one of these ways will be exclusively the right one. I hope that no reader takes the term 'tactics' as being in any way derogatory or pejorative, since really good execution on one key parameter can often deliver. The key to tactical success is really in the ownership of the tactics, and the absolute determination and commitment of those carrying them out. Just as in matters of war one has seen case after case where numerically far smaller forces, often less well equipped, have completely overwhelmed the enemy, so in achieving tactical business objectives the same rules apply. The problem really lies not in the exactness of the methods that are to be chosen and used, but in the ownership of the plan, and this ownership must be transferred methodically and skilfully from the leader to his team.

I remember when I was appointed as deputy chairman responsible for the Wilton site in the late 1960s. The site had been characterized by almost total lack of cohesion in the management team, and as a result we had lost all ability as a group to influence our work force. There was a common feeling prevalent at the time that the site was really run by the shop stewards. They were a tightly knit team who were absolutely clear about their aims. The problem was clear for all of us to see. The objective was not in doubt but we had always failed on the tactics for the simple reason that the managers did not feel that they 'owned' theirs. I remember chairing my first meeting of the works managers, who were the key management representatives on the site. They were all friends of long standing and I had worked with, or for, most of them at one time or another. As I took the chair one of them said, 'Well John, we're glad you've come, things will be all right now. Just tell us what to do and we'll do it.' My predecessors had tried every sort of management style, from the dictatorship style that my colleague was advocating, to the extremes of democratic consensus.

I remember replying, 'No, that's absolutely wrong, if I tell you what to do I know you won't do it because you never have in the past, so I don't see why you should start now. We're going to decide what to do together, and I think enough of you all to know that if you have actually taken part in the decision, and if you share the responsibility for it, you are going to be dedicated to it, and share the responsibility for making sure it doesn't fail.' From that day on things got better. We spent hours discussing the tactics until we were sure that we could live with them, and at no time, no matter what the pressures, did any of the team let the others down. I had succeeded in transferring the 'ownership'.

I have many mottoes which I have used in my business life, and one which never fails to irritate is that 'the best is the enemy of the good'. In companies with high morale there is an understandable wish always to do the best and to set the highest standards. Indeed the search after the best, as well as being the subject of many books, has very frequently been taken as the key to high morale. Certainly I do not wish to lead any business organization which does not aspire to be, ultimately, the best in its own field, and have always held the ultimate aim for ICI to be the world's best chemical company. But there is a trade-off between speed and ease of achievement, and the endless search after the consensus recognition of perfection. Indeed, in the sort of committed style of management which I seek so many people are involved that it is almost impossible to reach agreement on what is the best. Here the composition and balance of the team is a most important factor. Just as an exclusive diet of caviar would be boring and unhealthy, so teams need a broad mixture of abilities and personal qualities. Teams of superstars, each outstanding in their own area, seldom win, largely because their ability to analyse and criticize is high and their vanity and intelligence frequently make them bad listeners. This is almost the worst combination since their high intelligence and knowledge of their superiority in their own field makes it very difficult for them to accept any compromise in their own area of knowledge. Abandoning the purity of a position they know to be right is extraordinarily difficult, and the belief in the importance of the shared aim is often not high enough to make such a 'sacrifice' worthwhile. An interesting example of this happened at the Industrial Society Industry Year jamboree at the Albert Hall where three teams, one of young people, one of chief executives and one of trade union leaders, competed against each other to build a wall with lettered building blocks to form a slogan. I bet that the youngsters would win, purely on the certainty that they would see winning and the completion of the task as the prime aim, and would not have so much previous reputation and pride to risk – and so it was. The young team triumphantly romped home with the other two far behind!

Many years ago, during the Korean war, I was shipped out aboard a troopship, the *Empire Foy*, to join HMS *Amethyst* in the Far East. I had just left a long period in intelligence, and had not served aboard a surface ship of the regular Navy since the early 1940s. I found, to my horror, that I was the senior naval officer aboard and was responsible for the draft of about a hundred and twenty sailors who were going out to join the ships of the Far East fleet. The sailors on board were totally outnumbered by two thousand soldiers of proud regiments who were going to reinforce the armies in Malaya and Korea. A rather alarming number of my sailors were being shipped out to the Far East for their own good, and indeed some of them arrived under escort. Once I had got the whole lot on board and we had cast off, on what was then a six-week voyage, I got them together and said, 'We are sailors. Maybe this troopship isn't very much like the ships we served in and know, but we are going to win every single contest on board this ship. We are going to be the smartest, our mess decks are going to be the cleanest, and we are going to win every competition there is, because this is our element, and it doesn't matter if we are outnumbered by twenty to one, we know we can do it.' We did indeed achieve just that. We even, to my absolute amazement, won the tug of war, which once again taught me that concentrated, committed determination can overcome what appear to be insuperable physical odds. It was a matter of reinforcing our record on each occasion – one has seen the same thing with winning football teams. Ashore, of course, it was quite another matter and after each stop on the way out a number of my chaps would return, to catch the ship by the skin of their teeth, battered from their escapades in Port Said, or Aden, or Colombo. On board, however, which we had decided was our element, we won the whole time.

It is from this kind of discussion, iteration and involvement that the Japanese have derived their ability to win on the industrial front. Those of us who have worked with the Japanese and who admire their business achievements, as I do, know how long it takes the Japanese to reach a decision. One is lulled into a totally false sense of security by the apparently endless debate and the thoroughness of the involvement of people at every level of the organization in the decision, because when the action stage comes they move like greased lightning. Far faster than we do. Some years ago we licensed a process to build a paraxylene plant to the Japanese and as part of the deal put an engineer in with their design team. We were simultaneously building an identical one in the U K and we had each taken the decision to go ahead at the same time. After four months we were already breaking ground and priding ourselves on being well ahead of the Far Eastern opposition who, according to our engineer, were still endlessly debating items of the design and equipment. Imagine then our chagrin when not only did they complete their plant seven months before us, but also it worked at first go while ours suffered the usual teething troubles and only achieved its flowsheet some three months after start-up.

The Japanese do their planning while forming the plan. They get their commitment in the process of discussing the 'how'. When the whistle is blown – usually, from the point of view of a European, long after we would have made up our minds what should be done – they are able to move with a speed, concentration and understanding of each other's roles and problems which outshine even the fastest moving of European companies. It is, of course, a fact that this approach to management draws many of its strengths from the Japanese character, which in turn derives from the physical conditions under which that dedicated and hard-working race has emerged. In Japan the ability to work together in groups is admired much more than individualism, and the ability to lead groups and inspire them is considered, in my belief rightly, to be a much greater sign of manhood and effectiveness than the ability to lead by dictatorial methods and fear.

In the countries of the West the individual has always been king, despite, in the case of Great Britain, our national need to conform and our admiration of social prototypes. The fact that both by inclination and education we have sought to encourage difference and individual initiative, rather than the ability to work as groups, means that the achievement of this style of managing and working requires much more effort on our part and much more learning. We have to look no further than the field of sport to see how foreign teamwork is to the British nature. Real cohesion and the ability to work as a team only occurs as a result of great effort in their development. Be it cricket or football, all too often British sportsmen tend to perform as a group of different people, rather than submerging their individuality in order for the team to win. Only inspired captaincy and unremitting work can overcome this tendency in our national teams, and so it is in business also.

Other Western countries each have their own national characteristics, and some value cohesive working more than others. I would think that the United Kingdom is probably towards the extreme of the individual end of the spectrum, whereas Germany and the USA, while valuing the individual contribution, both show a considerable respect and regard for the ability to work together as teams. American industrial tactics are often signified by a series of 'programs', and despite the high individualism of that country, they still show an ability to organize, systematize, and deliver, which is in some ways a close parallel to the Japanese.

In the late 1960s, as I remarked earlier, I was given by I C I the task of trying to unite the management on a large and important site. As I said at the time, we could barely have organized a site, which depended for its economic success on the greatest possible cooperation between the various plants and factories, in a way which made this more difficult to achieve. We had at that time some seven profit-accountable divisions working there, and not infrequently one division's profit represented another division's loss. The divisions in I C I, although proud to belong to the group, all had different traditions and different ways of doing things, as well as quite different ways of accounting and approaches to technology. The problem that faced me was how to unite the management while accepting the realities of the business organization which the group wished to continue. I sought around at great length for various forms of educational and management training which we could apply ourselves to, to create some greater mutuality of respect amongst the different operating units, as well as giving me the opportunity to try to work with them in more detailed ways so that they knew the personnel director, Brian Jenkins, and me better as individuals and understood what we were trying to do.

After exhaustive searches through all the different training systems and management theories which were around at the time we plumped for the Coverdale System, which was a British invention developed by a management genius called Ralph Coverdale. From our point of view the course had many advantages. It was very action-orientated, it was a management system which, although it had its fair share of management jargon, nevertheless used English jargon rather than American jargon. It was short, lasting only three days, and it taught by exposing the practitioners to experiences from which they learnt, rather than trying to lecture or produce the 'ideal' model. The outcome and output of the course consisted of a number of important lessons, and I guess each one of us who attended it

took away rather different things. First, I gained an understanding of the importance of process, and process planning,
secondly a realization that listening is an art and a skill and
needs to be developed, and thirdly an understanding that
almost invariably businessmen seek to go into action far too
early – before they have actually discussed, analysed, and
decided what they are going to do.

We businessmen are an international race of little wind-up,
instant action men, and indeed so anxious are we for achievement that we are often well down the road on an inadequately
thought-out basis while others, more prudent than we, have
stopped to think. The lessons of the Coverdale course were
legion. Not only did you learn from practical experience while
playing what seemed to be rather silly games, that reflection
was better than action, but you also learnt that in teams each of
you has a role to play, and it is not always the most obviously
well equipped who can best work out the problem. I remember
to this day that we played one particular management game.
We were given a certain number of Lego bricks and were told to
design an edifice based on a rather complicated scoring system
for different characteristics of the edifice which we built. In our
team, as well as myself, we had an eminent construction
engineer, who seemed to us to be the ideal man to put in charge
of design. We also had a foreman who had three children of
'Lego' age and was an absolute expert with his hands and at
assembly. The tasks were allocated so that the construction
engineer would design, and the foreman would build, and we
set ourselves about the problems of planning. The designer
produced some elaborate mathematics, which we all debated
earnestly, tending, as I recollect, to ignore the foreman's inter-
jections and assistance as being unworthy of such a high level of
intellectual debate. The construction engineer started with an
in-built belief that the project was impossible and that there
were not enough bricks, and most of the debate set out to
demonstrate this. The foreman, understandably miffed at the
lack of acceptance of his contribution, withdrew from the
group. He went to the small table which we had set apart as our
construction site and started playing with the bricks. The design
team (where we were all following like sheep the logic of the
construction engineer, that the project was impossible, and that

it was a trap) decided that we should go to the directing staff and point out that we needed more bricks. While this was going on the foreman completed the building, which in the event proved to be the best submission of any group!

Apart from the many lessons in this simple homily, what happened next was even more interesting because the construction engineer, faced with this irrefutable challenge to his authority, lost his temper and stormed out of the room, announcing that he thought the whole course was nonsense, and that he was not going to waste his time any further, and intended to go home. The rest of us crowded round the foreman, congratulating him, and hurriedly trying to make amends for our own lack of respect for his abilities, and feeling extremely foolish at having followed what had been so clearly demonstrated to be the wrong theory. It was only after we had been congratulating him and seeking to expiate our own sins for some time that we belatedly realized that in losing the construction engineer, not only from the project, but also from the whole course, we had, as a group, had a major failure. In the nick of time a couple of us rushed out, grabbed a taxi, hurried to the railway station and were just in time to haul the still-smouldering construction engineer from the train. In order to persuade him to stay it was necessary to stop at several bars on the way, but eventually we got him back to the group.

In many ways just that one simple game contained in it practically all the lessons that one needed about teamwork, involvement, mutuality of respect, the ability to recognize contributions no matter where they came from, the importance of multiple skills, and the need to stay together, and produce a solution which was good enough. I am sure that our edifice was not the best possible, in fact I know it was not, but it was good enough in the circumstances, and the important thing was to have achieved the construction at an acceptable cost to the group. The group survived to live again another day and to carry out other exercises, and in other roles, projects and tasks different members of the team came to the fore and shone.

The big difference between the 'how' and some of the other areas that have been discussed in this book so far is that it is in the 'how' that all the management functions tend to be employed, although the actual functional skills, be they in production, development, engineering or information technology, are all involved. The 'how' is essentially a coordinating task as well as a leadership task, of a slightly different type from some of the subjects discussed earlier. It is absolutely vital to have project leadership for a task of any size in an industrial situation. The first task of the project leadership is indeed to work out the process by which the job will be planned, and the balance of the functional inputs which will be necessary for that exercise. Project leadership requires also a great degree of thoroughness to ensure that all aspects of the task are being covered by somebody, and the ability to coordinate and lead without dictatorship. It is in this area of industrial leadership that the free access to information is absolutely vital, so that people responsible for particular aspects of the task can adjust and align themselves to the problems that others are having. All too often the withholding of information is indulged in because of lack of trust in others' motives. There is a common idea that not revealing all the facts safeguards your power to manage your own affairs. The reality of course is that you are hampering your own chance of success, since information hoarding becomes a sort of group plague and in your own turn you will also lack the vital data you need to do your job. Equally, a time plan with very clear milestones, both of the planning process itself and of the task, is needed.

In many business functions movement is not immediately apparent and it is essential for the building up of confidence that there should be clear marks of achievement which you can recognize, tick off, and test yourself against. This is almost more important in the 'how' areas than in the 'what' areas, because, as I pointed out earlier, there tends to be great impatience, and a wish to get moving.

My company carried out an analysis many years ago of projects to erect enormously expensive new plants which had overrun in time and cost. In almost every case we found that the problem derived from starting the construction too early. When you have a final completion date of, let us say, two years ahead and on the site, apart from a bit of digging and the creation of a First World War front like Passchendaele, there is no sign of any building, it is natural that panic begins to set in and more and more pressures grow for something visible to be created.

However, the reality is that the ideal method of construction is to have everything planned and practically everything procured, and to delay the actual construction until all these matters have been resolved and the materials are to hand. Such techniques as Critical Path Scheduling can help to reinstate this form of courage in management, but nevertheless all too often we start too quickly. We seek to drive, rather than to lead. We need to use information freely as an enabling mechanism to help the many people concerned adjust to what is bound to be, even with the best planning, a changing scene. I like regular (not more often than once a week, not less often than once a month) progress meetings, which are designed to hold up the mirror so that we can all see where we are. I believe that there are great virtues in making these meetings short. The trap in progress meetings is the inevitable urge for each of us to examine in great depth what the others have been doing rather than trying to simplify so that the broad picture is more easily seen, and our own role in it is clearer.

Amongst my other responsibilities I was, for two years, chairman of the Confederation of European Chemical Industries, which dealt with an alarmingly wide series of political and industrial problems in the interface between what is, after all, Europe's most successful single industry, the chemical industry, and the EEC. I ran my contribution to this operation on the basis of a one-and-a-half-hour meeting a month, with three individuals, the director general of the British federation, the director general of CEFIC, a Dutchman, and my own ICI man in Brussels who did a lot of the progress chasing. We found, fairly soon, that as long as we kept the subjects broad we could communicate adequately for progress on about twenty or thirty different projects that we were running. We could ensure that each was in each other's mind, and that we knew who was the lead operator and the broad directions in which he was going. This required first of all absolute openness between us all, and an understanding of what the broad objectives we were seeking to achieve were, secondly a great degree of crispness and clarity as to who was going to do what in what sort of time frame. The minutes of our meetings never covered less than fifteen or more than twenty-eight subjects, and each subject was never allocated more than three or four lines, but it was enough to enable us to refer back and remember the issues. We could understand who was doing what and roughly how; we could check back that the achievement that we had set ourselves was adequate. This process also had the great advantage that we built up a steady degree of confidence in our own ability to move, and we were therefore able to develop the ability to accelerate.

The 'how' is also unique because, since no single route is necessarily perfect, it may be necessary if insufficient progress is being made along the road that we have chosen, to stop, completely re-route, and approach the problems in a different way. I have never believed that when looking at these sort of areas of operations it is absolutely necessary to hit the strategic target head on. Quite often I have found it impossible to achieve the precise route I had in mind, but it is better to be rolling and moving in the broad overall direction with the commitment of those who are, after all, doing the work than to be insisting on exactly one's own idea of what is required. Even so it is often the case that having started down the route you will find unexpected difficulties or problems, and then you have one of those interesting business dilemmas which form part of the attraction of my chosen career. Should you at this stage abandon, reinforce or re-route? Total abandonment is seldom the right solution, but even when it is, it is the most difficult single decision to take. Most of us have a great unwillingness, particularly if the commitment has been built up, to acknowledge that we have set ourselves a task which is unachievable. Indeed, there are very few such that exist. Nevertheless, from time to time either the external circumstances change, or we have overestimated our own strengths to such a degree that it is better to acknowledge that we have 'had it', and cut our losses. A particular example of this occurred in the Fibres operation where our aim of creating a large specialist polyester business proved unattainable. We invented some wonderful specialities but, alas, in each case the market was so small that they could not alter the overall state of the business enough to give us a hope of achieving the total turnaround we sought.

The most usual area, in my experience, where people hang on for the impossible far beyond the merits of the case, is where a new technology has been invented which the marketplace is

rejecting. Because the technology is your own, has been produced as a result of blood, sweat and tears and you believe in it,
you continuously reassure yourself that the marketplace is
wrong and that you are right. You make minor adjustments to
the technology and keep on offering it to the marketplace in
slightly different forms. Millions of pounds can be wasted in
this exercise, and it happens almost invariably because of lack of
understanding of what the real marketplace wants. It is very
difficult for technically based companies who are aware of
technical possibilities, but not actually operating in the marketplace, to appreciate what is required. These small preferences
almost invariably affect the technological solution to a degree
that one's own product and process may, or may not, be totally
inappropriate. ICI has always been very interested in the
introduction of new materials into the engineering and other
industries, and one of the problems here, of course, lies in the
fact that by definition a new material does not have design
engineers behind it who understand the consistency, stress and
other data which are necessary to use new materials to make
new products. In some cases the problem is even more esoteric,
since the engineering design data cannot be derived without
actually producing a sample product, and the cost of producing
a product for example, which is to be moulded rather than
assembled, is prohibitive.

In such a case, a real understanding of the customer's problems means that we have to produce, to the degree that is
possible, the same sort of tested and demonstrable design data
as exists for the design engineer, using his computer-aided
design system for the materials with which we are competing,
and we have to be able to assure him that the performance of our
products is of a comparable degree of replicability. Variability in
performance of materials is a fatal flaw, which no amount of
novelty is likely to overcome.

When deciding to re-route you have to consider abandonment as honestly and critically as you can. You should only
change your direction when it is quite obvious that the consensus of support for what you are trying to do has shifted. Quite
frequently a really determined crew can pull off a business
success in the face of apparently insuperable material and
market odds. The question of complete re-routing or reinforce-

ment is even more difficult. All of us invariably have a feeling
that one more mighty heave would do it, and that the reason for
our failure lies in insufficient determination, or that Mr X let us
down, or that really all we needed to do was to improve the
accountancy, or that unfortunately we always knew that the
production side was no good. It is surprising how often the
reinforcement of one particular selected area can suddenly
make the achievement of the strategic objective possible. The
most usual example of this is where the cost accountancy has
simply not been good enough to give the right messages to
enable the right deductions to be made. It is almost impossible
to achieve a good business success without the right information about the business to hand, and not only to hand, but to
hand quickly and available in the form of an analysis in which
one has confidence and which is a stimulus to action and
making things happen. So often this involves a detailed analysis
of the actual costs of one or more products from a whole family
of them which have been lumped together for ease of
administration. When examined you find, as always, that the
assumption that they all cost the same is wrong. Some will
involve more plant time, or cause more rejects, or involve
carrying more stocks both of intermediates and the end product, and this is usually the difference between profit and loss.
Reinforcement is also quite often the right thing to do in the
marketplace. We often underestimate the amount of selling
effort that is necessary to make an impact and expect, particularly in high technology, new products to sell themselves.
Certainly in the high-technology industries we all too frequently resist spending the very large amounts of money
necessary to launch a new product through advertising or
branding.

   We recently had an example in I C I, where we had looked at
how a whole area of our business had been performing for some
thirty or forty years. The cost accountancy criteria had been set
up many years before, and had in their day been considered to
be outstanding examples of a sensible way of allocating costs
and overheads across an enormous range of associated products. The system appeared to work well for many years, but
the business hit bad times and many changes had to be made.
We tried all sorts of injections of new blood and new thinking

into the operation, including new planning people, new marketing and selling techniques. The real key finally emerged when we put in a new accountant from a totally different background, who re-examined the whole basis of our costing, *ab initio*. Within a remarkably short space of time we found, as is almost always the case, that what we thought was a universally bad business contained some products which were in reality extremely good, and a minority which were extremely poor. The minority had concealed the performance of the good but because we had looked at the whole lot together we had failed to appreciate this. This may seem a very elementary mistake for a large and sophisticated organization to make, but I would caution against too happy a view that it could not happen in your own organization, be you a one-man band running your own business, or a large and sophisticated organization with multiple computer programs. Indeed the application of computer software to cost accountancy contains in the long haul the same sort of danger, because once the system is set up it will be extremely difficult to question the basic premises which may in the mists of time be almost forgotten. From time to time it is important to stand back and look again at the assumptions we are taking about any business activity. Human nature being what it is, it is very often easier for a newcomer to the business to do this than for those who have grown up in it. An excellent example of this occurred when the board instructed my division, Petrochemicals, to assume responsibility for the Nylon Intermediates business from the Dyestuffs division. The board's rationale was a technical one. Nylon Intermediates are an immensely complicated series of very large scale chemical interactions, far removed from the smaller scale sophisticated operations of Dyestuffs manufacture. From our point of view it was an unwelcome gift since it was losing money almost as fast as our division was making it. The previous 'owners' were convinced that their costs and equipment were fully competitive and probably the best in the world and that the problem lay only in the transfer price and rather poor relations with their main customer, the Fibres division. I recount the story in more detail in a later chapter, in order to illustrate a different point, but suffice it to say that all that was necessary to turn the business round was to apply a different perspective, and to set up new aims for those operating the plants. The problem was one of cost, as it so often is, and not, as had hitherto been assumed, one of price. At the same time we used the opportunity of the merger to try to create a wholly new organization, and to change the old outfit as much or perhaps even more than the new one. We changed the name to 'Petrochemicals', and looked anew at all ways in which the division was run, for already, even after less than three years in existence, we were becoming set in our ways.

Of the three choices that you have, when you have decided that your 'how' isn't going to make adequate progress, by far the most usual is to re-route. It is important that when you do re-route you should go through exactly the same process of discussion and involvement, and these require a more than usual degree of openness about why you are not succeeding. Since, by definition, somebody, or some people, have been responsible for the particular areas of your failure this is one of the real tests of whether your people are switched on and whether they have commitment to the overall strategic objective. The art is really one of timing; you must re-route while there is still a very high level of belief in the worthiness of the end, where you can demonstrate that you understand the reasons for re-routing and that the new route you are taking will avoid the rocks or the pitfalls which have caused your current problems. There must still be a degree of openness, and it must be before the awful stages of mutual recriminations and back-biting have set in, where the team begins to fall apart. It is at these times the leader can help most by 'throwing himself across the wire'.

In this situation everybody knows that the success that you are seeking is not being achieved. Dissatisfaction and back-biting will start. Leaders often feel that in such a situation they will lose their authority and ability to lead if they accept the responsibility. This is, however, usually the reverse of the facts. It is far better that you take upon yourself both the responsibility for the failure and the need for the re-routing. Curiously, provided this responsibility is shouldered generously, and with conviction, the invariable result is a strengthening of the leader's position rather than the reverse. People are mostly very honest with themselves and know where the faults and failures have been, so they seldom accept the leader's position as he portrays it – they do however give marks for taking the responsibility. From my own experience I can vouch that there is nothing worse than working for someone who runs at the first real conflict and then spends his time proving that he was perfect and was let down by the others (by inference you!). I have always tried to accept this accountability as my own, since it acts as a form of absolution for the group, and enables the energies to be turned positively, instead of negatively looking for the scapegoats. People are glad to have another opportunity to rethink and do better and, in their hearts, they invariably know that the wrong direction had been set together, and are grateful not to have their noses rubbed in their part of the responsibility.

Although I believe that the task of leadership of the 'how' is very much coordination and planning of the process, and indeed that the leader is an enabler as much as a driver, it is essential that if one particular area has failed the leader accepts and shares the responsibility. If the project is successful the credit should go to all but if the project fails the blame must go to the leader and he should be the first to pick it up. The reality, of course, is that it *is* the leader's fault, not because he could have been expected to know, for example, the intricacies of the computer model, or that there was some fundamental fault in the physics of the reaction, but because it was he who was the leader. He has been coordinating it, he knows and chose and presumably had some influence on the people and the tasks. It was in the final analysis his responsibility to have his antennae out and to have the sensitivity to realize the areas which were labouring, or hitting trouble. A bit of reinforcement or a second look at those areas is, of course, always permissible on the leader's say-so, and if he has failed adequately to appreciate the potential danger for which he is heading then it is right that he should shoulder the blame. Even more to the point, however, if he wishes to have the smallest chance of leading again another day it is beyond argument that he must accept the responsibility. If at that stage he merely shuffles it off he will find it almost impossible to pull together another team, and to engender in them the switched-on personal attitudes and commitment to the achievement of the task which is the essential ingredient. After all, every one of us knows that no one is infallible!

Very often the more excellent and skilled the professional functions are, the more difficult it is to coordinate them and the greater the pressure on the coordinating leader. Faced with a new problem the engineers will always want, as professionally they should, to advance the art. Simultaneously the computer people want to introduce a new technique and the production managers a new control system. Personnel, of course, sees the project as a golden opportunity to introduce new work practices and so on. So much innovation at the same time increases the risk of failure enormously and it is your unhappy task as leader to balance this risk against the equally real one that you will build an out-of-date, old-fashioned 'last of the Dinosaurs' – albeit one which works!

I have almost given up trying to count the number of times in which, in my own company, I have been told that we are going to build an exact copy of a plant that has been built somewhere else; in our jargon a 'Chinese Copy'. And yet when one actually goes to visit it one finds that the design has been 'improved upon'. Since one only takes the decision to build a Chinese Copy in order to be absolutely sure that the plant is built quickly and that the technology is known and will work, it is singularly infuriating to find that the experience so carefully garnered in one country or in one organization, has been rejected because others think that they know better. It is, however, very understandable that people want to do better and it is ultimately the responsibility of the project leader to make this balance.

However, the agreement to the investment has, to a large extent, been obtained on false pretences, since a carefully balanced decision has been taken to minimize risk and forgo the opportunity for improvement by doing things in exactly the same way. It can be impossible to build a Chinese Copy. The requirements of one market may not be the same as another, or there may be different environmental or other constraints from the time when the original, which you are copying, was built. Or there may be some new knowledge or hazard, or perhaps a safety factor. The conclusion that I have come to over the years is that it is almost impossible to build a Chinese Copy and that therefore it may be better not to fool oneself that one is going to achieve it. What one can do, however, is to minimize the changes that are sought if the objective is to have the plant functioning reliably as quickly as possible.

It is a fact that the risks associated with projects are seldom seen by those involved in them unless they have had a great deal of experience of similar projects which have gone wrong in the past. It seems extraordinarily difficult to transfer this bitterly acquired knowledge to others. For example, the experience of many of us would be that one should not build, in a lesser developed country, totally new technology. It is safer, and in the long run more effective, to build something which has been tried and tested, and is working elsewhere, so that the engineers, production people, chemists, and research and development people can lean on an exactly similar operation where experience has been built up over a period of time. Even though we would consider India very far from a lesser developed country, certainly from the viewpoint of the excellence of its managers, we have always put in tried and tested technology there. We have all seen the results which can follow trying new techniques far from home and the experts who invented them. This sad realization only comes after one has tried to accede to the wish of a lesser developed country, not only to have the very best existing technology, but to ensure that something of tomorrow has been 'built in'. It is understandable that developing countries are always frightened of receiving what they would describe, somewhat cynically, as the cast-offs of the developed countries. However, in a developing country one always has a host of problems to deal with which are quite different from those of operating in your own homeland. The infrastructure is invariably quite different from one's home base, the availability of really highly skilled help, in the form of consultants, construction firms, information technology experts, etc., is less and your own staff who are dealing with the problems are usually less experienced. Introducing totally new technology which has not been proven anywhere in the world is a very high risk business indeed. The risk is greatly increased if one's first attempt at developing some new form of modification takes place thousands of miles away from home, away from the inventors, and in a society without the usual support and back-up which you can reach at your home base. This is one area where project leadership requires the courage to appear to be old-fashioned and conservative. Every sort of blandishment is produced. 'The market is different' – and indeed it frequently is. 'The plant that is being built will not have as long an operating life because it is already out of date' – but so, frankly, is every plant that is built. After all, with the inexorable march of technology, the one thing that one knows the moment one starts up a plant is that it is about to be superseded by some advance somewhere else. The problem is to ensure absolute reliability of the achievement of the objective because lesser developed countries are very unforgiving of failure, even though they may themselves have contributed to it by their own requests and requirements.

Another area where bitter experience has taught me to be safe rather than sorry is in the whole area of multistage plant construction. Time and time again we have put up an incredibly complex multistage project with the argument that there is no technical risk since each stage individually has been tried and tested somewhere else. All too often the whole combination has never been tried and tested together, and it is here that the trap lies. At first examination, if a project is put up that consists, let us say, of five separate processes each feeding on to the next one, and with a single selling point at the end of the whole process, you would think that the highest level of risk would be five times that of each single stage. Indeed, even that would be pooh-poohed since established processes usually have a very high reliability indeed, and there is always plenty of statistical data showing the average time between breakdowns of each stage. The mathematical reality is, however, that if five stages are put together in a new combination the risk has been increased to the power of five, rather than by a factor of five, but one only learns this after one has carried out the exercise – when one has the benefit of hindsight.

I learnt this lesson the hard way many years ago when my division of ICI, the Petrochemicals division, decided to put up an Aromatics production complex. Aromatics might be described as the constituent liquid parts of crude oil. They are produced by distillation of liquids and form the basis for practically all synthetic fibre production. In addition they have many other uses when assembled in different ways by the skill of the industrial chemist. Aromatics had previously been produced mainly as a by-product of the refining industry. But in the early 1960s, because we had a large internal captive demand, the deliberate production of aromatics in their own right offered us an exciting new possibility. We were going to assemble five processes in a new conformation, all of which had been tried elsewhere. The scale of the whole operation was, for those days, enormous, and I was the commercial manager responsible both for the forecasts of our ability to sell and ultimately for the achievement of these forecasts. As it happened I was also responsible for buying for the division and this proved, in the event, to be a very happy accident. We were a highly skilled operating unit and justifiably proud of our production expertise. We were aiming to bring on line a million tons of capacity in one mighty bound, and no one foresaw that it would take us nearly a year before we had ironed out the problems and reached reliable operation. I had pre-sold most of the products of the plant since, understandably, the board had wanted assurance that we could indeed move these massive amounts of product. I speedily found myself in a situation where, quite often within a single week, I was trying to forward sell, or alternatively buy in, in a state of panic, tens of thousands of tons of one aromatic or another, as our plant floundered its way towards achieving balanced production. Believe me, an experience like that really does teach you to be cautious about multi-stage plant construction!

The reality of life is that if one has put up such a project it will eventually be made to work, and to work with the sort of reliability that one has to look for in any profit-making enterprise for which one is responsible, just as our Aromatics complex did in the end. However, all too often what is forgotten except by those who have gone through the horror of the start-up, is that it may have taken a year and a half or even two years to achieve that stage of reliability. Modern techniques of such concepts as discounted cash flow, coupled with reduction in rates of inflation, mean that if you lose the first year of beneficial production, all too often you have imposed a handicap on the project from which it can never recover. In absolute terms a mistaken investment has been made.

In the late sixties and seventies when world inflation was

relatively high, and there was a high intrinsic growth rate, the businessman was often saved from the consequences of a bad investment decision, or at least that was how it appeared. In those days inflation accounting was in its infancy and most people looked at their returns on a historic basis. A combination of high growth and inflation would always apparently dig one out of one's trouble. One was always paying back the money one had borrowed for the project in inflated currency and even if, as usual, the market forecast was wrong, growth would in time fill the plant up. The capital cost of a new plant would be quite disproportionately higher in the inflated pounds of later years, irrespective of technical advance. Small surprise under these circumstances that massive failures at the 'how' stage of operations were barely recognized, and that it was possible for inadequate tactical performance to be overlooked, or at minimum not to be subjected to exhaustive enquiry.

Those days have passed with a vengeance. Money is expensive and we now recognize world growth as being much slower than we thought it was in the past. There is an understanding of the effect of inflation on apparent performance. We are not going to be baled out in the future as we have been in the past; there is therefore a much greater need for achievement and reduction of risk at the 'how' stage of business leadership. The leader needs to recognize these changing external circumstances and the pressures that they put on achievement, and he needs to have a ruthless clarity as to what actually constitutes success and what constitutes failure. The achievement of tactical success by the use of vastly excessive amounts of money is equally horrendous. Risk can, of course, be reduced by building in 'belt and braces' the whole time, it can be reduced by carrying massive intermediate buffer stocks and it may be reduced by double-checking everything. But these life-belts in themselves may destroy the validity of the project or the business which you are setting up.

It is in tactical achievement that businesses succeed or fail and good tactical performance can often overcome deficiencies in strategy for a surprisingly long time. Really first-class low-cost production will retain you in business for a very long time. Really first-class distribution, which it is difficult for your competitors to emulate, will hold the counterattack at bay and give you a great deal of leeway, as long as you recognize the source of your safety. Despite all this, it is only by getting everything pretty well right, and above all keeping a high rate of tactical change and movement, that your business will succeed. Everyone in your business must be continuously trying to improve his or her area of operations, be it ordering procedures, safety, production, efficiency and so on. These are essentially all tactical matters, but it is through the multiplicity of such small changes that competitive advantage is gained. Industry and business are not about maintaining the status quo – they are essentially a race where unless we are out in front someone else will be. The race goes to the swift, but the race also goes to the sure-footed and it is the achievement of a balance between these two characteristics, plus the right choice between the new trail and the well-proven road, that lead to success. However, the task of the leader at the 'how' stage of things remains, as it does in the whole of business, the one of making it happen and that is derived from continual iteration, leadership of an enabling type, and the exercise of judgement with courage and honesty. Above anything it is achieved by teamwork and the commitment, skill and mutual respect of the team. Creating that is the leader's job.

5

All Change

Management is about change, and maintaining a high rate of change. There are special attributes required for this particular activity, yet there is also a natural, almost symbiotic kind of change, which can be maintained without paying particular attention to 'change management'. This differs from organization to organization and from country to country, and in this respect the United Kingdom suffers from some unique problems. As a country and as a race we take particular pride in our past and indeed are derided for living too much in it. Most successful British people wish to buy houses in the country, and to attach themselves to the countryside in a way which almost appears to imitate the patterns of life of the gentry in the eighteenth and nineteenth centuries. Here society has changed because we were not always so attached to the past. A feature of the Victorian era was a delight in the new and a willingness to see any amount of social upheaval based on economic change. Japan and Korea have been undergoing their own industrial revolution, and one can see many similarities to the social and other changes which occurred in the United Kingdom in the early years of the last century.

It is only in the United Kingdom that we have a particular love of the old and a seeming contempt for the new. Even today in Britain the word 'new' is not an automatic sales point. Almost alone amongst the world's developed countries we think 'new' signifies that the product is likely to break, that it is not adequately tried and tested, that it is gimmicky, possibly damaging to our fundamental values and probably unneeded. This is in stark contrast to the attitude to change of our industrial competitors. One of the most potent sales words in the United States is the word 'new'. In Japan newness and novelty are constantly sought and applauded. In Germany, which has some of the same attitudes as we do, nevertheless what is expected is continuous advance and continuous improvement. Nobody wants to buy last year's model, and they expect that this year's model should offer significant improvements on last year's. We should not, therefore, be surprised that the management of change in the United Kingdom is a difficult task as well as being a skill which both nationally and industrially we need to develop. Change management, like all aspects of management and leadership, requires understanding and attention, and a great degree of sensitivity to the needs and fears of the people who are affected by it.

Nevertheless, the management of change in every country involves similar problems and requires similar approaches. I have found the same sort of problems in India and the United States that I have in trying to introduce organizational change in the United Kingdom. The differences relate more to the stage at which people begin to worry and at which the climate is conducive to change, rather than to the actual problem of managing the process itself. The whole process is perhaps one which my years at sea led me particularly to appreciate and understand. I don't imagine for a moment that I was the only sailor who loved being at sea and dreaded returning to harbour. Life at sea speedily evolved into 'real life' where there was an absolutely unchangeable routine of watch keeping, where days merged into days, where the tempo of life reduced to one where one could savour the odd exceptional *bonne bouche* which was thrown one's way by nature. It was almost, in a way, like hibernation although I suppose that the pace of one's breathing did not actually reduce. You could savour small things like a particular record being played, or the sight of a bird, or a fish, or another living creature, or another ship. Many writers have described this process as monotony but, to my mind, life was reduced under such circumstances to the simplicities which governed our forefathers, whose work pattern depended more on the seasons and nature than the will of the individual.

It is not perhaps surprising that we, as a country which has seen so much change, find it so difficult to cope with. Even in my own lifetime I find the style of life which I and my family enjoyed before the last war almost the stuff of which historical novels are made. Unbelievable changes have occurred in the

United Kingdom over the last forty years and not all of them, in the view of some, for the better. I happen to believe that history shows that change in the aggregate is almost always helpful and beneficial. But the processes are certainly disruptive, and require adaptation to an astounding degree – adaptation which ultimately can only be made on an individual and personal level.

It is this aspect of change which requires understanding if it is to be managed. The reality of change is inescapable. If we do not change the inexorable forces of economics and shifts in the external world will force change upon us. One might say, under such circumstances, how much better to change before we *are* changed. But in real life this historical perspective is very difficult to appreciate, and we find most change uncomfortable. We cling to sets of values and conditions which we recognize and which are undemanding of our own commitment and effort. It is a fool's paradise, just as much as the hope that somehow one can get away from civilization, or that one can put the clock back. One cannot, and indeed one should not, because while it is foolish to throw away the past, it is the future that we can affect. The ability to create and manage the future in the way that we wish is what differentiates the good manager from the bad. This appears in its starkest form in this century in industrial change.

In years gone by changes were wrought on the battlefield by a small proportion of the population acting, very frequently, in the perceived self-interest of a minority of leaders. The lives of the majority of the people were barely touched. Today the battle is on the economic front and affects every one of us, but none more than the industrialist. It is he who is absolutely in the front line of the pressures for technological, economic, and social change. It is he who is left with the task of trying to manage the effect of these massive forces on the individuals for whom he is responsible. If you are to try to manage a rate of change higher than 'the natural order' of things in your own organization, a number of preconditions are essential. The engine of change is dissatisfaction with the present and the brakes of change are fear of the unknown and fear of the future. It follows that you cannot go too far against the grain; the grain of the people in one's organization, and their conscious or unconscious acceptance of the need for change.

I do not believe in the myth of the great leader who can suddenly engender in his people a vision and lead them to an entirely new world. I believe that the reality is more traumatic and more demanding, but we all know that there is no sub-stitute for being in a winning team, and are prepared to make quite a lot of sacrifice to ensure that our 'team' does win. While it is true that it is very difficult to lead change against the grain of the feelings of the people in your business, it is fatal to wait until those feelings have developed a large head of steam. The art is to discern the direction of the feelings and to instigate change before everyone is so frustrated and dissatisfied that they are boiling for revolution. Too much delay and waiting for certainty and you may acquire the dubious distinction of trying to lead a revolution, with the inherent danger of no longer being able to control the feelings of your people. I have to say that in my view very few people have 'managed' revolution. Forces are unleashed which are beyond the control of any individual and almost inevitably many innocent people are harmed. Moreover, although the benefits of revolution may work through later, they seldom have the immediate impact that is expected. One has only to look, with the perspective of history, at the French or the Russian Revolutions to see some indication of what a long time the high hopes that stimulate a revolution take to actually come to fruition – if indeed they ever do. In industry the time is never likely to be available for these hopes to have the chance of coming true. The rest of the world will have moved on, and the breathing space is never enough.

The requirement, and it is a tough one, is to recognize the basic dissatisfactions of people and if necessary even to heighten these, but always in an honest way. Our dissatisfac-tion grows when we know that we are threatened by the superior performance of others; other organizations, other countries, other products, or other individuals. This dissatisfac-tion can only be engendered by the broadest possible view of the circumstances surrounding our business and ourselves.

This broad view can only be built upon clarity and openness. People who work for organizations like my own, where the account books are open and where every man or woman knows whether we are doing well or badly and knows the nature of the problems we are trying to deal with, are much quicker to recognize the need for change than those who are kept in ignorance of such matters. I have never understood why some managers are so terrified of telling their people the full economic facts. I suppose it is because of the belief that if things go well they will be forced to share the good results, but surely so they should? In ICI we have, for a great many years, enjoyed a profit-sharing arrangement with our people so that a share of any good fortune the company may have goes back to those employed within it. Indeed, if the company does well it is right and proper that our people should share the rewards. After all it is they who have to bear the brunt of the personal effect on their lives, hopes and ambitions if things go badly. Not only do they need to know the actual day-to-day circumstances of the business, but they also need to have a very clear understanding of the external factors that are at work on the business. The policy really should be one of no surprises and indeed most changes that have occurred under my leadership have not come as surprises to those affected. In many cases I have been asked for months beforehand how long we can continue to carry a particular line, or a particular form of organization; and when the change is finally announced, hard though it may be, there is usually a feeling of relief. It is much more difficult to change things when everything is apparently going well. To be able to transfer the feeling that well though things are going they could be, and need to be, still better is a very difficult task indeed, but more of that later.

The reality of life is that while staying put is without doubt the most comfortable for the short haul, it is in fact the highest risk strategy of all. Sadly, one can see example after example where the company or the individual who was leading the race believed that they had found the ultimate solution and stayed with it too long, while somebody else was stimulated to greater effort and overtook. The outstanding example of this is the Swiss watch industry. After all, it was they who had developed the heights of perfection in mechanical and automatic watches. They believed they could look at the emerging competition from Japan as a direct frontal attack on them in their traditional field. They ignored, almost fatally, the development of the electronic watch and were nearly forced out of the battle altogether as a result. The world of industry is one of perpetual change not only technologically, but also as a part of the continuous ferment of the developing universe in which we live. These forces and processes are little known and little understood by any of us, but the end results certainly make themselves known and affect even the smallest aspects of our daily lives. It follows that if one wishes to lead change, rather than having to follow it, the first necessity is openness and open communications.

By and large in an industrial organization one's people should be asking not whether you are going to change, but how long it will be before you do. Wait too long and you have lost control, move too soon and you will lack the commitment which is vital to success. It's a very nice judgement and since, as a leader, one has the primary responsibility for trying to make sure that one's own team is out in front before the others, it's a judgement that requires a great deal of attention and thought. One's own ideas of change are not necessarily the correct ones and it is of immense help to ensure that all the people that will be affected by it are aware of the evolving external factors which are forcing you towards certain conclusions. The most obvious situation is plainly where a business goes into loss. There is really no excuse for people who work in a loss-making business being kept in ignorance of the facts. The reality of the loss is that the future and comfort of each one of them is under threat and it would be very arrogant to attempt to conceal these facts. Moreover, the people in the business are almost certainly already aware that they are operating in a loss position. After all they are bound to know whether the plants are working at full capacity, whether the repeat orders are coming in or not, and whether the customers appear to be happy, discontented or even nonexistent. Everybody in a business has a basic feel of the business, whether they are actually able to see the accounts or not. It may communicate itself in the grim face of the works manager or the chairman, but without question no one is in any doubt of the reality of the problems.

One of the unexpected problems I have found in being chairman, first of a division and then of a company, is the fact that so many people judge the position of the company by one's own apparent mood, even to whether one smiles or not. I remember once working for a leader who was an outstandingly nice but very shy man, who could never be prevailed upon to look others in the eye and to smile. Our business became poor and I remember pleading with him to look more cheerful as he walked around our offices because his attitude, while unchanged, was making our people more and more apprehensive, in my view unnecessarily. It was, of course, an impertinence on my part and moreover something which he was incapable of doing. It was silly to have thought that he could have changed his nature, but being the man he was he took it in good spirit and did not resent my attempt to help the situation. Indeed, he sought to rectify the problem in other ways, by opening up the books and talking more, though formally, which was his style. However, one of the penalties of leadership is indeed that people watch your mood in a way which you do not allow for, but must consider the whole time. I remember another occasion on which, in my anxiety to ensure that I spoke to a management course, I came straight off the overnight plane from America to address them. I barely had time for a shave before I appeared. A feature of ICI's management courses (this was one of the most senior) is a great deal of free and open interchange, and I had the usual rumbustious question and answer session. I felt very virtuous and proud until I got the feedback, which was that they were concerned that perhaps I was losing my grip! Entirely my own fault, but it certainly taught me not to assume that one can perform tasks beyond one's physical capability.

The corollary is also true. It is not much use expecting that you can convey only the bad news. Your people should be equally aware of the good news, and if you are making good profits they have every entitlement both to know about it and to press for their share of the reward. The essence of this has to be that when eventually the leadership enunciates the action they want to take, the background to this action should be understood, and, if conceivably possible, accepted by all those who will be affected by it. It would be illusory to pretend that they will be delighted. There cannot be, in the world of change, winners the whole time. People are very honest with themselves and provided that they are treated equally honestly will almost always understand and acknowledge the need for change. Indeed, it is interesting that one of Britain's great national heroes was

Captain Oates, who sacrificed himself for the lives of the others on Scott's Polar expedition. Surprisingly often when a group or company is in trouble, there are a number of people who will offer themselves as sacrifices, in order to ensure that the rest can carry on.

Not only must your people be aware of the need for change, but they must also realize the high risk involved in not changing. Everybody knows that the prizes go to the forerunners and not the laggers, and equally everybody knows when all is not well. In the really good organization people are continually on the look-out for these signs of losing the lead position, and will recognize them and start drawing them to the leadership's attention long before the competition have even realized that they are catching up. But if you enjoy a long period out in front these senses tend to become dulled. It is those who have enjoyed a monopoly position for a long time who become most unaware of the dangers surrounding them. Think what happened to the Singer Sewing Machine company: an example of a company which became synonymous in one's mind with the product it made. The generic name for a vacuum cleaner is still a Hoover, and yet see now the forms of competition which both these proud names face. Indeed, changing a monopoly without the force of competitive pressure is almost the most difficult management task known. Very few have succeeded in it.

How does one create the grain? Obviously information, as I pointed out earlier, and open communications and knowledge of the company's situation, particularly the competitive position, are key items. But there are other things that can be done. In ICI's case we have very frequently sent people to see the competition for themselves. A visit by a team of shop stewards and managers to your competitors in Japan, or America, or Germany, is often an eye-opener and certainly reinforces the beliefs that have been planted heretofore. Even a visit to your own organization in other countries points up key differences. Moreover, good organizations know that the status quo represents danger. The continual questioning of what is new and the showing of concern when little emerges in response to that question, helps to engender the right sort of attitude. When in my early days in the Fibres division I visited their plants and was told that they had no problems, I knew we were in deep trouble! First, because the business as a whole was in serious loss and the works did not know clearly the extent of their contribution to the problem, and secondly because if you are unaware of problems it is unlikely that you are putting much effort into changing anything. Management is about creating the new, but also about diagnosing and dealing with each problem before it becomes serious and unmanageable.

The task of leadership is really to make the status quo more dangerous than launching into the unknown. Target-setting helps in these areas, but the problem with target-setting is that it is a very difficult art. Set targets which are impossible to achieve and you switch your people off. Set targets which are too easy and you also switch them off. Set targets which are difficult but just achievable, and then ensure that you achieve them, and you will switch people on. One of the difficulties that we all face is that the scale of possible and necessary achievement is so far beyond what most of us normally manage. We have estimated for many years that in industry we get about thirty to forty per cent of what people are actually capable of. Probably the absolute optimum would be round about sixty or maybe seventy per cent, so there is plenty of scope for improvement. Moreover, living with success has all sorts of dangers and makes even these targets difficult of attainment. Nevertheless, the targets have to be related to what is necessary and what our competitors can achieve, and this in itself contains all sorts of other problems.

I remember when I set the aim of a thousand million pounds' profit for ICI. It was not a particularly sophisticated exercise, and not one which was the result of enormous amounts of staff work or even very large amounts of consultation. The figure was provable in all sorts of ways as being the sort of minimum continuous target number that was necessary if the group was to continue in the way which all of us wished to see. The thousand million represented ten per cent on our probable sales at that time, not by any manner of means an unreasonable return, bearing in mind that we are a high-technology company. It represented the sort of profit that my company had made in two previous high-earning years, adjusted for inflation. It also represented the level of profits which would enable us to increase our dividends to shareholders, which we had set as a major aim, and was also plainly the minimum consistent earning pattern to enable us to sustain the size and power of the company in its present form. But when it was produced as a target it seemed, and indeed I personally believed it to be, totally unattainable. I produced it as a result of a question at central council, when I was asked when I would be satisfied with the profits that we were making, which admittedly had shown a sharp recovery from the appalling levels which we had been achieving in 1980 and 1981, levels which would have led the group inexorably to a steady reduction in its size. Once the thousand million was expressed, even from such 'back of the envelope' calculations, it became a target, not only in the minds of our people but in the minds of the press, the analysts, and the leadership. But I have to say that it became such a target partly at least because of its apparent unattainability.

By a happy concatenation of circumstances we achieved the target in 1984, and in some ways I wish we had not, because the actual numerical figure was achieved at least as much by a set of favourable external circumstances as by our own efforts. Because the target had seemed to be so unattainable its achievement seemed to mean that we had entered the promised world where we were masters of our own destiny. Would that that were true, because yesterday's one thousand million is tomorrow's one thousand one hundred million. Yesterday's favourable circumstances are tomorrow's unfavourable ones, which lead us in turn to struggle more and more to stay in the same place. The fact is that very large numbers like these are beyond the comprehension of the people that we try to motivate. Even one hundred million pounds appears to be riches beyond the dreams of Croesus, and a thousand million pounds seems just plain greedy. No matter how much we have tried over the years to communicate with our people and to teach business realities, I find that the scale of the numbers blinds one to their relativity. This is made even worse when apparently one's own profit performance exceeds that of one's competitors, and increasingly we are asked, and indeed ask ourselves, how much we need before we will be satisfied. The answer is, of course, that the industrial manager will never be satisfied, and should not be, because the more money that is earned the more opportuni-

ties are open to one. The more chance of creating an uncatchable
lead over the competition, of developing tomorrow's world and
managing our own futures for ourselves, our shareholders and
our people. This may sound like the philosopher's stone but it
certainly is something which will switch most of us on and is
worth continuing to hunt for.

So much for the grain creating, which is based on dissatisfaction, and which is the major engine that enables change to take
place. Change is like some of the very best machines. The
forward power is backed or, more accurately, held in check, by
equally strong braking systems. These are more than capable
not only of not allowing the change to take place, but actually of
putting one temporarily in reverse. The fear of change is very
real, based as it is essentially on the fear of the unknown. It
doesn't matter that we may recognize the larger realities of
competition, or that we know that we are crewing the last
sailing schooner in the race (which is no longer a race) from
Australia, with grain for Europe. We may recognize that the
world is moving against our company and our team and we will
always, of course, blame 'them'. 'Them' being partly our own
leadership and even more our competitors, who we will always
believe, intrinsically, enjoy some sort of 'unfair' advantage
because we know that man to man we can knock the spots off
them.

For wholehearted resistance to change and the inevitable
results of such a policy one has to look no further than the
London docks. It was almost a conspiracy of resistance which
led employers to persist with casual labouring practices so long
after they had become extinct elsewhere, while the struggles of
the dock workers themselves to resist any new introduction of
work methods except at punitive cost exacerbated the situation.
It would be difficult to have more marked contrasts than with
the reaction of Rotterdam to changes in technology such as
mechanical handling of containerization. The results are easy to
see. London dockyard is now a development site for housing
and some new businesses – Rotterdam is Europe's largest port.

There is no easier area of self-deception than believing that
one's competitors are acting irrationally or 'unfairly'. In almost
every case that I have known, if one can only try to put oneself in
a competitor's place one sees that they are acting with the same

care and analysis as oneself but their starting positions are very different. We should not be surprised that German companies respond to stimuli different from British ones. After all, they are largely financed by banks, rather than by shareholders. Equally, American companies are under intense shareholder pressure for short-term performance, so it is not surprising that they quite frequently act differently from us. Japanese companies have very low financing charges, and above all are ceaselessly looking for a long-haul performance. That is what their banks, government and shareholders expect from them. All of these factors lead companies to act in different ways. Moreover, very frequently one's own assessment of a competitor's position is incorrect. What may appear to us to be weaknesses on his part may seem to him to be strengths, and vice versa. I do not mean by all this to imply that the competition is always totally rational – there have been occasions when an individual's prejudices or beliefs have forced his company in a particular way – but by and large it is sensible, before one concludes that one's competitors are acting irrationally, to try to understand what the explanation for their actions might be.

I spoke earlier about the problems of changing a successful organization, and the great difficulties involved in changing a monopoly. It is almost impossible to induce fear in these circumstances so one is forced to look for another motivating force. Because of the feeling of superiority that the successful organization will have there is always a tendency to think that the competition are still swinging by their tails, having only just come down from the trees. This sense of pride in the achievements of one's team can in fact be a force for change, but it is a much more difficult task to make it work that way. In these circumstances one has to turn the pride to dissatisfaction with the thought that if we are so good why are things going on just as before and not continuously improving? Can we really believe that we have achieved the ultimate end? If we are so good why are we not moving forward? It is a very difficult task to engender this belief and the art is never to lose the forward movement of change which has got you to the lead position. However, it is almost inevitable that over a period of time self-satisfaction will set in. The better life that you are able to enjoy as an organization will lead to all sorts of fat generating in all sorts of areas. You persuade yourself that your pre-eminent position needs reinforcement by outward signs of success, like planes in your own livery, prestige headquarters and advertising. You become increasingly intolerant of criticism and dislike press or other comments which you consider to be ill-informed because they do not adequately reflect the glories that you have achieved. There are a host of examples of this sort in the USA but sadly there are also timely warnings closer to home. EMI seemed at one time to be in exactly this position, as did Thorn. Even the merging of the two still produced the same conviction of invincibility. Rolls-Royce also had aspects of the same problem.

History is not full of examples of people who have turned this situation round once it has begun, but it is possible. Within ICI there are instances of outstanding individuals being able to change the climate in a successful organization sufficiently to keep it moving. Although it is very difficult to do, this can often be achieved by moving people in from other parts of the organization who are able to see that the Emperor isn't wearing as many clothes as he thinks. It pays to look with considerable scepticism at the successful parts of one's organization. Today's success is all too often tomorrow's failure and since the process of inducing self-criticism is so difficult, it requires even more effort and early targeting as being of prime importance. It also requires unremitting attention. The commitment and change of style of Jack Welch of General Electric in the USA following on from Reg Jones, a business hero if ever there was one, is the classic example of taking a successful company and making it better. In his case it was done by sheer force of personality and a belief that more could be achieved. It will usually require great tolerance to effect such a change. A great deal of sensitivity is required in all this since, self-evidently, the organization is being successful and too much unthinking criticism of it will merely get the positive aspects of what you are trying to do ignored, and you personally will be dismissed as being cranky and jealous.

Modest challenges to get change moving again are probably the most effective means of starting the thing on the right road. Putting in new people from other parts of the organization who may see the reality more clearly, requires of them a degree of sensitivity or they may be rejected and their ability to change things will be lost. One of the most useful attributes of a manager is his ability to induce change, and in any organization you will always find a number of individuals who are dedicated to changing things and have developed these skills. Skills such as the understanding of the human forces at work, the knowledge of the points of influence to press on, and an understanding of the process of change. To these must be added sensitivity, patience, and a willingness to be the agent of change rather than the principal. Such people form a most valuable network and resource, and it is most important that they should be nurtured and applied where they can be of most effect. They will always be a minority, but a minority who have an enormous catalytic effect on large organizations.

Fear is an intensely personal matter, and no two individuals' fears are the same. Fear cannot be dealt with in generalized terms. Although intellectually we may accept the forces that are at play and we may recognize that we cannot 'go on' in the way we have been doing, in the end for most of us it boils down to the more personal questions such as 'What is going to happen to me?' and 'Can I manage to cope?' It is sadly true that not everybody *can* cope, although we are often guilty of assuming that people are less adaptable than they prove to be, and indeed than they think they can be. I have been fascinated over the years to see the unbelievable changes that people can manage in their personal and professional lives, providing only that they are given the help and the time to adjust. Perhaps the most outstanding examples are found in people who make a total change of job and direction, such as one of our fibre technologists who retrained and made a happy and successful life as a master butcher, or the ICI director who went on to run the Ffestiniog Light Railway. Equally dramatic and rewarding changes, however, happen within the company. Outstanding technical people who find a new ability in a sales job, or the many people who transfer completely from one sort of business to another. Fibres men who find themselves in Petrochemicals, or explosives experts who find themselves in the world of plastics.

Here there is another Golden Rule. Change, or the prospect of change, will frighten everybody. In a situation where there are inevitably going to be some job losses it is surely better to try to reassure as many people as possible, even if you cannot reassure everyone, than to end up with everyone in the outfit being anxious. The first necessity of easing the fear is to make absolutely sure that everybody you know you will need, or who you are determined, barring acts of God, to retrain or find appropriate places for, is reassured. The unfortunate side of this is that some people are still going to be anxious, and sometimes unnecessarily. The biggest responsibility in managing change is to look after the 'walking wounded'. Not everybody can be retrained, not everybody is still young enough to adjust and not everybody actually wants to. Many people will seize the opportunity to follow some other way of life but even they do not wish to be shown the door with a shotgun. They have a right to be treated with dignity, to be respected, understood and helped.

The inability, or the unwillingness, to accept the new is not a crime. It does not necessarily diminish a man. But the sheer guts and determination, coupled with the stimulation of having to change and deal with new circumstances, can make a man or woman 'grow' perceptibly in stature. Each of us contains within ourselves reserves we have not dreamt of and hope we will never have to call upon. The fact still remains that, for a host of different reasons, there will always be some who cannot or do not wish to adapt. It is of the greatest possible importance that they should leave feeling that they have been understood, that they retain their self-respect, and that they are not diminished as people in the fight for life. This is an immensely time-consuming and rather harrowing job. Fortunately, in many large organizations like ICI, there are enough people who genuinely care for others and will take this sort of work on, and indeed derive much justified pleasure from successfully rehabilitating people into a new way of life.

It is an absolute responsibility of the business organization, if we are to continue in business for the future, that we should look after those who cannot adapt, and cannot look after themselves. By 'looking after' I do not mean merely the provision of money. What is at stake is not just whether an individual will starve, which is a rare occurrence in our twentieth-century Western world, but whether they retain their self-confidence and their belief in themselves as individuals.

Responsible companies will happily spend large amounts of time and effort in this area and it is essential that the managers and leaders keep their eye on the main ball. The great essentials in this process are time, compassion and readiness to shoulder the responsibility for the action. I have tried never to fire anyone without attempting to make them feel that the fault was more mine than theirs, that in some way the problem lay in my lack of ability to utilize their skills, rather than being any deficiency in them. This may cause them to resent you at the time, which can be painful, but it can sometimes bring long-term rewards. It may be many months or years later that the individual comes to see you to show you how successful he has been elsewhere, giving you the reassurance that in firing him you did not also destroy him. There is often a pleasing feeling that these human problems can be overcome with money, and while it is true that money in itself may help to ease some of the problems it is seldom, in my experience, the largest single hurdle. This remains the job of maintaining the self-respect of the individual, who feels that the convoy has gone on and left him, as the slowest ship, behind. He has been accustomed to being a member of the top task force, and he doesn't take kindly to being abandoned as a lame duck. Some will fight, but many will not, and these require help and assistance.

Change is a continuous industrial process, and if change is unfortunately achieved at the expense of the individuals that are known by everybody in your organization, you can say goodbye to the chances of keeping up with your overseas competitors. Damage to individuals will not be forgiven and will ensure that further adjustment is not possible. It may sound like the impossible, but the task is to create a degree of confidence that change will be managed sensitively, that those who cannot remain will be looked after, and will be helped to find other, hopefully even more satisfying ways of life. My own company has gone to the extent of retraining individuals and not just for the skills that we want, but for the skills that we know will enable those who cannot stay with us to get good jobs elsewhere. We have also had the devotion and hard work of many caring managers, who derive their satisfaction from knowing that they have managed change without unnecessary casualties.

I spoke earlier about the application of money to change. It is certainly a prerequisite. People who leave one's company before their due date are entitled to be looked after. ICI has always tried to avoid compulsory redundancy and so far has indeed done so. This has been largely as a result of generous severance terms which can be used to attract people to set up on their own, or follow different lines of interest to those for which we have employed them. I am constantly amazed and delighted at the range of experiments and differences that ICI has made in order to help people to adjust to the sort of organizational and business change which is not a result of our wishes or actions, but is an inevitable response to the economic changes in the world outside. We have retrained people to take on new jobs outside the company. We have given them contracts and helped to set them up as self-employed contractors. We have given them rights to inventions and helped them set up on their own. We have found jobs of every sort, shape and size and we have introduced new employers into areas we have vacated in order to 'take up the slack'. We have set up science parks and gardening firms. We have applied every sort of ingenuity and determination we can find to try to mitigate the problems, and have given very wide discretion and powers to the people who are on the spot to help.

Once the climate is right, and you have satisfied yourself that you can manage the people aspects of the change, a bit of symbolism will be of great help. I believe that change should start from the top, and that it is important to show that the top is changing faster and more radically than the rest of the organization. Hence it was that when I took over as chairman I had made up my mind that the board would operate more effectively if there were fewer of us. I also believed that we had too many levels in our hierarchy and that it was important to get rid of the deputy level which had crept in, as it always does at every stage of any hierarchical organization. We had deputy chairmen and deputy managers of every sort, indeed we had even begun to produce deputy section managers. In our case our act of symbolism was to totally change the way that the board worked and to reduce the size of the board very sharply. We also needed some overt signs that we were determined to change and that nothing was sacred.

Probably the most sacred part of the entire company had been our magnificent headquarters in London, on Millbank, which had been the very first thing to be built when the company had been formed by an amalgamation in 1926. We had already decided as a group that a smaller board required a smaller support staff, and here I must admit our ambitions for smallness exceeded what we were able to deliver. Most of us felt that it should be possible for us, as a group of eight, to operate with a support staff of about a hundred and fifty, but in the event this proved to be impossible. The lowest we could squeeze our-selves down to was about four hundred, from the twelve hundred that there had been hitherto. Even that involved devolving many of the responsibilities of the headquarters to operating units, and moving some organizations away from our headquarters. These projected changes in the board, and in the staffing of the board, enabled us to consider getting rid of our headquarters and we decided that we would try to sell it and establish ourselves in a more modern building.

No decision that I have contributed to or been responsible for in my business life has caused more criticism in some areas, or more support and enthusiasm in others than this one! It was looked upon by many as 'selling the company's birth right', finally demonstrating an entire lack of reverence for the good things of the past. By others it was looked upon as a bold, long-overdue, and imaginative step to free the operating units from the dead hand of bureaucracy. In the event the high hopes we had had of large capital gains from the selling of the building proved extremely difficult to achieve. Even worse, we suddenly found that far from there being a host of large new office buildings with the space available for a staff of four hundred, we were already out of step with the column, and most office buildings in London, even the large ones, only provided accom-modation for a hundred and fifty to two hundred people. Moreover, while we wished to change we did not wish to give the impression that the company had gone bankrupt. We believed, therefore, that it was essential that we retain some style in the building we went to, although by definition the style should not be of a kind which had been achieved by the mindless use of money. All of these things proved to be extraordinarily difficult to accomplish, and in the event we ended up converting one third of our existing building and refurbishing the other two thirds for sale or lease. As so often when one's original ideas are not capable of achievement I suspect that the end situation that we have reached may well be the best long-term solution for the company. It is even possible that it is the solution that we should have sought in the first place. One thing is certain, and that is that the symbolism of the decision really helped to focus the pressure for change, and was a clear indication to everybody that we were serious about what we had in mind.

Such acts of symbolism are frequently not too difficult to find and a good deal less painful in the achievement. There is almost always something in a large organization, either organization-ally or in smaller ways, that can be changed which will give very strong messages. An example of symbolism on a rather smaller scale was my wish to change not only the pattern of our meetings, but the venue. The day that I assumed responsibility as chairman, instead of meeting, as we always had done, in the ICI boardroom, an imposing but somewhat impractical room, we met in what had been my office. The boardroom had been designed in an earlier era to emphasize the power of the chairman and this was not at all the way that I wanted to run the company. I wanted our executive team to operate as a band of brothers, where discussion was free and uninhibited, where people could get up and walk around, pour themselves a cup of coffee, argue, draw things on flip charts, gesticulate, and generally feel easy and unrestricted. None of these things had been possible in our magnificent boardroom. Indeed, it was almost impossible to get an argument generated across the imposing round table which, while ensuring from one point of view that everybody could see everybody else, also ensured that the distances were so large that it was difficult to see each other close to. Other changes that I made were that when we met we sat in comfortable conference chairs, each of which had a small adjustable side table on which one could place a collec-tion of papers. There was no organization to where we sat, each person taking the nearest convenient chair. We had flip charts, tea and coffee etc. all available and we met, more often than not, in shirt sleeves. These things may seem unimportant, but in generating the atmosphere for change such details have a critical cumulative effect.

While the symbolism is important, one of the most difficult aspects of change management is to understand the cascade effect of change. Organizations and bureaucracies build themselves up by reinforcement, like more and more flying buttresses on a falling wall. Over a period of time these, which are not architect-designed, tend to force rigidity into the system. It is almost like worker bees building more and more cells, each of which strengthens the total size and dimension of the hive. It is extremely important that when thinking about changing things one should work out exactly where all these buttresses are and ensure that none are inadvertently left standing. If you do leave some the process of change will not be complete. This is another reason why it is helpful to start from the top downwards. In our case we started by sitting down and discussing together what we thought of the particular responsibilities of the board and how, ideally, the board would relate to its operating units. That then led, absolutely automatically, to new thinking and conclusions about the way in which we organized our discussions and our objectives as a group, and this led equally inevitably to changes in our control systems, our reporting systems and everything else.

In this process of change, small actions have a tremendous catalytic and change effect. This is particularly true in large organizations. I remember many years ago when I was responsible for our European operations, persuading the board of the day that in the future we should not look, as a board, at United Kingdom and European sales and profit figures independently. We should state that in future we intended to look upon Europe as our home market and would look at one set of numbers only, those being the total sales across the whole of Europe. This change involved an enormous amount of work and reorganization, but the effect of it was out of all proportion even to my hopes and expectations. Because these were the measures by which we judged success or failure, operating units based in the United Kingdom were forced to think in a European sense, and although the effect was obviously not instantaneous, looking back it was probably one of the most important single changes made at that time. An awful lot of change can be achieved by such catalytic interventions, provided that the interventions are made with great thought; and having clearly seen in one's own mind's eye the directions in which they will lead they can be most economical and effective methods of change. This view of ways of affecting large organizations is, of course, not unique to the change process but is a helpful general tool of management.

One last point in this whole area of change management is to be realistic about the time scale. Ultimately change is only anchored firmly when individuals have changed their perceptions and values, and it is important to be realistic about the time that this may take. Five years is absolutely par for the course for changing attitudes, and even that is only achievable if one is moving well within the established grain of thinking. The essence of change is to make sure that each change that is made is anchored firmly in position before you move on from there. While changing is a continuous process and indeed the habit of changing is one that one can become used to, nevertheless the big changes tend to occur in a sort of wave motion, and it is important that when the wave pulls back from the shore it does not go out too far. It is rather like the tide coming in or going out, each successive wave has to actually move the base line.

Even though this sort of catalytic change may seem slow and inadequate in response to the need, it does at least work. One has only to think of attempts to impose consultation and discussion from above to know that imposed solutions can be easily evaded. Equally such exhortations as 'You are to behave more commercially' or 'This is quite unacceptable!' have absolutely no effect whatsoever. In a position of perceived disaster imposition from above may work for a limited time, but even then speedily degenerates into internal dissension and bickering which is at best non-productive. Think of British Leyland's attempts to change labour relations in the sixties – or British Shipbuilders' head-on assaults on demarcation. Better by far to achieve some change which may self-accelerate rather than to expend all the available energy on resistance!

Although of necessity change requires a five-year horizon and therefore a five-year plan, it is equally important to have clear timetables for the constituent parts of the plan. When I was appointed chairman, with a five-year contract, I sat down and did a bit of thinking on my own. I allocated the first year to changing the board; the second and third years were, in my plan, to be devoted to trying to get the strategies of the operating units clear, and the fourth and fifth years to be devoted to trying to change people and people's attitudes, while pursuing the strategies that we had agreed in years two and three. Inevitably, in the event, other priorities overtook because some of the strategies that we were following were in themselves so demanding that they assisted the process of 'people change'. However, in every change programme there have to be the different components, the changing of the aims and objectives of the organization and the changing of the people within that organization. My 'people' objectives were, and remain, to make our company more customer-orientated, more market-responsive, and faster to adapt. At the same time I wished, and still do wish, to see ICI retaining the values with regard to people and their importance which have been the basis of our company. The mutuality of respect for each other that we enjoy, the ability to discuss and differ openly and without rancour, and the total belief that we must look after each other are the most precious inheritance that any company can have.

In the process of change it is equally important to be clear about those things that one wishes to hold on to, as well as those which one wishes to see changing. It is essential that one continuously reinforces the good aspects that one wishes to hold on to because otherwise, enduring though they may have been in the past, there is always a danger that someone will sweep them away in an ill-considered manner in the enthusiasm for general change. This is particularly the case in terms of dealing with the members of one's firm as a family. It is all too easy for people to think that in today's more rigorous competitive situation there is no room for the caring company. The reverse is the case, as ICI demonstrates practically every day. It is only the caring companies that will survive, and caring cannot be a 'con'; it has to be a genuine attitude of mind and an absolutely fundamental belief in every single person. It is the area that actually makes or breaks a company. It is only against the background of caring that continuous change can be combined with the maintenance of the company spirit and the ability to attract the best.

It is unfortunate that so much of the business world confuses caring, involvement and compassion with out-dated concepts of paternalism and treating your employees as if they are incapable of looking after themselves. True caring is a matter of respect for the individual and the individual's different aspirations, accepting them as his or her right and trying to acknowledge and assist them. It is neither helpful nor practicable to make people dependent on you and remove their self-reliance, but equally it is appalling business to be even more indifferent to their needs than you would be to a piece of machinery. Machinery would be inspected, listened to, oiled and maintained. Time is spent on each and every mechanical part. How is it that so many people begrudge giving the same degree of attention to the individuals who make up the company as they would give to a chunk of inanimate capital goods?

Too many people think that setting up successful organizations is just a matter of 'buying people' and driving them. You may indeed be able to hire people for money, but you can never run a company just by the force of money. The objectives and the company have to be seen to be decent to command the freely given spirit which will build an enduring organization, and an enduring organization is one which is able of itself to adapt continuously not only to the needs of today, but also to the needs of tomorrow. That is why change management is such a vital skill to be learnt.

6

Do We Want to be International?

One of the great paradoxes of business today is that superficially the world is becoming more and more a single market, while in reality national differences are becoming accentuated. The sheer cost scale of modern business is such that in almost every case we need to attempt to sell in world markets. This is particularly so in Europe, where the single markets of each country are quite inadequate to support a world competitive business, and where history has already developed in each country a degree of self-sufficiency which would be quite unthinkable in any single American state, or province of Japan.

Nevertheless, the differences between nations are as great as they ever have been and for British or American businessmen there is a particular trap, which is the growing use of English as the main language of international business. It is interesting, for example, that even in Peking the language of the International Business School is English. Operating in this milieu requires much greater sensitivity to national differences than we are accustomed to having. The mere fact that one stays in the same sort of hotel almost anywhere in the world, that one drives in the same sort of car, that it is now possible to call by telephone or telex directly from almost anywhere in the world, all give a superficial feeling of sameness. A sameness which is desperately misleading, and which must never be taken for granted.

The comment that Britain and America are two countries separated by a common language is uncomfortably true. I am always amazed at how admiring American people are of the verbal facility of many Britons, the wider range of vocabulary and the, to them, more elegant construction of the language. But the British using more words in a more elegant way does not make for better understanding between our nations. Even in companies which pride themselves on their internationalism, and ICI is one, it is amazing how frequently misunderstandings arise between the British and the American branches. Because we apparently speak the same language we tend to believe that we think in the same way and that the words convey the same messages. It is, of course, a peculiarly British characteristic to think that every man is the same under the skin, and that Eskimos are really only would-be Old Etonians wearing fur coats. The realization that Americans use language in a different way, that they are motivated by different things, that they apply a different perspective of history, and that they are the prisoners of different prejudices from ourselves, is something that we find very difficult to understand.

The main task of business is a long-term one. Overwhelmingly the prime responsibility is to try to ensure that the business that we have built up endures, and it can only endure by changing. The sort of business that I ran involves the deployment of very large amounts of capital, in rather inflexible plants, designed to serve particular markets. A fly-by-night approach to commerce is quite hopeless, not only because of the nature of the plants themselves, but also because of the commitment to research and the development of new products. Our aim has to be to try to develop a sense of mutual interdependence. We all know that in private life such relationships can only be built on trust, and a very full understanding and tolerance of individual motives and behaviour. The same is true in business. Under pressure for short-term performance there is an increasing tendency to forget this simple fact. But businesses are not disembodied entities, they consist of people. The individual banker who has lost money on a deal which you have made too keen will learn from that experience, and will seek to recoup on a later occasion. Good business should contain something for both parties and people who seek continuously to disadvantage the other partner soon run out of potential partners, in just the same way as the pyramid seller never achieves the nirvana promised by his theory. I am always worried when we do a deal which is too favourable to us at the expense of our business partner, because I know that the day will inevitably come when the position is reversed.

The point I am trying to make is that commercial matters

involve a great deal of rather sophisticated clarity of purpose, which individuals who act in these areas often do not think their way through. People do not always look far enough ahead to see the consequences of a particular course of commercial action. It requires understanding, sensitivity and perception to know what the long-term consequences of one's actions may be. For example, if you constantly seek to beat the market, it is almost inevitable that somebody is going to try to beat you, which may ultimately be very damaging to your company. If you try merely to match the market there is a clarity of aim and purpose behind your activities which may seem unadventurous but which actually will affect all the myriad commercial decisions which you take. This sort of ruthless clarity of analysis in the background of the way in which one approaches things is difficult enough to permeate through an organization of the same nationality, but it becomes much more difficult when applied to people of other nationalities and other backgrounds. Having a true company philosophy requires great patience, sensitivity and understanding. Most of us feel that in learning to speak another language we automatically gain with it a deeper understanding of the people. Nothing could be further from the truth. Some of the best trained interpreters in the world exist in the Soviet Union, but their actual knowledge and understanding of the different ways of thinking in other countries, and the national characteristics which lie behind the mere translation of the exact word, is a much rarer attribute, unless they have had the opportunity of living overseas. To develop the ability to work in a truly international sense it is highly desirable to have lived in a number of different countries and to have experienced at first hand the differences in them. Differences in small but significant things like shopping, diet, social behaviour and so on.

Language is not a computer program, and indeed the actual literal translation of words can cause offence out of all proportion to the actual intent. To the Anglo-Saxon there is a world of difference between being called a liar on the one hand, and being asked to verify the figures since they are at variance with those tabled by the other side, on the other. In other countries these distinctions are not so obvious, and offence can be given quite unwittingly if translation is too precise. Moreover, dealing with other nationals through a translator or an interpreter is no substitute for direct discussion, even if one's use of language is poor. Nothing is more frustrating than holding a meeting with a Japanese, and giving a short one-sentence reply which, when interpreted, takes six or seven minutes to communicate. At this stage one not only begins to lose confidence but can easily lose the train of what one has been saying, even though the interpretation may have been sound. It is very much easier, even if the language is imperfect, to be communicating directly. But above everything the task is to ensure that the individuals who are making the decisions understand what they are committing themselves to, or at least what you think they are committing themselves to. If the wording is imprecise or capable of two interpretations you can be sure it will be, and the only way to avoid subsequent differences is to test the agreement you have against a number of hypothetical examples. I can think of many cases where sitting down together and saying, 'Let us just see how the contract would stand up if the oil price fell to X, or if we found that we could not sustain our market position', will unearth either deliberate obfuscations or, more frequently, ambiguities which one may spend enormous amounts of time trying to resolve in the long term. It is necessary to check and recheck from every angle that one can think of, because business is based upon trust and trust is based, in turn, on clarity and understanding. It is particularly necessary to check ruthlessly in an internationally operating company because, in addition to the pursuit of a common business aim, large companies have an overlay of values and behaviour which makes it easy to believe that everyone understands perfectly what you have tried to communicate, when in fact they may not.

ICI operates on a substantial scale in India, a country where I was brought up as a boy, and there are many examples of the way in which ICI values and approaches have influenced the behaviour in our companies there, even though for many years there has been only one Englishman in a company with at least ten thousand employees. Indeed, the company has not been headed by an Englishman since the early 1970s. Shortly after the war we built a large explosives factory at a place called Gomia in the state of Bihar, to serve the Indian coal fields nearby. The centre of expertise in our industrial explosives area was at

Ardeer in Scotland. The plant was built, and the Indian engineers and work people trained by a wonderful team of Scots managers and work people, who spent a small number of years in this remote part of the world. To this day that factory in India, which has not employed a single Scotsman there, to my certain knowledge, for the last fifteen years, still solemnly celebrates Burns' Night every year. They pipe in the haggis and drink to the blessed memory in exactly the way that our expatriate Scotsmen did when they were there in the late 1940s. Such customs, which are of immense value in promoting feelings of unity in a large company, are too easily taken to mean that the method of working and the use of language will be exactly the same in both Britain and India. In reality nothing could be further from the truth. Indian people love to talk, discuss, examine and debate. The short, crisp discussion and decision makes them feel uncomfortable. They do not feel that the many ramifications that they would wish to pursue have been properly explored, while to a Scottish or English manager prolonged debate is taken as a sign of non-compliance, doubt and lack of enthusiasm.

Appalling problems can stem from this lack of understanding. For example, Americans tend to be very much more literal in their interpretation of language than British people are. A statement that nothing will be changed in a business relationship means just literally that to an American and the smallest deviation on unimportant matters, even if the deviations themselves are agreed as being desirable, is taken as betrayal of the original concept. British people tend to be more pragmatic and when they say that nothing will change, mean that nothing of substance will change, but that individual adjustments may be necessary to meet changing circumstances. Again, failure to examine what both parties thought they heard can lead not only to mistrust, but even worse, to the view that one party is not having adequate regard for the interests of the other and is treating them with contempt. That is no way to run a railway, let alone a multinational company.

These problems become of particular interest and concern when you get representatives of many different countries attending, for example, a senior staff training course. No matter how hard you try, the likelihood is that staff training courses will be devised and presented very largely by the staff of your head office or your headquarters, and therefore in ICI's case tend to be held in Britain. It is constantly surprising to find how different are the things that have been heard and remarked on by the people of different nationalities attending such a course, despite their apparent command of English, knowledge of the workings of the company, devotion to the values of the business, and their intimate knowledge, liking and respect for each other. I can think of courses where we have had a very specific aim to increase awareness of commercial opportunities, or to provoke discussion of our concerns about capital expenditure, which have been attended by overseas people who have thought that the objective of the course was in the first case personnel policy, and in the second one business strategy.

To deal with these problems in an international company requires a number of actions which we seldom take. I have already laid some stress on the desirability of having lived and worked in more than one country. Understanding the real differences between countries is much easier if these cross-postings can be made earlier in your career rather than later. They are also helped a great deal if the whole of your family moves with you because then the learning becomes a shared process. There is, however, some danger when families move as a whole unit, and it is perfectly possible to live in Japan for example, and make the whole of your life around the American Club, and the Country Club, never developing the friendships and understanding of the country which are after all the object of the exercise. When my wife and I lived in Germany while I was still with the Navy, and I commanded a ship which was crewed entirely by Germans with the exception of one other British colleague, I developed an understanding and liking for Germans and Germany which has enriched the rest of my life. I do not believe that this would have happened if I had just visited the country, no matter how often.

The wise decision that I took at the time (although in reality it didn't seem much of a decision since there didn't seem to be many other options), was to run the ship on exactly the lines of a German naval vessel rather than trying to get my twenty-five sailors to learn British ways. The ship was commanded and run in German, we served German rations and ate in the German manner. The officers and the crew all ate together, an excellent habit, but one which I had not seen anywhere else. Discipline was conducted in a very different way from the navy I knew. Sailors are sailors the world over and have a remarkable ability to find totally implausible and unlikely reasons for arriving back late and drunk from shore leave. The difference lay not in the ingenuity of the story which was comparable, but in the response expected from the officer. The story usually went along the lines of, 'I was coming back on board in good time, absolutely sober, when I saw an old lady who had fallen into the harbour. Without thought I dived in, dragged her ashore, and was lying exhausted by my efforts when a friendly passer-by revived me with rum, brandy, schnapps or whatever. Entirely due to this heroic act, I unfortunately arrived back late.'

In the case of the British sailor any sign that you had accepted such an implausible story was immediately taken as a clear indication that you were not fit to be an officer. You therefore applied a fairly mild punishment and an admonishment along the lines of, 'If you think I believe that you must think I was born yesterday!' In the case of the German sailor, questioning such a story was taken as being a matter of bad taste. The correct way of handling the incident was invariably to say something along the lines of, 'I greatly admire your dedication to the good name of the ship; however, as you know, orders are orders, and discipline is discipline.' You then proceeded to punish him with approximately twice the sentence that you would have given to the British sailor. The interesting lessons that I learnt during this experience were of far greater value to me in later life than any amount of reading or theory could possibly have been, and I was lucky enough to learn them while I was still young.

We try to cross-post a significant number of managers well before they are forty and it is important here to remember that posting to foreign countries is not just a matter of putting British people overseas. We invariably try to give experience of working in Britain to young foreign managers whom we consider to be of particular promise. It is also of the greatest possible importance to put people from overseas into other countries, as well as into Britain. Only quite recently have we begun to learn the value of posting, for example, a German to Italy, or a Frenchman to America. At the present time there are nearly as many overseas employees of ICI working in countries other than their own, as British people working overseas. In this way over a period of time ICI will, I hope, develop into a more truly international company, rather than what it is at the present moment, which is essentially a British company operating throughout the world.

In carrying out such postings there are obvious sensitivities about particular nations in particular countries, which do require some careful thought. It is also necessary to think about the character of the man, and in the case of international postings, his family, before choosing where somebody should go. All too often one finds the most amazing and pleasing surprises when people choose to go overseas. I remember sitting cross-legged on the floor of the flat which one of my British managers was occupying in Tokyo with his charming Lancashire-born wife who had never lived abroad before, hosting a party of his employees, all of whom were Japanese. The bath was full of cooling beer, the language barrier was immense, but the warmth, laughter, enjoyment and mutual regard of everybody at the party was a joy to see.

In overseas postings it is extremely important that the needs and wishes of the family should come first. It is a total waste of time and money to force a man either to separate from his family to pursue his career, or to subject his children to interruptions in schooling and so on which they themselves are not happy about accepting. It is always a very difficult judgement whether the advantage of having lived for some years as a young person in a foreign country outweighs the interruptions in the formal schooling schedule. Sadly this particular problem has become more acute as the need for academic qualifications for success in later life becomes overriding. The only people who can make the choice are the family themselves and they must, in addition to being given the choice, also be given the time to consider it. ICI believes in flying families overseas to see the sort of conditions they will be living in, and giving them the chance of talking with those who have lived there for some time.

It is surprising how courageous and adventurous people are, and I never ceased to marvel when working in the North-East of England at the way in which the Japanese wives of some of the employees who were seconded to my division adjusted and settled down in a land and culture so totally different from their own. It was always easier for the men, because after all they were dealing with business problems of a type which they understood and were familiar with, albeit from the other side of the looking glass. For a Japanese lady, however, suddenly to find herself pitchforked out of her small house, probably a long journey out of the centre of Tokyo, or Osaka, into a house on the edge of the Yorkshire Moors must be the most incredible change to adapt to. If you add to that the fact that the Japanese find English particularly difficult to learn and make themselves understood in, I always felt that such women were true heroines. One can, however, overestimate one's own assessment of the problems and when I talk to them either in the United Kingdom, or when they are back in their homelands, the vast majority of them have looked on the whole thing as a tremendous and enjoyable adventure.

There are other dangers in the cross-posting business. Sometimes, in our anxiety to give broader international experience to people we place them in jobs which are either beyond their level of competence, or to which they cannot adjust. A bad report under such circumstances can be particularly damning, even though the man in his own setting would have been well able to handle promotion at a national level. This all really adds up to a need for great sensitivity, both in selecting and following up individuals who are plucked out of their natural habitat, and I suppose when considering the whole area of international operations the very first lesson is to listen and listen and listen again. Not only do you need to listen, but you need to show that you have heard and understood, and are taking whatever action needs to be invoked.

The area where it is probably necessary to move in most quickly is where there are signs that levels of trust are breaking down between different parts of the organization, one of which is of a different nationality from the other. It is a depressingly frequent event and, more often than not, derives from misunderstandings. Any firm with an American subsidiary must have experienced on the one hand a continual suspicion at the British end that the Americans wish to have nothing whatsoever to do with the main group and are interested in unilateral independence – regardless of the cost to the rest of the group –

which on the other hand is mirrored with equal intensity on the part of the Americans, who are convinced that the sole aim of everybody outside America is to force them to operate in a way which is inappropriate to their country. No matter how many times you tell them that you do not wish to introduce British management style into the USA they are convinced that every move you make is a step in that direction; an effort to introduce greater centralization and rigidity in order to curb their freedom of action. This syndrome has, to my certain knowledge, occurred in practically every company of every nationality that operates in the USA and is, I am sure, something to do with American culture and the very high value that they put on headroom. It is a classic example of lack of trust on both sides and although it would be foolish to pretend that either side's suspicions are never justified, even when they are not, suspicion still seems to abound. The same thing can, of course, happen in relations with customers of other nationalities, but there the reaction on the part of the customer is quick and brutal and he has his own remedy. Perhaps because of this, customers of nationalities other than our own tend to get the sort of attention and consideration which we do not by any means always give to those of our own nationality. Trust, once it begins to deteriorate, quite suddenly flips over and becomes a sort of galloping corrosion of suspicion which is very difficult to halt. Trust is tremendously difficult to build up and all too easy to destroy, so it is worth taking all sorts of actions, even if they appear to be finicky, to avoid losing it.

The biggest source of deterioration of trust is always misunderstanding, and misunderstanding can happen on the telephone all too easily. A conversation on the telephone never enables you to judge whether you have been understood. You cannot tell whether your remarks are being greeted with incomprehension, incredulity, hilarity or sheer disbelief, reactions which are easily gauged when one is working face to face. Moreover, telephone calls are usually of quite limited duration and people hate admitting that they don't understand. It may be useful to ask whether the listener is sure that they understand what you have said; although, while once in a blue moon they may admit that they don't, more often they will not because they have formed their own impression of what is required from the words you have used. If you make a practice of recording some of your telephone conversations you will be surprised how often you will find that you have either been imprecise or that your words have been capable of more than one interpretation. This situation is easier to avoid in a face-to-face meeting where it is much more difficult for misunderstandings to occur, but even here they can begin to develop when both sides are communicating imperfectly. Understanding between different nationalities needs checking in every way possible, but particularly by asking each other to repeat what actions we believe we have been asked to take. Understanding can be checked again by getting regular reports of what actions have actually been taken in pursuit of the agreement that you thought you had reached. Confirmation in writing of the salient points of a telephone conversation can often catch misunderstanding before it begins to burgeon.

It is particularly important in international relationships within a company to make it 'safe' to expose misunderstanding. No one feels comfortable working in an environment which is different from his own national one and people in such circumstances are very hesitant to display ignorance. After all, every individual has pride and if to personal pride you add the pride that one feels when one is representing one's country in an international milieu, it is even more difficult to relax sufficiently and take the risk of appearing to be foolish, uncomprehending, or even uninvolved. It is absolutely essential under these circumstances to make the exposure of misunderstandings legitimate and to ensure that no one feels that he is being subjected to hostile treatment.

I remember many years ago visiting a factory in India where a serious industrial relations problem had arisen with our people. As is so often the case, unfortunately the industrial relations problem was partly of our own making. The area was one of very high unemployment and there were large numbers of educationally highly qualified Indians who were unable to obtain work. We had set up the factory from new and had thought, therefore, that we would attempt to choose only very highly qualified people for all the jobs, no matter how menial. We therefore found ourselves in a position where we were under-employing the capabilities of our people and moreover they felt that we were letting them down because they had expected promotion opportunities which simply were not there. Their frustration manifested itself in a series of confrontations with the management, who became increasingly demoralized; the factory then entered into a depressingly familiar spiral, where relations between both parties deteriorated, trust vanished and local management and their people spent most of their time sniping at each other. While the root causes were different, I had just come from dealing with a rather similar situation in the United Kingdom, and when I was talking with the management was able to point out that their problems were not by any means unique, and that the remedies which we had applied in Britain could conceivably apply to them as well. The realization that other people in other parts of the world had to deal with similar difficulties eased the problem of discussion enormously and within no time we were merrily working together to try to resolve a common problem, where each of us could bring something to the party. We could do little for the over-qualified staff that we had recruited, except try to ensure that we listened to them more sympathetically and attempted to see to it that some promotion opportunities occurred. The solution lay, rather, in the attitudes of the management who had to realize the source of the problem and deal with it with sensitivity and sympathy. The realization that others had had the same experience and that acting in these softer ways was not necessarily a sign of lack of manhood helped a great deal. We introduced considerable training of the management and within eighteen months the problems were easing and the factory had many years of peaceful operation thereafter.

I do not believe the true international company yet exists, although some of the oil companies and IBM are perhaps closer to such a picture than most others. The idea of the international company is something of great social importance for the world at large, as well as being an absolute prerequisite for business success. There are sadly all too few activities where people of every nation work together in harmony and mutual respect for a common and honourable goal, and the international company is one of them. The days have gone when each theatre of the world, separated by large geographic distances, could isolate itself from what was happening elsewhere. When I was a boy at school in England it used to take nearly two months to get a reply to a letter written to my parents in India. A long-distance telephone call was a near impossibility. Nowadays no matter where you are it is possible to communicate almost instantly with even the most distant parts of the world. Quite apart from the business prerogative, anything which increases understanding between people of different nations can only help in the long term. I have sought deliberately to internationalize our board by obtaining high-quality non-executive directors of different nationalities to work with us. We have gained immeasurably by this but the day of the true international company will dawn when instead of the majority of a board being of one nation with, perhaps, non-executive advice from other countries, we will be operating in a truly international way. Hopefully by then the board of the international company will reflect the measure of its operations.

Just as we have sought to spread our business where the markets of the world are, one third in Europe, one third in the Americas, and one third in the Far East, so one would hope in the years ahead that the board of a company like I C I would be constituted, in approximately equal proportions, of citizens of the same areas by birth. We are sadly all of us a long way away from that but we are moving in the right direction. Our Belgian operations are run by a Frenchman. Our Italian operations are run by a Swiss. Our Australian company has a Canadian as the chief executive officer. Our worldwide speciality chemical business, based in America, is run by an Australian. We have almost as many third country nationals working in other countries as we have Britons. These things are steps in the right direction, but there is no question that if we are to be successful in the markets of the world we need a much greater understanding of, and sensitivity to the habits, values and mores of other countries than we have at present.

7

Catalysts and Judo

I have always believed in what might be termed the techniques of 'mild' management. By this I mean that small interventions, carefully thought out, can have an effect far out of proportion to the amount of effort involved in the actual intervention. They often start a greater degree of movement, and generate a stronger self-accelerating trend than one anticipated. In my mind's eye I have always likened it to making a small movement near the centre of a see-saw which makes a much more obvious impact at the end. While the theory is great the practice is extremely difficult to master and always opens up the danger of that most difficult of management positions, the fear that people are being manipulated. The lines between manipulation, management and leadership are fine, but devastatingly clear in the minds of individuals. Manipulation, or the fear of manipulation, arouses more antagonism and is more antipathetic to business success than almost anything else, and yet the really skilful manager has to take actions which can lead to such accusations.

Let me give an example from my own personal experience. Many years ago, when I was a division chairman of ICI, I and other division chairmen became concerned at the lack of integrating mechanisms being used by the main board. We felt that we perceived a vacuum in the way in which the company was coordinated and led. After attempts to explain our concerns we decided that we should try to fill the gap by setting up our own meeting of division chairmen at a level below the board. There had always been great fears of such a step both on the part of the main board members who felt, perhaps with some justification, that this might be an attempt to usurp their authority, and also on the part of the division chairmen, who feared exactly that reaction and the consequences that this

might have on them personally. We were extremely fortunate at
the time in having, as the most senior division chairman,
Donald Emmerson who was of an age when it was quite clear
that personal ambition could play no part in leading such a
move.

He and I, who shared the problems of leading two of the
larger raw materials suppliers to the company in the shape of
the Heavy Organic Chemicals division and the Mond division,
were painfully aware of the consequences of the perceived lack
of coordination which was taking place. We therefore took the
lead and with the agreement of the chairman of the day (who in
retrospect showed the tolerance for which I CI is justly famed,
and a great deal of personal courage to boot) set up our meeting.
The meeting was quite successful in enabling us to sort out the
problems which lay within our own jurisdiction and speedily
established itself as something more than just a talking shop.
The fact that all the division chairmen were prepared to give
their time to attend and that we felt that something was to be
gained from such meetings, which were held quite openly in
Millbank, was tribute enough to the concept.

The division chairmen's meeting was set up in about 1970 and
was staffed by a secretariat that was provided from one of the
operating divisions. For administrative convenience it was usually provided from the chairman of the meeting's own division.
We issued and circulated minutes, took decisions and operated
in a perfectly open way. However, as time went on we became
more and more concerned at our inability to influence company
policies, which we saw as increasingly preventing us from
doing all the things that we thought were possible. I left the
meeting of course when I was appointed to the board, but as the
'new boy' I remained in touch with it and became a sort of
unofficial liaison officer between the board and the chairmen. I
am not sure that my colleagues really approved of this, since to
them it must have looked rather like keeping a foot in both
camps, but I still believed it was important to try and link the
thinking of the division chairmen and the thinking of the board
more closely and tried various ways to achieve this. A sort of
grumbling dissatisfaction continued for some time on the part of
the division chairmen and a degree of concern began to develop
in the board at what they perceived to be a focal point for

trouble. I was the organization director of the day and sought many different opinions about how we should resolve the problem. My own solutions tended to be of a classical, organizational type, setting the division chairmen's meeting up as a formal part of the company structure, delegating specific powers to it and so on. There was absolutely no support from my colleagues of the day for such an approach. When Roland Wright became our chairman he instituted the habit of an annual get-together with the division chairmen to discuss the company's activities and prospects in the round. At one of these the whole issue surfaced in quite a dramatic fashion, with a fair amount of feeling being generated on both sides of the controversy. We appeared to be at an almost total impasse. The division chairmen felt that they had a contribution to make which the board did not wish to hear, and the board were unwilling to delegate to the division chairmen, as a group, a substantial part of their own responsibilities.

Roland's solution was a brilliant one, and in the finest tradition of what I would term 'catalytic' management. I remember being deeply disappointed when he advocated it and saying that it fell so far short of what was required that I did not believe that it could possibly have any effect: how wrong I was. The solution was that the division chairmen's meeting should continue to be their meeting, it should not be entered into the company scheme of organization and it should not have any delegated powers. However, the secretariat of the meeting should be provided by the secretariat of the company and the minutes should be circulated to the members of the board. The secretariat of the company would be available to help with organizing any follow-up action which might be necessary. The agendas of the meeting would remain under the command of the chairman of the division chairmen's committee, himself a division chairman. Attendance at the committee could only be at their invitation, and to this day even if the chairman of the company wishes to speak to them, he gently sounds out the chairman of the committee to see whether they would be prepared to invite him. This right of managing their own affairs is, in my view quite rightly, fiercely defended.

The system was set up, and has worked very well ever since. It contains the best features of the loose organization, while having given a degree of authority and status to the meeting from which it has benefited. It has proved to be of immense value, both to the board and to the division chairmen, as a means of communicating, coordinating and understanding each other's viewpoints on many difficult issues. I always regarded an invitation from the committee as a three-line whip and it took precedence over any of my other activities. At the same time the division chairmen are able to ask and obtain the attendance of any board member whose actions or activities they feel are not having the results that they should, and this can be done in a pleasant and informal manner. This one small 'mild' management intervention has acted in the catalytic way of bringing the board and the division chairmen closer together and has enabled us to coordinate our affairs in a way which a harsher intervention could not possibly have achieved. My own solution of setting the meeting up as an integral part of the organization would not have resolved the interface problems, instead it would have led to endless debate around the lines of demarcation and the specific responsibilities that each had retained to themselves. What was achieved was a degree of flexibility in our approach to problems, and a degree of adaptability which has enabled us to withstand many changes and remain together as a team – a really first-class example of a catalytic input.

Catalytic interventions are very often about communications and communications systems. Another example which springs to mind was during my period as deputy chairman at the Wilton site. One of the many problems of industrial relations is invariably the lack of accurate and fast communication. Industrial relations matters are very often as much about misunderstandings as they are about points of principle. They are quite often about issues which themselves are not of great importance, but are the fuse which allows dissatisfaction to boil over. I have even known industrial relations situations in which the problem has been to find out what the strike is actually about. The actual pretext for the strike could be solved quite easily and quickly but was, in the event, merely the trigger point which enabled a whole range of other, cumulative items to build up. Resolving the trigger point does not, under such circumstances, resolve the strike.

A catalytic intervention that I made at that time was to put in a personal intercommunication system where all the works managers on the site could communicate on a private-line system, a sort of primitive 'conference phone' arrangement. As soon as an industrial relations problem occurred on one plant, which might flash over to the others, we had an arrangement that we would activate the system and the works managers concerned would, as a prime responsibility, keep the rest of us informed of the state of affairs. The effect was almost instantaneous because all of us knew as much as each other, and because all of us were involved in the tactical decisions, and understood them. A degree of unity formed around the works which was far more effective than the systems we had had before. Previously the works manager would have reported to the site manager or, while I was there, the deputy chairman responsible for the site, and he would have informed the other works managers as he felt fit. An open communications system enabled the works managers to relate things that were happening on one part of the site to things that were happening on another. A good example of an area where quite a small investment but a major change in a way of dealing with things produced long-lasting results far out of proportion to the time and effort involved in the action.

Unfortunately, many of us are all too familiar with what one might call reverse-catalytic reactions, in other words, a small, unregarded action which worsens an already bad situation in a dramatic way; the extra turn down on the relief valve which finally causes an entire situation to explode; the inadvertent pushing of something one step too far which brings the whole situation to the boil. What we fail to think through is that for every one of these bad effects it is possible to have an equally powerful positive one. Is this manipulation? I think not. But what it is, or what it calls for, is a degree of sophistication in deciding what intervention to make, and a degree of determination and clarity to make minimal interventions which are facilitating or enabling interventions rather than limiting ones. Catalytic interventions are an art; an art that can only derive from a real understanding of how both individuals and organizations work. It is not a subject which can be taught by sociologists or behaviourists, but it is a subject which any thinking manager really needs to address him or herself to. It is an area, interestingly enough, where women managers very often intuitively think and act in these ways, while men tend to go for the more 'macho' and obvious. A problem with catalytic management initiatives is that to the majority of people they appear to be quite inadequate responses to problems which worry them, and indeed in many cases are seen almost as being an attempt to evade dealing with the core problem. They are, in fact, far more than that.

Another example of catalysis which I think is extremely important and where the world is littered with bad examples, is in the whole area of takeovers and absorption into organizations of new parts or partners. This is an area, I must admit, where participation in some social science training taught me a great deal. In the late 1960s a number of people in ICI became very interested in behavioural training and there was a growing move to send senior managers to the USA to take part in T-groups. These were in a way the forerunners of the encounter sessions which have been described so many times elsewhere, but were an attempt, by a process of psychological immersion, to teach managers sensitivity and more about how their styles were perceived by others. Excellent though the aim may have been, I am bound to say that I found the methods distasteful and started, perhaps because of my own inhibitions, with a prejudice against the whole idea. At the time I was the personnel director of the Heavy Organic Chemicals division. A band-wagon was growing on which, while nobody was forced to go to a T-group against their will, there was a strong feeling that you were something less than a man and a good company servant if you refused. The inference was that you had something to hide, or that you were such a psychological mess that you couldn't face up to it. From my point of view the thing was made even worse by the fact that wives were encouraged to go along and I felt this to be an intrusion on individuals' privacy and rights which was beyond the company's legitimate interests.

I had made up my mind that I certainly wasn't going to allow anybody from my division to go unless and until I had experienced a T-group myself, and so in a thoroughly unhelpful frame of mind I set off. The T-group took place at a splendid American country club called La Costa in California. The surroundings were magnificent with every conceivable luxury available. On the course that I attended there were only three non-Americans – two of us were British and from I C I, and there was a South African from Shell. All the other participants were Americans, all had brought their wives, and the whole thing was conducted in a sort of 'pressure cooker' atmosphere which encouraged degrees of revelations of internal motivations and feelings which I found embarrassing and distasteful. However, that has little to do with the example of what I did in fact learn. We were formed into groups and after going through the wringer of examining what our motivations were and what we thought of each other (including, in our case, at least two complete breakdowns of individuals), we took part in a game with other groups which was called the 'takeover game'. Much though I disliked the internal sessions, the 'takeover game' taught me more about the dynamics of teams and the problems of takeovers than any other experience that I could possibly have had; the rest of the week was worth it for that alone. I would hasten to say that the rest of the week was not one of great personal suffering but seemed to me to be rather far away from what I conceived to be our business needs at that time, and moreover was stretching continuously over the line between public and private life, on which I have always had very strong views.

The 'takeover game' had been blocked out as a day in which two groups together would agree how to apportion their time. It looked like a non-event about a non-problem, because sensibly one would have thought that two minutes in the bar would have made everybody decide to go to the beach or the swimming pool and that would be the end of it. In the event it proved to be an almost impossible task. It started by each group independently deciding how we should spend our time and then sending two delegates to explain our position to the other group and to negotiate on our behalf. Paradoxically my colleague from I C I and I were both chosen by our own separate groups to negotiate with each other on this epic problem. We found little difficulty in agreeing between the group of four representatives what would be a sensible course to take, though this had involved a degree of compromise and even some difference from the negotiating briefs we had been sent out with. When we went back we found that we had been rejected by our original teams. From such an unpromising beginning things went from bad to worse. Having experienced total failure during the whole of the morning at agreeing together how we should spend our time, the second half of the day involved one team being given the right to allocate the time of the other team. This was even worse. By the end of the day we had spent the entire time in high emotional argument and had achieved no concrete results whatsoever.

What were the lessons? The lessons were that if you wish to amalgamate two groups you can only do it by actually setting out with the aim of creating an entirely new group, in the composition and design of which both parties are equally involved. Even more to the point the taker-over has more obligation to change than the taken-over. It is up to the person who has the power to accommodate to the other, and the degrees of change involved to the taker-over must both be, and be seen to be, at least as great as to the team which is being absorbed. In addition to these points a further point emerged and that was, rather obviously if one thinks about it, that the weaker of the two parties, he who is ostensibly being taken-over, will accept things which he himself asks for, but will not accept things which are imposed upon him. I have had many subsequent opportunities to put the lessons that I learnt from this rather silly game, which at the time seemed to be one of the biggest wastes of a day I had ever spent, into practice. I have to say that the lessons seem to me to be as valid and clear today as they were when I had spent some time thinking about and dissecting in my mind the actual game that we had played.

My first opportunity of putting these ideas into practice occurred during my chairmanship of the Heavy Organic Chemicals division. I have mentioned these experiences briefly in Chapter 4, but it is perhaps more interesting as an example of catalytic management. In those days the manufacture of nylon and terylene, both in a past era high earning inventions, was shared between three divisions in a rather haphazard way. This reflected the development of the business rather than any technical or commercial logic. As an attempt to address this problem I was asked by the board to take over the intermediate plants which were being run at that time by Dyestuffs and

Fibres. Thereafter the theory was, and still remains, that everything from the basic oil refining to the polymer stage would be
done by one division while the actual polymerization and
spinning would still be carried out by Fibres, who were close to
the customer and understood their business. There was a lot of
technical logic in the change of organization. The Dyestuffs
division had considerable skills in the fields of organic chemistry and running fine chemical manufacturing. Our own skills
lay much more in the very sort of large-scale, capital-intensive
operation that the manufacturing of nylon had become. The
same applied to the manufacture of terephthalic acid which was
just being started up and developed as the raw material intermediate for the manufacture of polyester fibre.

I was helped in this absorption by the fact that it was well
known that my own division had made no predatory bid for the
other organizations and indeed had argued that we did not
want it because we believed that the diversion of management
effort from our own fields of activity would be damaging. Of the
two business absorption problems the absorption of nylon was
the most difficult. The business was in heavy loss, the people in
the business had believed for many years that they were cost-
effective, competitive producers and that the problems lay
further downstream in our Fibres operations and that, because
they could not make an adequate living, prices had to rise.

Arthur Taylor, my deputy chairman, and I on having been
told to take on the nylon operation decided to make a start by
doing a tour of the competitive nylon producers to see what we
could learn. Ten days later in a bar in America, after a day of
discussing nylon production with some American producers, I
remember us both saying almost simultaneously that we knew
what the problem was. Far from being the most cost-effective
producer it was apparent that we were actually relatively ineffi-
cient. Other producers were able to live with current prices
better than we were, something was wrong therefore with our
cost structure, and the happy assumption that if we couldn't
make money nobody else could was wrong. It was, in fact, an
arrogant assumption of superiority over others who were in fact
doing better. The problem therefore was to get something in the
order of £100 a ton off the costs. That stage of the analysis was
easy. All it required was a fresh approach to the problem, with

an open mind which was unfettered by responsibility for the historic position in which the business found itself. How to do it, however, was a different problem altogether. This was where my experience of the 'takeover game' came in. It was quite apparent that we could not go blundering in telling people who felt that they were the ones who knew the business and the technology what we felt was wrong and how they should go about putting it right. It was equally apparent that they had not been set the task of reducing their costs in a way which had gathered their commitment.

Before the night was out, between us we had made a number of decisions which we subsequently carried out. First of all we would change the name of the division to indicate that we wanted to create an entirely new organization combining both the old Heavy Organic Chemicals division, of which I was the chairman, and the two new parts that were joining it. Secondly we would find more places in Heavy Organic Chemicals for senior management from Nylon and Terephthalic Acid than we would place in the reverse direction. And thirdly we would install a 'gate-man', in other words put in one manager, the best man we could think of from our outfit, and we would instruct the remainder of our division that there was to be no approach to these new businesses except through him and with his consent. We were not going to have our functional experts treading across and arousing antagonism by displaying their greater expertise.

We chose as our gate-man Dr Rab Telfer, who subsequently became the chairman of the division, and is now pursuing a later career as the director of the Manchester Business School. We could not have made a better choice. He was a man of great technical confidence and considerable sensitivity in dealing with people. He understood what we were aiming for and he spent enormous amounts of time and energy gaining the commitment of his new team to the concept that they could indeed reduce their costs. We did not, at that stage, explain the full enormity of how much we felt they had to take off but we did indicate a number which, despite being almost immediately rejected as quite impossible, had been easily surpassed within two years. The energies of the people in the nylon business were turned totally on to demonstrating to the new organization that they were a *corps d'élite* and highly competent. At the same time when they hit problems which were outside their own experience, or where they could not see a way through, they could always call on the help of the remainder of the division. There were inevitably a number of jobs to be reduced, but we ensured that the reductions occurred evenly throughout the whole organization and that at least as many of our own people left as the new people who had joined us. The whole process worked extremely well and it all had its basis in a single, theoretical, management game.

I have had many similar experiences subsequently, when I have tried to do the same thing. The latest experience of this technique occurred when we acquired the speciality chemicals business of the Beatrice Foods Group: the largest single acquisition that I C I has ever made. This group consisted of ten highly specialized and successful companies who had been assembled together into a loosely coordinated speciality chemicals business by Beatrice Foods over a period of time. They were in different areas of business and did not appear to have a great deal in common. I C I's interest had really been in trying to buy an established outlet in the new materials business and we had been interested in a particular part of the Beatrice Group for some time. In the event it proved easier to buy the lot and when we got them we found to our delight what a jewel we had. Again we put in a first-class gate-man and we instructed the rest of the company that they were not to approach the Beatrice Group, they were to wait for the Beatrice Group to come to them. It was a rather different situation in this case, because the relative sizes of the two businesses were such that we could not readily demonstrate an entirely new organization, but we did try to show that the specialities business, which we had recently set up, would be modelled more on the Beatrice way of doing business than on the traditional ways that I C I had been using.

There is remarkably little written about the process of taking over and absorbing companies. I know because at the time that I was asked to absorb the nylon operations I read everything that I could find that had been published on the subject, which was not a great deal! This is odd as it is one of the areas of activity which is most common at the present time and every financial analysis has revealed how few takeover bids succeed in achieving the hopes with which they have been launched. The reasons lie almost entirely in the management of people and the subsequent ways in which teams are coalesced to form a new and better team which puts together the strengths of both the old teams. If this is not done with understanding and sensitivity, prolonged and unconstructive internal conflict can reduce the intrinsic strengths of both.These are all examples of what I would term the catalytic approach. Mild interventions which seem to be shirking the main object, but which have the effect of releasing energy and gaining commitment to the actual achievement, albeit in a slightly longer time scale. But there is another management approach of a totally different type which is equally effective, and this I term managerial judo.

Judo is always described as using the power of the opponent to defeat himself, and the name is therefore perhaps not the most felicitous choice for what I have in mind. Judo in my managerial terms is where you utilize the force of the dynamic of what is going on and by diversion turn it in a positive way instead of a negative one. There are many examples of this technique, but perhaps the easiest one to describe is the whole problem of internal pricing. I have never known a large or a small organization which doesn't have endless problems about the prices at which an intermediate that is manufactured in one part of the company is transferred to another. It is a source of almost endless belly-aching and can produce a fantastic head of managerial and emotional steam. It is a problem which ICI has always had in spades!

As a chemical company ICI is integrated right the way through from its own oil wells, sources of salt or limestone to the end product. In consequence most end products have gone through a number of stages inside the company. Many years ago it was plain that if we were to understand the relative economics of various parts of the company, and the relative profitability of those parts, we had to attempt to transfer at commercial prices – but what is a commercial price? In many cases the intermediates that we make are not readily traded and in cases where they are traded it is not always apparent what discounts are available for very large 'tied' customers. Typically, in a chemical business, raw materials may amount to nearly half of the total bill, therefore a mistake in buying can invalidate the whole process further on down the line. Since reinvestment decisions are invariably made on profitability it is small wonder that there is no more critical area of debate than that of inter-merger pricing.

For many years we operated a set of rules drawn up by one of the most commercial of ICI's main board directors in the past. We agreed that the aim should be commercial pricing and set out an appeals procedure which could be followed in the event of failure to agree. Initially this worked well, because there was an implied failure on the part of the operating units if they were unable to agree what the commercial transfer price should be. Over a period of time this effect began to weaken and a whole new corporate game developed. It was much easier to claim that one's failure to reach one's profit margins or projections had been due to an arbitrary and ill-considered judgement by somebody else, than because of one's miscalculation of what the real price should be. The arbitration system that had been set up increasingly tended to resolve the problem by halving the difference between the two opposing points of view. The game to obtain competitive advantage within the company therefore became one of increasing the difference of view rather than decreasing it, since if you could demonstrate a ridiculously low (or high) price, dependent on whether you were a buyer or a seller, there was a chance that the process of cutting it somewhere near the middle would still give you a competitive advantage. We had inadvertently set up a dynamic which led to more and more escalations and differences of opinion, and also the development of bitterness and ill-feeling. The board found itself spending enormous amounts of time on the whole issue.

The judo solution to this would have been to have issued a new ruling which said that in any case that went to arbitration, the arbitrator would choose one or the other case submitted and that in no case would he arbitrate between them by seeking an intermediate position. All the energy which had gone into trying to prove unduly high or low prices would then be directed to trying to avoid the consequences of a disastrous decision to one's business, since most businesses cannot live with uncompetitive prices. In fact we solved the problem by other, less harsh methods over a period of time and inter-merger pricing arguments occur very seldom now. The judo approach is in many ways almost the reverse of the catalytic one, although in some cases the approach may be rather similar. What would have been necessary in the example I have given would have been an apparently irrational firm statement of how the matter would be dealt with. This would have had to have been based on careful thought and analysis of the likely reactions of the parties concerned. Very frequently the use of the judo technique leads to further decentralization and giving those who will be affected by decisions the responsibility of taking them. The placing of clear responsibility on those most affected very often changes the dynamics of the argument.

Another example of this relates to those services which are common to a number of parts of a business and are frequently grouped together with the name 'centralized functions'. Such things as centralized purchasing, or a centralized computer service which provides the concentration of expertise which no individual outfit on its own can afford to carry. Many of these seem to be more efficiently run as a single grouping serving the whole gamut of the businesses. If the centralized functions are a part of head office and therefore 'belong' to the board you have united everybody in the company against them. One thing that everybody knows is that the board is incompetent and out of touch and that head office is a cost centre and not a profit centre. There is the maximum mileage to be gained from complaining and no mileage whatsoever from acceptance. Moreover, centralized functions are threatening because there is always the belief, in the outposts of Empire, that they are spending their whole time making value judgements on the way that the business is conducted out in the sticks, and rushing to report to the boss on how incompetently X or Y or Z carries out this or that or the other specialist function. We have found remarkable success in putting centralized functions out to one of the operating units to run on behalf of others. Confidence is greater because the other operating units feel that these functions are now under the control of people who they consider to be more profit-motivated than the board (incorrectly I hasten to add!), and also because each operating unit is already likely to be managing something on behalf of the others. This produces a high degree of mutual interdependence and a greater willingness to collaborate with the function concerned in the knowledge that lack of collaboration may be reciprocated in an area for which one is oneself responsible. There is a degree of balance, therefore, which the head office relationship with operating units or associated companies is never likely to achieve.

Another example of the judo technique, which I am bound to admit I find very difficult to follow, is the constructive use of time in industrial relations matters. I have always been an activist in this area, and I have never been happy to sit back and believe that time may affect things – I need to know what is being done to resolve the situation. There is, however, an equally experienced view which says that time is a major factor in industrial relations disputes, and I am bound to say that experience seems to show that this view is valid. My own compromise position on this is that I am prepared to wait in an industrial relations dispute, provided I know what I am waiting for and provided I am convinced that there is nothing more positive that can be done to influence the result. Time is a major element in such matters; there is a time when these things can be settled, and there is a time when they cannot. The erosion of time in itself affects people's views and people's thinking on subjects. It is a good example of a sort of passive judo approach but one where, as in all the subjects touched on in this chapter, the key is to have thought out both the forces at work and the probable course of the forces that one is either using or releasing.

There are innumerable other examples, both of the uses of the catalytic approach and the use of the judo one. Each of us uses them consciously or unconsciously depending upon our previous skill and experience. A trivial example which every one of us has used is to set a clear date for the reporting back of work in which one is engaged oneself. When I took over as chairman of ICI, I announced almost immediately the date of a meeting with the chief executives of our companies throughout the world, where we would announce how the board was going to work. Working against this self-imposed deadline certainly concentrated our minds, and forced us to move at a pace which we might not have chosen if we had not known that we would have to face the public humiliation of saying that we had not been able to clear our own minds sufficiently to meet it!

The difficulty is that in these matters the fact that you have thought the thing out at all can leave one open to the accusation of manipulation. In the case I have just cited I explained to my colleagues why I wanted to set the date, and we all agreed that it would form a useful forcing mechanism for us. Had I done it purely on the basis of 'This will make us buckle up' and not communicated my thinking, I believe I could have been accused of manipulation, even though the action would have been exactly the same. These techniques are vital if the results are to be achieved, but equally it is important that they are not used in a hole-and-corner, or back-street sort of way. People have to understand what is being aimed for and the feeling that one is being manipulated by forces outside one's control has to be avoided at all costs.

8

Boardmanship

Almost everywhere in the world the title of director carries with it an image quite different from that of the title of manager. In almost every country an appointment as a director is viewed as being different in kind, in power and in esteem, even to that of being a manager of a very large organization. The fact that directors come in all shapes and sizes, from those with tiny enterprises with a turnover of a few thousands, or even hundreds, a year, up to the very largest, and the fact that many general managers in large organizations have far more responsibility, and control far larger businesses than many directors, hasn't weakened in any way the mystique of belonging to a board. The public's view of directors in the United Kingdom is not always a very flattering one. There is a considerable suspicion amongst many people that directors spend their time living high on the hog on expenses, and manage to carry out a lot of their duties on the golf course, or entertaining in far-off sunny climes.

Despite the romantic views and the fact that, for example, the Institute of Directors in the United Kingdom tends to be looked on as being of much more importance and significance than the British Institute of Management, it is surprising how little guidance is available to people who become directors. Books by the thousand are written on management – reminiscences, advice, and management theories are all propounded, and schools of management are available throughout the world. For all the advice available you would think that the task of management was incredibly simple. One only has to follow theory Y as opposed to theory X, or one should employ the Blake Grid, or the precepts enclosed in Peters and Waterman's book, *In Search of Excellence*. There are almost as many theories of management as there are managers, and of course this is the problem. Each one of us has to develop our own personal management style that suits us and the people with whom we are working. Whatever one can complain of as a manager it is not shortage of advice. Management consultants are there for every conceivable part of the manager's job. But you try getting advice, guidance, a course, or a specialist book on the skills of being a good director of a company, and you will find almost nothing except a great deal of mystique.

It is fair to say that the change from being a manager or CEO of a business to joining the company's board, is one of the most profound that a businessman is ever likely to experience. The jobs are quite different and require quite different skills. It does not always follow that the best executive manager will become the best director, and, indeed, I have sometimes wondered whether we should stream and select directors quite differently to the way we stream and select chief executives. Not only is there little external guidance about the changes required of you, but all too often no one inside the company guides you either. To a considerable degree the advice, help and counselling that you receive depends on the chairman's view of his responsibility for helping in the education of his fellow board members. Even if he is interested, with the best will in the world it is a tricky job to undertake.

In law every member of a board shares a co-equal responsibility for the future of the company. The chairman's legal position is very little different to that of the newest board members. Moreover, board members are chosen from amongst the most successful executives of the company, and are invariably men of mature age and considerable experience. Even the most robust chairman must find it very difficult to take on the responsibility of guiding mature people on how to do their job, particularly mature people with a very considerable personal track record. There is therefore an understandable tendency when you first join the board of a public company for everyone to assume that you will 'pick it up as you go along'. Just as in the rest of industry, guidance, counselling and the minor but helpful and significant interventions from your boss which help to develop skills, experience and confidence, are sadly all too rare.

Individual help of this sort is also very rare on the boards that I have served on. The natural corollary should be that the board ought to spend some time, reasonably regularly, discussing amongst themselves how the board is actually working, in what ways the process can be improved, what the role of the board actually is, and how it can be more effective, but this occurs far too seldom. In ICI's case at least twice a year time is set aside for the board to discuss privately, as a group, the worries that any members may have about the board's efficacy, or achievements, or whether they are addressing the right problems and so on. Painful though the discussions may be, they are the only way for the group to operate more effectively. Time is spent looking at the work in hand to see how it is being done. Has too much time been spent discussing a particular part of the work, or perhaps some decisions had been taken without sufficient preparation and need to be looked at again? Boards do not easily set themselves the sort of criteria of success that they would unhesitatingly apply to every other part of the business. Yet unless a board continuously criticizes the way it is working, is clear as to what it should be seeking to achieve, and its members able to learn from each other, it is extraordinarily difficult for it to improve its performance.

All boards are differently organized, and many have totally different views of their role, and the ways in which they relate to the company as a whole. There are endless arguments about some of these aspects. For example, there has been prolonged debate in the United Kingdom as to whether the role of the chairman and the chief executive officer should be divided. One group argues that it should, while the counter view is held equally passionately – that a one over one relationship is bad for both parties, and confuses the line of responsibility. Amongst the many companies where the role of chairman and chief executive officer is combined in one person, one can think of Reed International under Lord Ryder, Grand Metropolitan under Sir Stanley Grinstead and until very recently, Guinness. Those where the role is divided or where the organization has changed are perhaps more numerous, but examples that spring to mind are BICC, Glaxo, Beechams and, more recently, Thorn EMI. Neither system is a panacea for success. One can cite examples of companies run in both ways succeeding and failing, and so the debate runs on.

Many boards and board members seem to me to be quite unclear as to whether they are merely a coordinating committee, attempting to coordinate the individual aspirations of the constituent parts of the company, each of which is represented on the board, or whether their primary responsibility is to the group as a whole. In companies where the board is essentially a coordinating committee, in many cases the directors are permanent chief executives of their individual businesses. It is asking too much of human nature to expect them to sacrifice the business for which they are personally responsible for the greater good of the group. This type of board tends to be less effective, since there is an inevitable aspect of trading off with each other – you support my olefine cracker and I will support your pharmaceutical investment – or whatever it may be. Even when this is not done consciously you are nevertheless acutely aware that you are always in competition with each other for both people and money. In this type of board you will only succeed by compromise and achieving agreement. There is no doubt whatsoever in law what the position is. As I remarked earlier, once you join the board of a public company you have a clear legal responsibility to that company as a whole. Quite frequently the aspirations that you have for your own bit of the business may be at variance with those of the group as a whole. For example, a very powerful executive in charge of a low-growth, unexciting profitable business, who is always able, by his political skill and his single-minded devotion to his particular business, to pre-empt an undue share of the resource of the group, is plainly not carrying out the proper responsibility of a board member. It was notable for example that when I analysed the way that I C I's capital investment of many billions of pounds had been spread around the group between 1970 and 1980 the differences in the capital base of the company at the beginning of that period and the end of it were barely discernible. Since many of the businesses had been in trouble, and others were merrily investing on very low returns, it must say a good deal for the persuasive skills of those responsible for some of the 'bad businesses'. Yet they are more likely to be looked upon as heroes and admired for their skills, than deplored for misdirection of the group's resources.

For many newly appointed directors the sense of uncertainty

stems not only from the changes in role, but also from the apparent lack of any personal control systems. As a manager your responsibilities are quite clear. You have a responsibility to your business which is usually expressed to a superior, who is well versed in the art of making it clear what he wants, in what areas he is seeking improvement, and whether he considers that you are doing your job well or badly. You also have a responsibility to your people and they have, even without formal organization, a thousand ways of making their expectations of your leadership clear. A good leader will seek in every way possible to understand and listen to the expectations of his people. But even if he doesn't make the effort, I have never known any organization where the hopes and expectations, many of which may be quite unrealistic, were not plainly there for all to see. Moreover, the manager feels a deep load of responsibility. He feels pressures from those above him, pressures from the business performance and the profit and loss statement, and pressures from his people.

Life tends to be very different when you are promoted and join the board of directors. Since the responsibility is collective it can be quite difficult to shoulder your share of that responsibility. When I first joined the ICI board I came from being the chief executive of a large division which had fought its way back from a very poor profit position to a somewhat better one. In the division I was the clear leader. I could demand help, service or advice from any one of the twelve thousand people who were employed in the division in those days. If I didn't feel that I had enough advice I could hire in consultants, seek advice or buy services elsewhere. I felt a heavy load of responsibility. I felt that the future of my people and my business rested entirely on my shoulders, as indeed to a large extent it did. In addition I knew that my ability to meet their expectations for future investment and growth of the business depended on a level of performance which would be difficult to achieve, but without which I thought I was unlikely to obtain the financial support that I required from the ICI board.

When I joined the ICI board after a couple of weeks' leave, I found that I had no personal staff at all. I had a secretary, and a driver. The support staff for the board responded to other board members and in those days, if I wanted some accountancy help I would first have asked the finance director, who might or might not be willing to help. At least I would have informed him before approaching any of his people. I felt only a small responsibility for the divisions that responded to the policy group of which I was a member, because they had their own chief executives and my role was merely to help and advise. If things went wrong the chief executive was blamed, not me. The company appeared to me to be doing reasonably well. My role in helping to form the policies for the company as a whole was very much as the junior boy in a team which did not spend a great deal of time discussing the total balance of our business. The main instrument of control was the capital programme, and here you were judged not by the degree of sacrifice that you made for the group, but by your success in getting the favoured projects of your own organizations through.

One of my first feelings on joining the board was surprise and almost relief at the sudden release from the constant feeling of pressure that I had felt before. It seemed to me then, and still does now, that it was wrong for anyone to be able to react in this way. As a director, although your responsibilities are more diffuse it is still quite clear where they lie. The director's first duty is, clearly, to the shareholders for the maintenance of their investment, and to ensure that they get a relatively good reward for it. In theory he gets his feedback about the feelings of the shareholders from the share movements and from the Annual General Meeting, or by shareholders' direct representations to the board. In practice, though, the accuracy of this feedback is far from satisfactory.

Share movements very frequently have more to do with expectations about the economy, international exchange rate movements, or the relative performance of other forms of financial savings and investments such as government bonds, than they do with the relative performance of your business. Even if your business performs reasonably well in its own sector, the whole sector may be out of favour, or the fashionable money may be going into some other area, with enormous price-earning multiples. One has only got to look at the American boom in bio-technology companies some years ago, to see that the share price and the price–earnings ratios are poor guides to the satisfaction, or lack of it, of the investing public in one's business performance. Moreover, shareholders are remarkably unwilling to use their undoubted rights to comment on, or criticize, the performance of the company. It is surprising, in the welter of questions that one gets at Annual General Meetings, how few actually relate to the performance of the company, or the decisions taken by the board in particular areas, unless disaster has struck, when, quite rightly, retribution tends to be swift. Even letters from shareholders, which are always welcome, tend to be on small matters rather than large. When analysed as a group they may give indications of the general mood of the shareholders, but there is nothing like the immediacy of the pressures of one's boss or the expectations of one's people. Shareholders' views are in any event frequently formed by financial analysts, or their money is invested by institutions, to both of whom one has, as a director, only very infrequent access.

The press, and the financial press, also have a large effect on forming shareholders' attitudes, and most managers will have had very little direct experience of handling the media. The chairman and the finance director will certainly be meeting representatives of the press, or financial institutions and analysts, on a weekly basis. A new member of a board of directors may see such people only once or twice in a year, and this hardly replaces the pressures of a boss, and direct and individual responsibilities.

Secondly, of course, the director has responsibility to the business, but, and here is the nub of it, to the business as a whole, and not to any individual part of it. I have always been opposed to boards of directors which have 'representative' portfolios, where the board members are individually answerable for particular businesses. I believe that such arrangements tend to develop a Persian market aspect, where one board member will trade off support for another's pet project, for the same favour returned at a later stage. I do not mean that this is done explicitly, but rather that there is a pattern of behaviour where the responsibility for the whole business gets fuzzed and left with the chairman and the finance director, and every other member of the board looks after his own patch in the happy belief that maximizing his patch will automatically result in the maximization of the whole. I know from my own experience how difficult I found it to speak against certain investments in Petrochemicals, which I knew well from previous experience, when I was a main board member and responsible for the Fibres division. I was not actually seeking investment in fibres at that time, but I was uncomfortably aware that I needed the good will of my colleagues, including the Petrochemicals director, to continue to carry the losses which I knew we would have for some time. If you are in that situation you don't deliberately set out to antagonize people, and in many cases a defeat by your fellow executive directors is looked upon as a personal failure.

The director's responsibility is to the business as a whole. But there is very little that a board of directors can do to influence the immediate short-term performance of the company. That lies in the hands of the executives of the individual businesses, but even there the time scale, except by the application of the crudest possible control methods, tends to be fairly long. The directors and the board are, after all, concerned with the balance between long- and short-term performance – a constant and increasing problem to which all of us have to pay more and more attention. The institutional pressures are invariably for an ever improving short-term performance, and these are pressures which are felt and seen. However, the first responsibility of a board of directors is to ensure that the company in the long haul can survive and that the investors' money is not hazarded through the pursuit of some temporary short-term advantage.

Nowhere are these judgements more obvious than in the long lead time, high-tech industries, of the sort in which I have made my living. In many cases it takes more than ten years, and the expenditure of tens of millions of pounds, to bring an idea from the laboratory into the marketplace. At any time during that ten-year period the short-term performance can be maximized by shutting down the development of the project, and yet without a continuous stream of new products, new businesses and new opportunities the company will wither on its feet. These are decisions which, uniquely, have to be taken by the board and can only be taken by looking at the group as a whole. You can only make the investment for the long haul by holding back a number of people, and forcing them to contribute more than they receive in the short haul. During the period of my chairmanship of ICI we have been deliberately holding back investment in the heavy chemicals end of the business in order to have funds available both for the 'effect' chemicals, which we believe have greater future growth opportunities, and also to make funds available for the rapid changes in shape which we felt we needed to achieve by acquisition. It is very difficult to decide when a business is approaching its maturity and should be ruthlessly turned into a cash generator, but the main task of the board and the director is the balance of the business. For each part of the business that moves ahead there has to be a balancing part that is held back.

The responsibility to the business also involves a share of the responsibility for the financial strategy of the business and the balance between financial risk and financial prudence. Again, a manager has been in the happy situation of leaving this to somebody else to look after, indeed most managers are very intolerant of what they see as financial caution. They don't realize the lack of flexibility that very high gearing gives, and they do not think of the fact that it is only balance sheet strength that enables companies to withstand the rigours of a severe economic onslaught. This was the situation that I met shortly after joining the board of Reed International, which had always maintained a high gearing. When some of the major businesses began to hit trouble, particularly the paper businesses and our operations in Canada, we found that we were not generating enough funds to maintain our interest payments and necessary capital investment, or to continue to pay our shareholders at the sort of rates they had hitherto expected. The only recourse lay in borrowing more money, but the gearing was already high and the more we borrowed the more we were looked upon with suspicion. As the market became more suspicious, the cost of borrowing money increased and the availability of funds decreased, except on short-term, high-price loan, and the more precarious the whole thing looked. Getting out of a mess like this is not quick. You have to sell parts of the business in order to reduce the gearing, but invariably the easily sold parts of the business are the best earners, with the best prospects, so it is all too easy to end up in a situation where you have sold all your best businesses, have got your gearing down, and are left with the businesses that caused all the problems in the first place. The remedy is not to get into the mess initially by keeping your gearing low so that your balance sheet is strong and you can continue to borrow at good terms, and cover the sort of down-turns in business which everybody experiences. This is increasingly a difficult problem of balance, as international banks become more and more aggressive in marketing their services, and the illusion is created that there is a plethora of money just waiting to be taken up without regard to the problems of repayment.

Another difference between the director's responsibility and the manager's is the necessity for directors to establish a balance between the demands of several different constituencies, customers, shareholders, employees and the environments in which the business operates. This concept of responsibility to a group of stake-holders in the future of the enterprise is one which my company tried to develop energetically some years ago, and is one which I believe is necessary to have constantly in one's mind. It is all too easy to see that, at certain periods of our recent economic history, companies have serviced their employees' interests far better than they have their share-holders'! It is also easy to see areas where the interests of the stake-holders, in the localities in which we operate, have not been adequately looked after, and it is the establishment of the balance between these four different groups that lies uniquely with the board of directors.

As a new director one is very conscious of the pressures from some of these groups, but less so of others. The employees have a myriad ways, including organized trade unions, in which to express their wishes and expectations in terms of reward. The customers have time-honoured and extremely effective ways of making their dissatisfactions felt and their expectations known. The shareholders' reaction is, however, less direct and less easy to disentangle from the market movements I referred to earlier, and the stake-holders have few direct financial means of expressing their disquietude. However, if the shareholders, and the localities in which you operate, withdraw their support for your company, your company is finished, just as surely as if you lose your customers or fail to attract any employees. A company like mine can operate only with the willing support of the local inhabitants where we are established. If they do not trust the safety of the operations, or if they believe that insufficient attention is being paid to the environment in which they live, they can close a plant down, or inhibit its operations just as surely as if the business runs out of money. Trust in this area is elusive. It can only be built up over a long period of consistent concern, and clear demonstrations that the company behaves responsibly. You can be let down by a stupid mistake or a badly phrased explanation, but above all you can be let down by not attempting to ensure that your neighbours and employees are in your confidence, and are aware of exactly what is happening.

Lastly, the director's contact with the people in the organization differs markedly from that of a manager or an executive. The manager or the chief executive of a business is in constant day-to-day touch with his people, and has every opportunity of seeing how they work. He knows, on a day-to-day basis, how individuals are relating to others, and he knows the problems that are arising in every part of his field of responsibility. It is very much more difficult for a director of a public company to get that immediacy of feel. First of all, whenever he appears it is a special occasion. Try as you may to 'drop in' on X or Y or Z, it is soon known that you are around. Also, since many of your responsibilities can only be undertaken with your colleagues, you simply have not the time to be always 'dropping in' on people. Even if you could, the director's job is not to instruct and manage. It is simply to direct and therefore you are always looking for small signs, and trying to get the feel of the enterprise. Any businessman who has been involved in manufacturing can tell, just by walking through a factory, whether it is well or badly run, and whether performance is satisfactory. The signs are there for the experienced eye to see, whether it is a ship-building yard, a car factory, a chemical works, or a coal mine. The attitude of the people – the way they look at you, the way they smile, the relationships you observe between people, the way in which people are working, the cleanliness and order, the sense of purpose – all of these enable you to make an instant judgement which is very seldom wrong. Every person who visits a Marks and Spencer store knows that it is a well-run company. The staff are cheerful and helpful, the stores are clean and ordered, the managers are approachable and go out of their way to demonstrate that as a customer you are valued, and everyone shows that they have pride in the establishment. The

Christmas bazaar where you enter a rented hall and find cheap and shoddy reject goods piled up high with bargain offer prices on them, and are served by scruffy-looking characters in duffle coats, does not create at all the same impression. Just as we are accustomed to judging retail stores by these sort of almost intuitive means, so the industrial manager is able to detect the difference between the well and the badly run in whatever field of business it is. A bad safety record or a dirty factory with piles of rubbish lying around are by definition dangerous and reflect poor management and an unhappy work force. Such judgements are different from knowing who has contributed to the good performance, what the particular abilities of the certain individuals are, or, even more importantly, what their expectations of you are as a director. You no longer feel this specific pressure. You can feel concerns and dissatisfactions at the performance of the board – usually that they are not giving enough support to the business, or not putting enough investment in; but that is a collective dissatisfaction or expectation, directed at another collective body, which is quite different in its effect as a driving and motivating force, from that which you felt as a manager or chief executive.

I mentioned earlier the change in working conditions that occurs when you find yourself promoted to a board. There are other major changes as well. A considerable amount of the new board member's time will be dedicated to board meetings, or meetings of committees of various sorts. The rest of his time is almost entirely at his own disposal. It is up to him to decide how to allocate it and what balance to choose between meetings, influencing and pursuing specific objectives, travelling in order to tune in, checking progress or the overall temperature of parts of the organization that he is staying in touch with, taking part in external activities to fill in gaps in his own knowledge or experience, and so on. Time allocation is always a major problem for every senior businessman and is a very necessary skill to develop. The director of a public company has both more constituencies that he needs to keep in touch with, and more choices that he can legitimately make, than those in other positions in the organization. In addition, a lot of these time allocations tend to be self-accelerating. For example, acceptance of a series of public speaking engagements on behalf of

customers can speedily become a flood, and one where an
inability to comply with a request has the exact reverse of the
effect that you are endeavouring to create by offering to speak in
the first place. It is unlikely you will get very much help or
guidance in these areas from your peers, or from the chairman.

ICI attempts to lay down some clear criteria for board members. For example, we believe very strongly that it is helpful to
the company and to the individual if he can be a non-executive
member of one, or at most two, other boards. We have pursued
this policy deliberately because it is one way of learning the
many differences of approach in different boards, so that we can
adapt in our continuous reviews of our own performance, and
profit by others' experience. A feature of ICI, and hence of the
ICI board, has been that practically all of our people join as
graduates directly out of university, and so tend to have worked
within only one company. We badly need fresh air from outside
and the realization that others cope with problems in different
ways from ourselves, or perform as well or better, with
apparently less back-up and less hassle than we indulge in.

While one may have some guidance on the allocation of major
blocks of time, such as non-executive directors' jobs, external
conferences, courses etc., it is the day-to-day and week-to-week
allocation of time that constitutes both a major opportunity and
a hazard. In essence, the job of the director is to place his own
company within an external context that he can judge from his
experience. Directors are not chosen only for their mix of skills
but more particularly for their experience and judgement. It
cannot be restated often enough that the job of the board is all
to do with subjective judgement, based on the members'
individual and collective experience. No amount of staff work,
or rerunning facts through the computer, will take the board's
decisions for them. If the course of action that has to be taken
follows so logically from a mathematical analysis, it is almost
certain that the decision is being taken too late. The job is to
discern trends, and to match the opportunities and skills which
exist within your own company with the growing opportunities
which you see in the changing world outside. In this area I
contrast ICI's late entry into the seed business, when the trends
in agricultural development and genetic engineering were clear
for all to see, with that of Ciba Geigy or Shell Chemical who

entered the business ten and fifteen years ago out of a belief
which would have been impossible to have proved at the time.
They got there first, and when they entered the field were able
to pick and choose, and to enter relatively cheaply. We have
paid a high price for missing this chance, and, while we are
determined to catch up, it would obviously have been much
better to have taken a smaller risk earlier on, than to be forced
into a large investment when others have already established
their positions.

While reading exhaustively and meeting people from different walks of life and countries helps, there is no substitute for
seeing for yourself, and no real alternative to continually widening your field of acquaintance. The information that you pick up
through such things, and the different perspectives that you get
by looking at what seems to be a familiar landscape from a
different angle, or viewpoint, are of inestimable value. A fair
amount of directors' time is therefore spent in ways which
might be considered, by direct analysis, to be a waste of time.
They certainly cannot be judged on a quantitative basis, but
they can be judged on a qualitative one. The degree to which the
director brings to the discussions of the board new information,
new viewpoints, relevant appreciations of what or how others
are thinking about problems, is a pretty good guide to whether
he is spending his time productively in these areas, and keeping
his personal experience tuned in and up to date.

It is all very well to speak of the changes in responsibilities,
pressures and back-up that occur when you join a board, but
what people want to know is what they should actually do, and
how their skills should be developed and applied. An awful lot
of advice in this area depends on the way in which the board
operates, and how the board organizes itself under the
guidance of, and with the help of, its chairman and its non-
executive directors.

Your collective responsibility extends to trying to make sure
that meetings are adequately prepared and the right information is presented in the best possible way. Ultimately, this is the
clear personal responsibility of the chairman. Invariably he can
do with help. Boards of directors get far too much information
and, no matter how hard you try, it is very difficult to prevent an
overload in this area. Moreover, we are all individuals, and

differ in the way in which we like to process information. While I am a fast reader, I also like visual presentations of figures rather than tables, but I have worked with people who are the exact reverse. At different times in my life I have worked with two outstanding leaders who could only create mental pictures through the medium of numbers. They had an instinctive ability to correlate numbers into a sort of pattern, and whereas in my own mind I use numbers as a sort of coarse scale to check whether my pattern is true, in their case they could only conceptualize the other way round. I remember in one case I used to have to deliberately work my conceptual ideas into figures in order to communicate with him.

It is well worth while putting a great deal of thought into the presentation of information to your colleagues. If you cannot communicate adequately the main points that you want to get across on two sides of a sheet of paper, you have almost certainly not thought the problem out properly. You can support your single sheet of paper with as much or as little data as you feel is desirable to back it up – and here boards of directors have their own likes and dislikes. Some consider a single sheet of paper an insult, whereas others are grateful to have the problem presented in such a concise way and without a plethora of back-up data. It is actually very much more difficult to write short papers than long ones.

I remember that at one time I was given the job of chairing a committee of my peers from the different operating divisions of the company. They were all extremely busy men and they viewed the task they had been given, of helping me, with some understandable reservations. I and my staff sweated blood to ensure that we never presented a paper to them which was more than two pages long. As a result all the papers could be read properly in the car on the way to the meeting, and we supported the basic facts with a large number of visual aids. The meetings were amongst the most successful that I have ever run, because, as a result of the thought and effort that we had to put into condensing subjects down, we were almost invariably discussing real problems and were working close to the nub of the problem. A good guide is to think what you would want yourself if you knew nothing about the problem, but were required to give advice, or a judgement upon it, in a relatively short discussion time. It is far better to produce a concise document which can be expanded orally, but will have been properly read and understood, than to take the easy way out and send a fifty-page report complete with tables and diagrams! The latter is an implied insult to one's colleagues. It is, after all, always available to them if they wish to ask for it, but it is quite unrealistic to think that they are going to spend that amount of time on going into the details of a problem which you are presenting to them, unless they have specifically asked for it.

A large amount of industrial life consists of setting oneself private and personal objectives for achievement. I have never much liked the systematized approaches to this, such as management by objectives, because I think they have a degree of artificiality about them. However, I know that in order to make any movement at all I need to have a clear series of personal aims, whether they be for what I would hope to make as my contribution to a meeting, or what I hope to have achieved during a year's work. For at least the last twenty years, at the beginning of each year I have taken a few hours out to write down on a postcard, which I keep in my desk drawer, the six hopes and aspirations that I have for achievement during the coming year. They may be very large, like the achievement of a particular deal, or the selling or purchasing of a particular business, or they may be quite small in absolute terms but important to me, like getting such and such a committee to work properly, or improving my understanding of some part of my business. This personalized approach to setting some standards for achievement is one of the ways from which you can derive most satisfaction, because it is when you look back at the end of the year that you realize that your effort has been purposefully directed, and that you have actually managed to move further towards your aims.

It is equally important not to go in to a meeting without some clarity in your own mind as to what you are expecting to achieve from the meeting, and what you think your contribution should be. Plainly in setting objectives for individual meetings, one has to be more flexible, since there are a number of other people involved. Nevertheless, if you merely go because the meeting has been called, with little personal aim, one should really ask oneself why one is going at all. If you are merely going there for appearances' sake, then you should begin to ask whether your attendance at the committee is necessary at all, whether you are using your time in the right way, whether the business that the committee is allegedly carrying out is sensible and well directed, and if not, should you do something about it? The chances are that if you feel that you are there purely for show, so do most of your colleagues. Until somebody makes the comment the system is unlikely to be changed, and you will all be collectively responsible for wasting time and extremely expensive and rare skills.

Inevitably, boards do have a certain amount of formal business which has to be conducted. We refer to this as 'boiler plate', and the objective should be to try and ensure that as little time as possible is wasted on it. Boards of directors have, of course, to accept minutes of the finance committee or the allotment committee. They have to pass some formal resolutions and it is important that, as a board member, you should have read the papers and know what you have agreed to. Trying to breathe life into a board debate on such sterile subjects is a waste of the board's collective time, and 'boiler plate' should be segregated from the important subjects of the board meeting, and should occupy the minimum amount of time possible.

Sadly, it is perfectly possible for boards of directors to meet regularly and never discuss any creative business at all. I suggest that to do so is a severe abnegation of both personal and collective responsibility. After all, the job of the board is all to do with creating momentum, movement, improvement and direction. If the board is not taking the company purposefully into the future, who is? It is because of boards' failure to create tomorrow's company out of today's that so many famous names in industry continue to disappear. We should never forget that industry is the most ephemeral of all institutions. It is only by constantly trying to look ahead, and consciously ensuring that the company is being positioned for the future, rather than merely dealing with today's problems, that the company – and you with it – can have any future.

My own experience is that boards need to set themselves very clear tasks in exactly the same way that individuals do. Every year we spend some time setting out what we consider to be the twelve most important tasks that we, as a board, should have worked towards during the year. We then take time out a year later to review what progress we have made, at the time when we are setting out next year's targets. These targets are not the obvious things like improving the profit, or improving productivity. We take these as read as being the day-to-day momentum of our business. Our targets tend to be specific tasks which we, as a board, believe we should address ourselves to, and where we require to convince ourselves that we have taken measures to effect change. They could be, for example, to improve the allocation of information technology to the commercial aspects of our business. By which we would mean that we would have at the back of our minds a whole host of developments such as the ability for all sales offices in the world to accept and pass orders by electronic mail, or to tap into a common database on customers, or to have instant access on the latest credit positions of people with whom they may be doing business, right the way through to such objectives as trying to ensure that we tie our computers in with those of our customers, and obtain competitive advantage that way. They could be to provide a more effective operating organization in another part of the world. The key thing is that they have to be tasks that the board, as a group, can affect and have agreed that they can tackle, and they must be aimed at improving the long-term direction and momentum of the business.

We also review, on an annual basis, our progress both as a company and as a board. We review how the company has done against its own previous best in a whole variety of areas, and we also review how the company has performed against the direct competition in our own sector. All too often it is only by measuring against your own achievements that you can really see clear movement. There are so many factors obscuring competitive comparisons, such as exchange rates etc., that it is difficult to make these accurately except over a fairly long period of time, when trends are both evident and overwhelming. In addition to measuring our aims and progress in this way, we also attempt to carry out fairly frequent process reviews of the ways in which we formulate our discussions and allocate our time, prepare our papers and generally manage our internal affairs. These reviews are usually rather painful, certainly for the chairman! While we try to do this fairly regularly, on a

formal basis, we have also found it invaluable to set up circumstances where we can have such discussions on an informal
basis, usually when we have a buffet lunch on our own.

We organize most of the collective board work into one week
of the month so that the remaining three weeks can be spent
travelling, or on the various external areas where we are concerned, but during board week itself we spend almost the whole
of our time together. We always try to have at least one informal
lunch together during this week where we help ourselves from
a buffet and are not interrupted in any way. We look on this as
an opportunity to let our hair down, to gripe and moan, or
occasionally, if nothing is burning any of us up, just to chat and
enjoy each other's company. Above everything, boards have to
spend a lot of time together, and have to know each other very
well. Keeping in step with each other has to be almost instinctive, just as it is in the Brigade of Guards; but, like the Brigade of
Guards, keeping step only happens as a result of effort, training, time and commitment. These are things that one has to
actually put into the task, even though the payoff appears to be
much more indirect and obscure than one has been accustomed
to as a manager.

There are only three ways in which you will know if you are
being a successful board member. The first and most important
one is that you must actually feel responsibility, you must
actually feel that you are sharing the future of the company. You
must be conscious of that responsibility, and it must produce in
you at least some degree of worry and concern. If none of this
happens, the board is not working correctly and neither are
you. As a member of the team it is up to you to try to initiate the
changes that are necessary until you do all feel this pressure. Of
course, the chairman will feel a different level of pressure to the
rest of the board, because ultimately it is his responsibility to
organize the board to deal with these things, but unless the
weight is shared there is something radically wrong with the
organization and performance of the board and your performance within it.

The second way in which you will know whether you are
performing satisfactorily or not is whether you believe that you
have been able to affect the general direction in which the group
is going. It is no use looking for individual scalps that you can

dangle from your belt. Those days have gone. It is through being able to change the group's thinking, and to get your ideas accepted and supported, that you will have the satisfaction of knowing that you are being effective. It is a peculiar sort of satisfaction because you have to exchange the pleasure of being the captain of your own ship for a share in the responsibility of manoeuvring the whole fleet. The good news is that the group as a whole can achieve much more than an individual part of it, but the bad news is inevitably that the group as a whole is slower to move. Because the burden is shared, your best work may well go unrecognized and is unlikely to be recorded in any history book! This calls on qualities of patience, perseverance, dedication and belief which are different from those in other fields of business.

A really good board of directors works together. When they are working together they are much greater than the sum of their parts, and can surprise themselves at the profundity of some of their thinking, or the changes in direction which the interaction of the group will produce. There is a real satisfaction to be derived from this. Even when going about their business individually they are still supporting the group as a whole. Companies only react to unified direction and there is nothing worse for a company than a feeling that the board is not united and is heading in a number of different directions at once. Comments such as, 'The board policy is X, but I happen to believe Y', are immensely harmful to the unity and sense of direction of the group. This is why it is important that board policies should be simple and that they should be supported by the board members. It is yet another example of the major adjustments that the individualist, who has made a success of running a specific part of the business, has to make if he is to be an effective board member. To some degree he has to subordinate his own personality within that of the group.

The third and most difficult way in which you can learn to judge whether you are an effective board member is to analyse ruthlessly your own interventions in discussions. A degree of introspection is required here and, above everything, a very considerable amount of honesty and integrity. Are your comments constructive or destructive? When you look back on the debate, did you help the debate move forward, were you building on others' ideas, or were you merely reiterating the position from which you started, with growing ill-will? Did you talk too much and try to dominate the discussion? Had you thought out your interventions? Had you listened? Had you read the papers? Did your thinking change during the discussion, or did your preconceptions never waver for a moment, therefore possibly wasting everybody's time? This sort of analysis of one's contribution in a group is helped greatly either by some help from the chairman, or by asking one of your peers to watch and help you improve yourself. It can be embarrassing, and sometimes you may not be very happy with the results, but if you want to work for a really good organization with a bright future, if you want to be effective and help in the process of making things happen, then surely a small amount of embarrassment is not an unreasonable price to pay. After all, you have just been promoted to one of the most important jobs in the country, and if you don't want to 'make it happen' what are you doing there at all?

9

The Emperor's Clothes

If the change from being a manager to being an executive director is a big and traumatic one, there is little doubt in my personal experience that the task of becoming a non-executive director of another company is the biggest learning experience of all for the professional businessman. When I actually think of the difficulties of being a good non-executive director it amazes me that any of us bother at all. It certainly cannot be for the money since in the United Kingdom non-executive directors are, in my view, extremely poorly rewarded if they do the job properly and perhaps over-rewarded if they are merely 'there for the beer'. This has sadly been the pattern for quite a long time.

Most of us who take non-executive appointments in other companies do so for personal reasons, usually linked with the wish to fill in some particular form of missing experience. The value of working, albeit for a limited time, in a totally different environment with a different culture, different ways of doing things and facing different problems, is in itself a substantial one. Seeing that things can be done in other ways causes one to question the practices 'back on the ranch'. But for most of us, I think that we choose a non-executive directorship to learn about some specific area of operations that we are dissatisfied with in our own company.

The first non-executive directorship that I took outside ICI or ICI's subsidiary companies was when I was invited by Alex Jarrett to join his board at Reed International. I admired Alex in any event, but at that time Reed had a formidable reputation as an acquirer of companies. It had been built up, under the leadership of Lord Ryder, by a process of aggressive acquisition and occupied the sort of position in many people's minds that Hanson Trust does today. I joined partly, I must admit, because I was flattered to be asked, but also because I believed that acquisition of companies and disposal of parts of the group were skills which were little exercised inside ICI but which would form an essential part of the armoury for the repositioning of our businesses in the future.

How right I was in that assessment. But the lessons that I learnt at Reed were not at all of the type that I had expected! They were immensely valuable and they taught me many hard lessons about acquisition, but for me they certainly did not provide the answers to my questions about why some people are extremely good at this skill and others so poor. When the time came for me to leave Reed (and there is always a time when one should leave a non-executive directorship) I was invited and chose to join the board of Grand Metropolitan. Here again my reasons for joining were linked to a vision of the way in which I felt that my own primary company might develop in the future, and a wish to learn some relevant skills.

Grand Metropolitan were looked upon as being extremely able operators in the field of services and indeed had set out to develop branded services throughout the world. I believed then and believe still that ICI, which had grown up primarily as a manufacturer, should move increasingly into the field of providing services. Our customers are overwhelmingly other industrial companies. What we provide them with is not merely raw materials, or specified products in a bag, but the solving of their problems. As knowledge expands and expertise is continuously developed it is becoming more and more the case that no single organization can do everything to the highest world standards. Both in the fields of water treatment for industrial use, and in lubrication of specialist machinery, ICI operates service companies that are well used by small and large organizations who rely on our greater knowledge and expertise to ensure that these minor but essential aspects of their operations keep going. Anyone who operates a boiler needs treated water, but if you use only a single package boiler to run your plant, while you may totally depend on it for all your output you don't expect to maintain in-house the experience and expertise of the Electricity Generating Board. You hire a service. I believe that the chemical industry is increasingly the facilitating mechanism for much advance and therefore we need to acquire more knowledge and understanding of how successful service industries work.

It is an interesting fact that people are prepared to pay more for services than for goods. If a company is wrestling with a problem its solution has a definable value; the bigger the problem the more they are prepared to pay to have it solved. The source of the problem itself may be quite small but extremely complex – there is little relationship between the effect that a loose bolt can have and the cost of replacing it. But if we do not know where the bolt is, or that it is loose, the cost of tightening it is quite out of proportion to the damage which may be caused. You only have to think how grateful you are to the man who gets your car back on the road when it has broken down. The job may have involved great skill but perhaps only a minimal adjustment. It was this belief that led me to accept the invitation to join the board of Grand Met, and indeed I have learnt a lot about the differences between service and non-service organizations through working with my colleagues on that board.

Finally, it may be merely that you desire to have a change and to have the opportunity to see your own operations from a different perspective. All of these are in my view good and adequate reasons for seeking a job as a non-executive director. Turning the coin on its head, however, why should anyone want to have a non-executive director? Throughout the world there has recently been a growing debate on the value of non-executive directors and whether there is a need for them within companies. Let me say, unequivocally, that I believe in seeking the strongest group of non-executive directors that a company can obtain. The value gained from the differences of view and background far outweighs the time and trouble involved in trying to ensure that they can contribute their best. The most obvious examples of this are where you have a non-executive director from another country. They are able to give you insights into how problems are perceived in that country which you cannot gain without that background of nationality. The reactions of your competitors or customers in Germany or Japan are more likely to be accurately read by a German or a Japanese than they are by a Briton or an American. I can also think of examples where all the in-house directors of I C I have taken one view, based largely on their perception of I C I's technical competence, which has been called into question by outside directors who have a broader perspective. Be clear, though: unless the board as a whole sets out to use the skills of its non-executive directors and genuinely wishes to make use of them, it is very difficult indeed for a non-executive to play a full role. It is the boards that function openly, and are seeking constantly to improve the performance of their company, that gain most from having non-executive directors as members. As members of such a board they can perform practically all the roles that I have outlined in this book so far. They can be most potent agents for change, but they certainly have to be so through the use of catalytic intervention rather than by the use of the blunderbuss. I can think of many examples where too trenchant a criticism has merely aroused all the defensive instincts of the executive members of the board and resulted in almost total rejection of the advice. It is a good man who, after boarders have been repelled, actually sits down and says that they may have had a point after all! Rather there is a mutual self-congratulation and delight that the attack has been withdrawn. One certain way to ensure that advice is rejected is to prescribe exactly how the problem should be dealt with. Nothing is more irritating in any company than to hear someone pontificating about how things are done in his own. A good degree of diffidence and a very definite willingness to hold back from trying to prescribe solutions, but rather to point out problems, seems to me to be the most effective means of moving ahead.

When the advantages of employing non-executive directors can be so great and when the personal advantages of being one appear significant, one well may ask why the role should be a difficult one to fulfil. Here, of course, you hit a host of problems. First of all, as I pointed out earlier, every member of the board shares the same legal responsibility for the future well-being of the company. But the amount of time that the non-executive director can be expected to spend on this task is relatively small. Typically most non-executive directors will put in perhaps three working weeks a year, usually accompanied by fairly consider-able amounts of work in their own time, reading or studying, visiting or listening – often when going about their other business.

Experiments have been done with non-executive directors giving much larger periods of time – say three or four months of their working year for example – but these have generally fallen down, not because the logic was wrong, but because it is extremely difficult for any executive to commit himself for a third of his time to a company unless he has no other calls on his time.

Part of the problem arises from the difference between part-time involvement in a company and full-time, and part from the fact that the very value of a non-executive director is that he comes from a different culture. He therefore has a different way of looking at things and is not so easily tuned in to the customs and practices of the business to which he has been appointed. There is no way in which he can hope ever to have the detailed knowledge of the business that the executives have – nor should he. However, he does have to have a helicopter vision of the business and is expected, through the use of a database which is seldom specifically tuned for his needs, to be able to sort out in a very broad sense the wood from the trees.

When the situation is changing fast, as it is nowadays in most businesses, these occasional swoops, where you get a sort of momentary snapshot view of the business, to be followed perhaps by a few written papers and a lot of numbers over a period of six or eight weeks, followed by another swoop, are a less than ideal way of remaining adequately in touch with fast-moving circumstances. It is difficult enough, therefore, to be able to make the analysis of the problems that you believe the business is facing. On the other hand you may be lucky enough to be able to bring specialist knowledge to bear on specific problems where your own experience is directly relevant.

However, the problems of diagnosis are as nothing compared to the problems of actually making things happen when you have finally made up your mind what you believe the problems are. Let us start with the most obvious one. You are unlikely to have been appointed as a non-executive director unless the chief executive and chairman of the company actually like you, at least at first! Even though, increasingly, chairmen seek the services of a head-hunter to obtain really top-class candidates, they will still want to be reassured in their own minds that the chemistry is right. Moreover in most cases, certainly in the United Kingdom, we operate in a fairly small and incestuous circle, where practically all of us in the upper reaches of business know our colleagues and competitors. Even if we don't know them well on a personal basis, we certainly know them by reputation and are almost bound to have bumped into them somewhere.

It is seldom, in my experience, that people like people who do not like them. You therefore start off in the potentially difficult situation where you like and probably admire the chairman of the company whose board you have joined, and with reasonable luck those feelings are returned. Therefore, even if you think he is making a right mess of things, you certainly do not wish to cause undue pain and suffering. Indeed, you are very conscious that your ability to influence him and his company will depend on giving advice in a helpful and constructive way, rather than in a critical and destructive one. This process can work well in a situation where neither the chairman nor the company has real worries about their business position, but all too often it is the non-executive director who has the unhappy task of blowing the whistle, and demonstrating that the company is in serious trouble. Hence the title of this chapter – The Emperor's Clothes – for it is the non-executive director who, above all, is best placed to observe that the Emperor he is serving actually hasn't got any, or at best many less and of a different style and cut than the Emperor believes.

In the fairy story I do not recollect its being easy to persuade the Emperor that he actually wasn't wearing any clothes, and certainly on most boards of directors the task is equally difficult. After all, every one of your colleagues has been involved in putting the company where it is and if, in our view, serious problems are looming which are not being dealt with, it is a bit much to expect them all single-mindedly and with speed to accept your analysis – based, as it is bound to be, on less profound knowledge of the circumstances. Indeed there may be a suspicion that you only joined the board for your own greater glory and are merely seeking to make an impact rather than a serious point. This problem may be described as a chairman/ chum-man one and if it is severe when the company appears to be in a steady state, it becomes even worse when everyone in the company is, possibly belatedly, aware of the problem that the company may be facing. At that moment quite suddenly the non-executive director is expected to achieve almost unbelievable and certainly unachievable acts of leadership, and to produce solutions to problems which are quite beyond his 'part-time' capability. Such was the situation in that ill-fated company, Carrington Vyella, which ICI had backed into as a defensive measure and then found itself as a majority share-holder with a self-accepted imposition that we would not use our majority position on the board. The ICI non-executive directors had consistently drawn attention to the dangers which the company was running. The chief executive, however, had made it plain that he considered that as long as the company was performing to the average of the textile industry perform-ance we couldn't really expect anything better, and 'something' would have to happen if the situation deteriorated. As we all know the situation did deteriorate, and the 'something' that happened was that large numbers of textile companies went out of business. At that stage – long after it was possible to take the remedial action that had been avoided for too long – the board turned expectantly to the non-executive directors, of whom I was one, and expected us to resolve the problem.

The non-executive director has a very small range of weapons and powers although he has a wide range of responsibilities. It is in learning to deploy these limited assets that the problems of becoming a good non-executive director lie. All too often you only get one kick at the ball – and you have to learn on the run. There is no school where you can learn the art of non-executive directorship, and I have not seen any book which gives the sort of practical advice that is so badly needed at this stage. Moreover, although you may be lucky and serve with a board where the chairman will spend quite a bit of time explaining to you what he is seeking and possibly even produce a written note on his expectations, all too often a warm welcome and a press announcement is all the advance briefing that you are likely to get. Non-executive directors tend to play a dispropor-tionate role in companies that are in serious trouble. The stage at which the takeover bid has been launched, or the stage at which the banks are about to withdraw support, or the stage at which it is obvious that the chairman or chief executive, or even both, need to be replaced are ones where the non-executive director is expected to deliver what is in many cases virtually undeliverable.

Moreover, it is important that the non-executive director should recognize what he cannot do. He cannot develop a strategy for the company, since that has to be worked out by the executive team who will be responsible for its execution. This is not to say that he cannot make contributions in this area because his difference of perspective may well enable him to see that the strategies which are being pursued are unattainable, or that the position of the company is simply not strong enough to support the company's ambitions. I remember Howard Macdonald and I struggling with this problem in Reed International. The essence of the dilemma was that Reed had a total of five businesses, four of which were strong and one was at best a cash cow but was difficult to get out of. All the businesses were in totally different fields and we did not have either the financial means or the management strength to expand them all simultaneously. Each of the Reed executive directors was the chief executive of one of the five businesses. We spent many days away together as a group discussing how we should proceed but it was almost impossible to agree on which of the businesses should be allowed to go ahead and which should be sacrificed for the others. It was easier to get a consensus amongst the non-executive directors, but we were all uncomfortably aware that, because the executives had to be able to believe in the courses of action they would be committed to, there was no way in which we could impose our decisions upon them. This applied particularly to those who had to sacrifice or hold back their businesses in order to allow the group as a whole to advance.

The most frustrating situation of all is for the non-executive director who is aware either that there is no strategy, or that the strategy being pursued is inadequate, and yet he cannot succeed in persuading, or leading, or teaching the executive team to work out something realistic, despite the fact that this is one of his major responsibilities and roles. Little wonder, therefore, that the job is so difficult to do – and even less wonder when you look at the paucity of reward and the expectations of others as to what a non-executive can and should deliver, that it is so difficult to obtain good ones. You must remember that a non-executive director is expected to spend only a limited amount of time in the company, and must not interfere or get involved in line management matters. At the same time, with much less involvement than the executives, he is expected to contribute as much or more than them to the success of the company. It is an unreal equation and expectation.

At best the non-executive director may gain a board quite a lot of time to deal with pressing problems which they themselves have not been aware of. Shortly after I joined the board of Reed International, Howard Macdonald (who joined at the same time) and I, from our quite different approaches came to rather similar conclusions. We formed what must have been a most irritating chorus of advice to our colleagues, but they were open-minded and willing to look again at the position in which they found themselves. Because of this I think we were able to gain some precious time for the resolution of problems which otherwise might possibly have overwhelmed the company. Neither of us could do much to resolve the problems. Those tasks, and many of them were very difficult, had to be carried out by the chairman and executive directors of the company itself – but what we could do was to draw attention to possibilities which perhaps they had not seen or to dangers of which they were certainly not adequately aware.

By now everybody recognizes the problems of expansion by acquisition. There is a momentum in improvement in profit which can be achieved by buying companies with a smaller profit to earnings ratio which steadily improves the performance of the acquirer. But eventually the day of reckoning comes. In the end one has to settle down to work the assets which have been acquired, and one has to deliver the improvements out of generic growth. This happens – if only because the company has grown so large that it is almost impossible to buy anything large enough to have any effect. It is, moreover, a common belief that in some way acquisitions can be made to pay for themselves. This is very seldom, if ever, the case. You simply cannot buy companies with their own money. Nothing comes from nowhere and improvements in a company's performance can only come from actual changes which are applied externally. You can add two and two and make five, but you have to be clear in your own mind where the extra one is coming from. It is this sort of rather banal observation, which can be totally infuriating to successful operators, that the non-executive director can contribute.

Very often the non-executive's contribution in this Emperor's Clothes area is to fire the warning shot. He may point out that the time has come to stop repeating a business stratagem which had operated well in the past; or sometimes that the favoured growth business is about to go ex-growth. One of the most common industrial problems is that of 'the bridge too far'. One has repeatedly invested in a particular sort of product ahead of the market and each time the market has caught up and paid for the new investment successfully. But the day comes when the market is about to be saturated and it is a very good management indeed that can see that danger coming up for the next investment they wish to make. There is always the feeling that the existing investment is going to be all right and it is only the one after it that may hit trouble. This is just the sort of area where the difference of perspective of the non-executive director may enable him to warn of the discontinuity which those closer to the business cannot see.

Sounding the warning, however, is not in itself enough. It may be satisfying to the non-executive director to be able to turn round and say, some years later when the investment has proved to be a poor one, that he pointed that out at the time, but that is not discharging your responsibility. Your responsibility is actually to try and prevent the mistake being made and this is where you suddenly find that you may be a good observer of the Emperor's sartorial tastes, even an extremely accurate observer, but unless something can be done about it you have failed, and the tools for effecting the change are inadequate for the job.

Let us look at some of the other areas which constitute the constructive role of the non-executive director. I suppose the second one is what I would call the 'oil can'. This means the multiplicity of small interventions one makes in an attempt to make the board work more effectively as a group and ease frictions, or even to raise the level of friction to one which will enable traction to take place. This is an area which requires enormous skill and great knowledge of one's colleagues. On many occasions I have felt that the chairman of the company is losing his colleagues' support, or that they have unspoken criticisms or concerns which for various reasons, noble or otherwise, they fail to express. It is a difficult judgement. After all you do not wish to be leading the revolution against the chief executive, particularly as such a revolution is likely to be thoroughly unhelpful to the aims of the company; but equally you cannot allow the chief executive to plough on in a situation where he has lost command of his colleagues, who are sitting festering with views which they do not know how to get out on the table.

Equally the chief executive may need help in building bridges and finding ways in which he can explain his concerns. The 'oil can' role is one where I have had many occasions to be grateful to my non-executive colleagues for drawing my attention to areas where they have felt that I was not adequately covering unspoken concerns which were existing elsewhere. This can happen even in the most open of boards where infinite trouble is taken to try and ensure that problems are dealt with cleanly and in the open.

The next role of the non-executive I call 'The Bank of England'. In the past non-executive directors tended to be chosen from the great and the good, and the mere fact that a 'name' was on a board was taken as reassurance that the company was reputable and well run. Alas, one has seen too many cases where individuals have allowed their names to be used to give a spurious degree of confidence to outsiders. The fact that you are a non-executive director of a company does mean that people will expect of that company some particular attribute which they believe you can bring to it. There is an expectation that your previous track record will be exemplified in the performance of the company. It is not unusual when people begin to worry about a company for them to take solace, either directly or indirectly, from the composition of the non-executive directors on that board, and this is a fact which one has to take very carefully into consideration when deciding whether to serve or not.

However, there are quite often occasions when this confidence from outside the company can be of great value. In my experience, when external investors, or the banks, or the press begin to get worried about the progress of a company they very frequently contact the non-executive directors for some reassurance. This can be used positively to gain time to enable the executives to continue dealing with the task in hand. In a way it is like holding an umbrella over them so that they can continue to work more effectively. Hopefully this sort of action is not required too often, but be sure that if you are a non-executive director of a company that hits trouble it is your reputation which will suffer, as much or more than that of the company concerned. This is a consideration you should bear firmly in mind before you decide to serve and it should be continuously borne in mind all the time you are serving. Reputations can be lost overnight, but it takes you a lifetime to build one up.

The next role is what I would describe as the 'Father Confessor' role. The chairman of a company has a remarkably lonely existence. Even in the friendliest and most open of companies there are many subjects that he cannot discuss with his executive colleagues on the board. You cannot discuss your views of individuals with another executive colleague. Often you cannot discuss your own plans, thoughts or fears. You have a responsibility to keep the confident face of leadership to the fore, but you may need to lean on somebody. You may be uncertain of a decision which you may wish to sound out with somebody who cannot have any possible axe to grind – and that is where you look to the non-executive director. You may look to him in general terms, or you may look to him in specific terms.

Non-executive directors on the ICI board are selected from a wide range of constituencies. We aim to have a continental European, we are lucky enough to have a senior and respected Japanese businessman, an American businessman, a distinguished banker, two well-known British industrialists, and an individual who has had a long and distinguished career in public service and is currently employed in the media. To each of these I was able to look for specific advice in specific areas. It is extremely important when designing the composition of a board to look carefully at the areas where you cannot produce adequate 'in-house' experience. It is a great advantage to be able to obtain informed advice from people outside your own company and to be able to select them on a totally open basis.

This is not always easy to achieve within one's own management tree. You are selecting from within a limited group in a competitive situation. Some people may well be switched off if their reasonable expectations of promotion are not met. None of these considerations apply to the non-executive director, where you are as free as the wind, in fact the problem is almost the other way around. If the broad job description is that you want someone from the financial field, a moment's thought will show you the vast range of differences that such a choice can cover. Equally the decision that you need Japanese or American input is in itself only the beginning of making the choice and selection, which should ideally cover a number of areas where you are seeking the benefits of external advice. For example, when I CI had decided that it wanted a Japanese director it was also trying simultaneously to develop a business supplying the electronics industry. It was not a giant leap of imagination to decide that it would be helpful if our Japanese, as well as having all the necessary personal chemistry, internationalism, large-scale operating knowledge and so on, also had some knowledge of the electronics industry. We were lucky enough to be able to persuade just such a man to join us.

The Father Confessor role is an extremely valuable one, which it is a privilege to be able to extend; and in many cases it is not confined to helping the chairman. The knowledge that non-executive directors brings is available to every member of the board. On the boards on which I have served the chairmen have felt that I had specialist knowledge in areas which were likely to be of use to them and have sought advice from me on a great variety of subjects. This, after all, is the area where one can really return the friendship of the chairman of the company in which one is serving.

There will obviously be occasions where you will feel that you have to give advice which is not palatable to him, perhaps regarding the relationship that you see developing between him and one of his board, or on any number of other subjects. You are in a unique position to do this. You do not have money at risk. If the position that you occupy becomes untenable you can always leave, and you owe it both to the man and to the company if you feel that he is heading for trouble to warn him in plenty of time, albeit tactfully. I need hardly say that there are occasions on which this can be highly counterproductive, but nevertheless it is a part of the non-executive director's role and cannot be ducked. Concerns, either about individuals or about the chief executive himself, must be aired to him and it is essential both to your reputation and your peace of mind that you perform this simple duty.

The last role of the non-executive director is, I think, the most difficult and unpleasant of all. I call it the 'High Sheriff' role. It is extraordinarily difficult to replace a chairman or chief executive of a public company before disaster strikes. There can, however, be a necessity to achieve the removal of somebody who, perhaps for good reasons, is no longer able to perform adequately in good time and without harming the company, its shareholders' or its employees' interests. It is almost impossible for executive directors to carry out this very unpleasant and fortunately infrequently required task.

One of the reasons I like the model of a separate chief executive is because you always have cover if one man is removed. The problem of replacing a chairman and chief executive as one individual is an extremely difficult one, even given that the non-executive directors exercise their skills and responsibilities to the letter. The High Sheriff role is extraordinarily difficult. The mere removal of a chairman or chief executive is a relatively easy task, but if in doing so you leave a vacuum you are in desperate trouble and have failed the company and its shareholders. It is not an accident that in two recent British cases where non-executive directors have moved in and removed the chairman and chief executive they have found themselves placed in the unenviable position of having to assume the chairman's role themselves because of a lack of suitable replacements within the company. Both the cases of Beechams and Thorn EMI show this dilemma in its clearest possible sense. It is one of those curious laws of nature that people who are not performing adequately and need to be removed have very seldom produced adequate cover under them, seeming to have assiduously avoided the development of competition on their own patch, while the successful man is frequently supported by a large number of potential successors.

If the execution of the task is difficult the timing is even more so. From the point of view both of fairness and of practical expediency there is a great temptation to leave the execution of the High Sheriff role until the failure of the individual concerned is plain for all to see. This makes both the justification and execution of your act easier. Unfortunately by that time it is really too late. It is when it is apparent that the course on which the company is set and the ability of the chairman to deal with the problem concerned are inadequate, that the real need for the execution of the High Sheriff role occurs. At these times there is every temptation to 'fudge' the issue or to avoid it altogether; the execution is difficult and one is naturally concerned with the possibility that one's judgement may be at fault. Remember, moreover, that by definition the man that you are having to replace is almost certainly somebody that you like and is responsible, so to speak, for choosing his own executioner.

It is small wonder, therefore, that this task has been very seldom carried out at all, and it has even less often been carried out competently and in time. This despite the fact that the knowledge that you can execute the High Sheriff role is one of the main sources of reassurance to external investors when they see your name as a non-executive director on the board of their company. Although this is an absolutely necessary role, it is certainly no part of my ambition to write the definitive book on the subject. It is an area where I am exceedingly self-critical of my own abilities and skills. Both in the United Kingdom and in the United States of America non-executive directors are being expected to perform this task more and more frequently. Sadly, and perhaps this is a warning to anyone who is seeking a career as a non-executive director, it appears that this aspect of the role, which can only really be looked on as constructive in the longest possible time scale, is likely to grow in the future. With this in mind, unless you are prepared to play your part in such a decision, you should think carefully about whether you wish to take on the job at all.

While dealing – albeit superficially and with limited enthusiasm – with this difficult subject, I should perhaps raise another problem which faces the non-executive director and of which I have also had practical experience. I have referred on a number of occasions to the inadequacy of the tools and weapons at the non-executive director's disposal, but this is not strictly speaking an accurate portrayal of the position. The non-executive director has one weapon which is of such absolutely fearsome consequence that it is rather as though the infantry were armed only with the atom bomb! This weapon is the act of resignation from the board, either individually or, even more damaging, collectively. The weapon is a real one and is constantly at the back of the mind of any non-executive director of a company that is badly run, or where he is sure of his prognosis of disaster and yet unable to effect adequate action to avert it.

There are undoubtedly occasions on which the threat of resignation will finally force some action, but the threat can only be used infrequently. One of the important principles of business is never to threaten anything unless you are really prepared to carry out the threat. This applies even more strongly to the non-executive director. Moreover, a non-executive director could not operate effectively if he was continually threatening to resign – there would be bound to come a time when both he and everybody else concerned would be glad if he did! The difficulty with resignation from a board is that the actual time when one can do so without precipitating the very event one is trying to prevent is very limited indeed. It is therefore an extremely difficult weapon to use.

I have had personal experience of this problem and on each occasion have delayed too long, so that I found I had thrown the weapon away. If things are really bad and the external perception of the company is poor, it is very likely that a resignation by one or more of the non-executive directors will precipitate the final collapse of confidence in the company by customers, shareholders, investors and lenders. Should you precipitate the collapse of the company by your resignation you have plainly failed in your duty as a non-executive director. Therefore the threat has to be used early on in a deteriorating situation. It can only be used as a means of drawing to the attention of your colleagues the urgency of your views of the position and the very high risks you feel they may be running.

Just as joining the board of a company may give some reassurance to people both inside and outside a company, so the act of leaving is likely to have the equal and opposite effect. It therefore has to be most carefully thought through. You must have a very clear mind as to exactly what you are trying to achieve and what the possible consequences of such an action will be. On the occasions when I have been forced to contemplate such drastic action, I have resorted to what is for me the unusual step of writing a carefully thought-out evaluation of the options before me and the likely consequences of each of those options. I have always discussed the matter carefully, first of all usually within my family, and then I have sought the advice or opinions of the other non-executive directors concerned. All too often you find that they are in the same position and contemplating the same sort of action. Of course a collective approach to the board is very much more likely to have the effect that is required than an individual one. Every action has its equal and opposite reaction, and one of the measures of poor performance as a non-executive director is if the non-executive directors become ranged against the executives. There should be an interchange on most important issues and if you find yourselves forming into two opposing teams that can only be bad news for the company as a whole.

I would not like to leave the impression that the non-executive director's job is all problems or that it is unrewarding, for I actually believe the reverse. Anybody who operates a business is an artist, for the skills of business are closer to the realms of artistry than science and any artist must be continuously seeking to improve his technique, his palette, his range of colour and his skills of application. It is in this broadening experience that the rewards of doing the job come. While I know no more difficult role I also know no other stimulus which causes one constantly to think and re-examine and contemplate matters which one has taken for granted over many years. There can be no external experience more likely to broaden one's thinking, or to cause one to appreciate real advantages or good aspects of one's own company which have hitherto lain unregarded, than experiencing the operation of another business.

The learning experience never ends. You are mixing with another team who are perhaps playing in a different league or even a different game, and are certainly playing to different rules and values from those that you have applied in your own field. There is from such an experience a continuous stretching of one's imagination and one's critical capabilities, as well as a continual enrichment of one's skill base. It is, I suppose, not so surprising that so many of us seek non-executive jobs and that despite the difficulties of 'making it happen' and the poor financial rewards, we find in them satisfaction, self-growth and a breadth of new experience which more than compensate for all the difficulties.

10

The Top Job

Of all the jobs that look different from an outside viewpoint, the top job must surely take the blue ribbon. It is only when you become aware of the range, scope and incredible responsibility of the job, that you realize that there is an almost limitless opportunity to be ineffective, unless you are totally clear about how you are going to set about it. The problem itself is manifestly an enormous one, which is not eased by the fact that it is a very fortunate chairman who has any significant hand-over from his predecessor, even if the incoming man is prepared to listen. After all, for many years you have watched the mistakes and blunders of your predecessors. You have always been aware of the things that have gone wrong, and have always believed that more could be done, or that things could have been done in different ways, or more effectively.

What you have not been aware of is the enormous scope, in a chairman's life, for diversity of attention, and the fact that, for the first time in your business life, there are no limitations of any sort on how you can spend your time, or to what you should address your attention. The people with whom you should work, the way in which the organization is set up, even the basic objectives and form of your company, are all available to you as a clean sheet of paper for the first time. Well, not quite clean of course, because the company has already been moving in different directions, it already has a number of employees, a sense of values and so on. However, in reality there are practically no limitations to the ambitions and objectives which you can set yourself as the top man, and very few limitations to the objectives which you can set your company. You can borrow more money, change the people, buy and sell parts of the company, change the technical base, acquire other companies in other countries. Superficially at least, you have boundless opportunities, which match the boundless responsibility you now hold.

Moreover, to compound the problem, after long years of waiting you have suddenly reached the pinnacle of your ambition. Without the benefit of the full breadth of knowledge which can only be gained by holding the job, you have already formed a number of ideas about what you would like to do, almost invariably in terms of correcting what you see as being the mistakes of the past. You are conscious that you need to 'grasp' the organization immediately. You must move quickly if you are to convey the image of determination and clarity that you will need if you are to establish your leadership and achieve your ends. Furthermore, the responsibility lands on you suddenly, almost without warning. Neither you, your colleagues, or your company are likely to take kindly to you spending your first three months in a secluded location, doing what you really ought to do, namely thinking. It is important to do as much thinking as you can before you get the job, but it is even more important to pace yourself and your workload, so that you allow yourself time to contemplate and reflect on what you wish to achieve, and how you intend to set about it.

The very first question that anybody asks the leader of a large corporation is how they do it. How can one man impress himself on people in eighty or ninety countries, numbering in all, perhaps, two hundred thousand? How can the influence of one individual actually make any difference to the company as a whole? How can one individual be responsible for, and have any worthwhile knowledge about, the sort of problems which are facing his people in areas as diffuse as Ecuador, Auckland and Aberdeen? If he can't have any effect on the company as a whole, what on earth is he doing there anyway? All of these, and many more questions, have to be resolved to your own satisfaction if you are in fact to achieve what is expected of you.

You must be clear in your own mind that there is no way that one man can manage an enormous company. The job of the chairman, or chief executive, is to 'manage' his colleagues on the board, and to manage the company through the board. I have always believed in the concept of added value, in an organizational sense. Namely, that every level in the organization should only exist if it has some unique role, responsibility, or capability to add to that which people below it are capable of doing. The only job in the entire company where it is totally clear where the added value lies is probably that of the chairman and chief executive.

There are certain ineluctable responsibilities which lie upon him, but above everything the entire question of the board. Only he can develop the board as a collective organization, handle, select and motivate its members, and manage its work. The style and way in which the board works will have an enormous effect on the group as a whole, and the content of what it addresses itself to will decide to a large extent whether it is successful in influencing a large organization. The actual way in which it works depends entirely on the chairman. There is an almost limitless range of behaviour in any board of directors, and, at one time or another, one experiences practically all of them. One has seen boards which are purely ritual dancing, dealing only with the legalistic boiler plate, where no decision has ever been taken, and where everything is 'fixed' before it ever appears. Equally well, one has seen boards at the other extreme, where the entire time is spent on seemingly endless, fruitless debate, which is never pulled together and turned into decisions. Indeed, if decisions were taken it is very doubtful whether there would be any mechanism to check on whether they were followed through.

In between these two extremes, board behaviour can cover every sort of note on the keyboard. Boards can be used to solve problems, although this is rare. It is, in fact, probably the best use of the combined talent you have, for remember that the board of directors of a company is very probably the most experienced, and almost certainly the best paid group that you have. If they can't solve problems it is a little difficult to see who can. In order to solve problems information has to be shared, and not only information, but doubts, fears and questions. Boards can, in their ways of managing themselves, run the whole gamut between construction and conflict. Somebody has to intervene, to manage that balance.

These matters cannot be decided collectively. There may be a collective will, or precedents about the ways in which certain things are dealt with, but finally it is only the chairman who can decide the style. Only he can judge in what way the board can be most effective as a group, and how effective their influence will be on the company as a whole. The board's working style will have a cascade effect throughout the whole company. For example, I have mentioned my predilection for looking at trends in a graphical way. Shortly after the start of my chairman-ship we obtained a very fine piece of equipment, which enabled us to 'interact' with the financial data presented to us. We had formerly received this as a book, in tabular form, which involved very large amounts of work by each of us to try to discern the trends which lay behind the tables. Thanks to modern technology, and some splendid support work by a number of our people, it became possible for us to sit in front of a screen and, for the first time, see the development of the trends in the individual businesses and economies in which we were interested, and also to indulge in a certain number of 'what if' questions on the run. We found to our surprise that suddenly the whole of our business became alive to us all. We were all joining the discussion, forming our judgements and views, and were able to express concerns that we had about aspects of the business in a lively way. It proved to be a very useful board tool.

We did not promulgate any instruction to the company as a whole that such a method was to be used, but it soon became known that we were looking at numbers in this way, and one or two people wished to see what we were actually doing. I suspect that this was a fairly sensible and basic defensive urge, rather than any particular wish for imitation. Once seen, however, the process began to sell itself, and to our surprise we soon found that a number of other parts of the company were using the same sort of equipment, albeit in different and more adventurous ways. Therefore a process was set up, without any dark intent, in which we, and a number of our businesses, began looking at the database in similar interactive ways, and learning from each other. A very good example of a situation where a matter of selection of style had effects far beyond those which were originally intended.

The point I am making in all of this is that, above everything else, the management of the board, and the board working process, is the unique and specific responsibility of the man at the top. One is lucky if one understands this when one is given the job, and one is even more lucky if one's first fumbling attempts to influence these unique 'added value' areas meet with success. Because most of us learn from our own mistakes, you may well find that you are only just beginning to under-stand the opportunities and hazards of top leadership long after the original chances have gone. It is very difficult to learn from another's mistakes, because only the individual knows exactly how he set his objective, and can analyse exactly where his ambitions failed to materialize.

Besides this major management role there are, of course, a number of other responsibilities which fall inevitably on the top man's shoulders. One major concern is to ensure that succession to his job, and to the top jobs in the company, is assured, and this is no easy task to carry out. The chairman also carries the responsibility for ensuring that the board is actually taking the company somewhere. It is surprisingly easy to fall into the trap of thinking that the maintenance of the status quo, the maintenance of an adequate level of profitability, and defence of one's market share, are enough. Alas, this is far from the truth. The company that is not clearly progressing is equally clearly losing ground to the competition. Clear strategic direction, worked out by the board as a whole, is essential. Although, as I pointed out earlier, this strategic direction and thinking has to be derived as a group, there is no question but that the man at the top must have his own clear views as to the sort of company he wants to lead, and where he wants to lead it to.

Another field which cannot be shirked by the chairman is the problem of projecting, both inside and outside the company, the company itself, its values and its worth as a whole. This, like all the other parts of a top job, is not easy, for one addresses many different audiences, all with different interests, fears, and perceptions. The message that you are about to shut down a loss-making business may be very good news for your shareholders, or the financial analysts, but is likely to be very bad news to the community in which you operate and to your employees. It may also be very bad news to the government of the country in which you operate. Yet all of them have to be communicated with, and persuaded that the steps you are taking are desirable and necessary, and will be carried out, bearing in mind the many different interests that are affected. This problem cannot be solved by blandness. It is very tempting to try to avoid making any positive statements to anybody, hoping that it 'will all be all right on the night', but of course it never is, and you land in even deeper trouble.

On really important issues nobody can speak for your company except you and, although you may get a lot of advice, the choice of words and sincerity of the presentation will rest on you. A congruence between your own values and feelings and those followed by your company in its approach to business is absolutely essential. Any divergence between the two causes immense difficulties, and will show in a quite alarming way. I have been lucky enough to work, during practically all of my industrial life, in a company which has ethical and moral views almost identical with my own. I have seldom, if ever, been put in a position where I have had to defend a company position which I did not feel at ease with in my own mind. It is, however, perfectly possible to be appointed to the top job of a company with whose values and positions you are much less happy, and which you are setting out to change. That must be the most horrible of problems to have to deal with. For example, the incoming chairman of Guinness plainly has a major problem of house cleaning and change of attitude to contend with.

In addition to these difficult tasks there is a major responsibility for the way in which the board works, which depends very much upon the chairman's wish to balance the board between boiler plate and problem solving; between information and sharing of doubts and fears; between constructive debate and the airing and earthing of conflicts; between overkill and excess verbosity, and a style so disciplined that the more introverted members of the board are never heard at all. In all of these areas the chairman has to understand what is known in my business as 'process'. 'Process' is the study of how groups interact and how work is planned, in fact how to actually do work, rather than the task itself. It is not an easy concept to grasp, and once grasped is even more difficult to learn to read and influence. The chairman has to be the head of the board process, and it is worth his spending almost limitless amounts of time, worrying and teasing out the way in which the group interacts, attempting to flush out the hidden and unspoken comments, which are so often the cause of process difficulties. Before the ICI main board goes away for one of its regular strategy discussions 'off campus', an enormous amount of time is spent working out the balance of the meeting, and how it should be carried out. It is essential that the time is used to best effect, and this means structuring the meetings so that there is an adequate input of fact, and time available to stimulate lively discussions about it. The conditions must be right, so that the whole purpose of going away, and meeting in casual clothes, without the paraphernalia of a board meeting, is to enable fluent and open interchange to take place. This aim is completely lost if the two days are filled up with a series of presentations by staff members, which are so carefully honed and polished that it is almost impossible to get a finger nail into the edge! The aim is first of all to have discussed with everybody what are the key issues they believe should be aired and considered. After attempting to ensure that each issue starts from an agreed database and definition of the problem, the aim is to let the thing flow. Letting things flow is an art in itself. The place where you meet, the distractions that are around, the relative comfort of the chairs, the style of the presentation, the size and scope of the meals – all affect the issues. There is invariably a light lunch and eating is concentrated on dinner. Time is left free after dinner for resting and relaxing, because, after a day of intensive meetings, people tend to 'run out of puff' by about six or seven in the evening. At any time that the meeting appears to be circling, or the members seem to be getting tired, or losing interest in the subject or debate, the chairman speedily moves in and closes off. All these apparently trivial matters, which are so often left to staff members to see to, without intervention or guidance from the chairman, are what constitutes the planning of the process, and it is the process planning which actually enables the business to be done.

The chairman is also responsible for the creation of the mood of the board; not always an easy task, since, being human, he may well have moods of his own. Nevertheless, it is up to him to keep the board working, to ensure that subjects are addressed properly, that all the differing views are actually heard, and that the board doesn't fall into the all too frequently observed trap of spending its time 'playing games'. Board time is immensely expensive and, comprising as it does the time of the most highly paid and highly experienced people in the group, must not be wasted. Board discussions have to be useful and conclusive. The conclusions have to be different, on a sufficient number of occasions, from those which were anticipated. If the board acts in a predictable way in every case, then it is not being put to the right use. If it has become a rubber stamp, and never ever affects or reverses a decision, changes its mind, or behaves in a totally unexpected way, then the board has ceased to work properly. If that is the situation nobody is to blame except the chairman, and nobody except him can rectify it.

In order to rectify it, he has to recognize what has happened, which in itself is not too easy. It is easy enough to know when a board is working well, when the results of its labours are showing through in a well-run, happy and competitively successful company, and when you have the pleasing and exhilarating feeling that you are working well as a team, managing to really thrash things out, and are taking good decisions which are having the effects you are hoping for. It is very much more difficult, however, when you leave your meetings frustrated, when you do not seem to be shifting either your own or the company's position, and where the level of conflict has gone over the edge from being constructive to being dysfunctional. Most chairmen have had experience, to a greater or lesser degree, of situations where they are conscious that their colleagues are dissatisfied with the collective way in which they are tackling things, and are looking to him for help in resolving problems which are harming the reputation of the board within the company, and which, in turn, may cause the external image of the organization to suffer.

It is, unfortunately, all too simple to know when one is in that situation, but it is all too difficult to be able to work patiently back to see what is the root cause, and what are the simple things that one can do to try to put things right. In this, as in so many other areas, the only person who can actually put things right is the chairman. While he can get a lot of help from his colleagues if he creates the conditions under which they can have an open discussion as to why they are in a mess, the remedies still lie within his hands. Only he can actually take the initiative which can begin to break you out of such an unfortunate position. The interesting thing is that boards do have a sort of collective 'feeling'. It is very seldom that half the board are happy and feel that things are going well, while the other half are worried, dissatisfied and fearful.

I hope I have said enough already to indicate that, besides the sheer fascination of the opportunity to try and lead a large organization, the problems lie very much in the balance and selection of the actions and activities that you undertake. Therefore the art of being a good top leader is really one of breadth of understanding, absolute clarity of aim, and lightness of actual intervention, always making sure that the interventions are on key points which can be shifted in the way that you hope. Besides the sheer power, the necessity for analysis, clarity, and subtlety, many of the actions that have to be taken in a top job demand great courage. The stakes for which one is playing are so high, and the consequences of failure are both so public, and so damaging to so many people, that the job itself places great demands on one's willingness to continually take risks. The irony is that it is perfectly possible to, so to speak, cease pedalling and coast downhill, or even some way uphill, with the momentum that the company has, but this failure of drive will only reveal itself at a later stage. Almost every decision that is taken from the top involves risk, and has to be taken on a personal basis, even though you may seek a great deal of advice. Failure to take the risk means failure to do the job as well as the job – and your organization – demands.

The very first problem to which the new top leader must address himself is what he would see as being the best size and composition of his board. I have always believed that there is a golden rule as far as the size of a board is concerned. If you analyse how even the largest and most complex organizations work, I have yet to find any organization in the world which is not ultimately managed by a small group, rather than a large one. A large group almost inevitably leads to a small sub-group actually doing the job, and the small sub-group, from the analysis that I have done of companies and other organizations, cannot be less than three, and is seldom more than seven or eight. The range in between depends upon the complexity of the organization, rather than its size, and the style, predilections and energy of the people constituting the top management.

History teaches one that groupings of five, plus or minus two, are much more effectively made into teams than larger ones. The military organization, and practical experience of working in groups, all seem to show that the optimum size for ease of communication, development of mutual trust, ability to share common objectives, and ability to coordinate with each other without excessive intervention, lies in this range. In particular, small groups are more likely to remain as a single cohesive team, whereas large ones almost invariably break into smaller sub-groups, which tend to get involved in internal politicking and fragmentation of effort and drive.

The speed at which a company can move depends, to a large extent, on the speed at which the board itself can move, for, while boards can seldom create the opportunities which exist for businesses further down the line, they have demonstrated over and over again their ability to stop such opportunities being seized or developed. My ideal board is an enabling board, which adds value to the effort of people below and enables everyone, from the top to the bottom of the company, to give of his best and to utilize the very large amounts of headroom and opportunity that he should be given. To achieve this it is really essential that the board itself should be a team. It is impossible to act as an enabling mechanism if there are unresolved fundamental differences between different parts of the group which shares the responsibility for the direction of the company.

Great power, in a hierarchical sense, can very seldom really act as the engine for a large organization. What it does do is to give a tremendous power on the brakes, to stop things happening. There are some examples of groups of people who have been driven by the sheer determination and energy of one man, albeit mostly working with the grain of the group; but experience seems to me to show that they will always be defeated by the association of free men working together in concert, under broad direction and enabling leadership. Outstanding examples of companies propelled, as far as one can see, by the sheer willpower of one man are IT & T under Harold Geneen, CBS under William Paley, and more recently the revived Chrysler under Lee Iacocca. The sadness is that the first two did not survive the removal of the driving force, and indeed, some of the force of drive was plainly misdirected in the later years. This is one of the reasons why great hierarchical power tends to be, in my view, dangerous. No matter how great the man may be, he becomes less adaptive with time, and tends to follow those areas of success which have worked for him in the past. He repeats a particular action once too often and, almost inevitably, disaster strikes.

In addition to having a great keenness for a small executive board, I also have a distaste for boards which contain more than one level within them. As I pointed out earlier, the legal responsibility is totally shared, and I therefore find it extremely difficult to understand how it is possible to operate with tiered responsibilities within a board. I have little patience with the concept of senior and junior directors. The top job may have to be split, because of the sheer problem of load, but I certainly do not like an intervening layer of deputies, who stand between the ordinary board members and the chairman.

I believe a flat organization at this level is essential, both in terms of keeping the team moving together, but also in terms of the example further down the line. After all, if a board of eight to fifteen people cannot organize themselves, except in a tiered hierarchical way, what chance have you got of manning tightly down the rest of the company? At one time, in ICI, there were five hierarchical steps between a director of a division, in itself a responsible job, and the chairman of the company. The irony was that this contrasted with only seven such steps in the line from the shop floor to the divisional director. In my own case I progressed from work study officer in 1957, to a director of a division in 1968. This period of eleven years contrasts with the nineteen years I have spent on boards at the differing levels we used to have. I am bound to say that I believe, both from the company's point of view and my own, more time in the engine room and less on the bridge would have been a better plan!

The essence of a board working together is that it should be like Nelson's 'band of brothers'. There should be mutuality of trust and understanding between the members of the team, there should be a shared objective, and above all there should be so much sharing of perceptions and values that each can coordinate with the other, almost without having to discuss an issue at all. This idealistic way of working, which most of us far prefer if we can achieve it, is made more difficult by the introduction of an intermediate layer between the chairman and his colleagues.

One of the areas about which I am still very uncertain is the never-ending argument about whether the top job should really be two jobs or not. I have seen successful examples both of a combination of chairman and chief executive in the one, and an admittedly smaller number but nevertheless very successful examples of a situation where a non-executive chairman has worked well and happily with a chief executive. Dalgetty, in the United Kingdom, is perhaps an extremely good example of a company that operated well with a non-executive and highly professional chairman in the shape of David Donne. Moreover, many of the companies that John Cuckney has run have had the same attributes. There is no doubt that if the top job of chairman and principal executive officer are combined in one, the job is a killer. The outside, representational role is immensely time-consuming, and tends to be an inescapable, self-accelerating function. The better known and more successful you are at projecting the image of your company, the more you are requested to do so. Time management and allocation between the representational and the executive role is very difficult, since the latter requires very large amounts of time to be spent on the preparation of the work, and the management of the board as a whole.

There are real advantages to having the top job split between two people. It is easier to replace either one of them under such circumstances if some disaster happens, or if one or the other begins to be 'off the boil'. It is extremely difficult to replace a combined chairman and chief executive. You take a double risk for a start, and the actual mechanisms of replacement are difficult to effect. It is relatively easy to draw up the fields of responsibilities of two people who share the top job. The non-executive job should be primarily directed to the management of the actual board, and the external environment, as well as ensuring that mechanisms are in place to develop strategies and clear policies on the many issues for which a board has responsibility. The other, the executive role, is then responsible for seeing that these policies are carried out, and actually managing that process. The chairman is responsible for seeing that the board checks that their policies have been carried out by the chief executive.

The difficulty in such organizations is one of split responsibilities. An organization of this type calls for a degree of integration and understanding between the two top people which is often difficult to achieve. Moreover, it can fall into the trap which the Americans dislike so much, of a lack of clarity as to who is ultimately in charge, and where the buck actually stops. It is a fuzzier organization and, while it does have some highly desirable characteristics of flexibility, it lacks some of the crispness of having the whole thing tied into one person. Certainly such an approach is an unpopular one in America, where again organizational theory seems to be rather starker than in the United Kingdom.

Having tried to do the job as a solo effort for a number of, perhaps in retrospect, less good reasons than I thought at the time, I suspect that the strain of doing it on one's own may well not be worth the candle. If you have the job of chairman and chief executive in one you rely totally on your own sensitivities as to the real feelings of your colleagues. It is all too easy to lose the feel of the mood and to move into isolation without meaning to. At that stage the capacity for leadership is severely limited. If there are two of you, you have double the chance of evading this situation. However, I have even seen examples where both the chairman and the CEO have lost this feeling, and once lost it is very difficult to recover. On balance, in a UK environment, I think I prefer the top job to be split, but again this is a matter which rests with the chairman. He must decide what he thinks would be the best organization for the company and the board, after giving the matter careful thought. The difficulty of such an internal debate is that it is extremely difficult to understand clearly the pressures which one is imposing upon oneself, and there is a natural tendency to overestimate one's ability to handle things.

Having decided whether the top job itself should be split, and how many directors you are going to have, you then turn to the interesting problem of the non-executive directors. The most important thing here is to make sure that you have a 'critical mass' of non-executives. The job is difficult enough anyway, but becomes almost impossible to carry out if they are hopelessly outnumbered by the executive directors. I have always favoured approximate parity of numbers between the non-executive directors and the executives. Whether you have a majority of execs or non-execs is, I think, largely a matter of preference on the part of the chairman, and will be dictated in part by the complexity of the company and the custom and practice of the country in which you operate. Predominantly non-executive boards are the norm in America but are a rarity in the United Kingdom.

The sheer size and complexity of ICI makes it very difficult, I believe, for the board to have a majority of non-execs, so I opted for approximate parity of numbers between the executives and the non-executives. Here again, it is important to be clear about the role that one expects the non-executives to play, as well as the specific gaps in the board balance that one is seeking to fill.

One of the first things I did on taking over as chairman was to
write, with a colleague, the draft of a paper which we debated at
length amongst ourselves as to what we were seeking from our
non-executive colleagues. We started by considering, as ICI
had in the past, the particular areas where an internal board,
promoted from career executives, were unlikely to have
adequate experience. There are some very obvious examples of
this. We needed access to people with experience of government, overseas territories of which we did not have deep
personal experience, the City (where, with the exception of the
finance director, most of us felt that we were in a rather alien
land), the educational establishment (who affect so greatly the
future of our company), and other types of business which
faced different demands and problems from those with which
we were familiar.

Having decided the areas where you believe that differences
of perspective and view would be useful, the numbers that you
might be seeking, and the ultimate composition, you then have
to look at the balance of the board as a whole. The balance has to
be created in a number of different ways. It is a bit like trying to
play three-dimensional chess, a skill which I am bound to admit
I have never learnt! First of all, and quite obviously, you need a
balance of basic skills. In ICI's case a balance is needed between
commercial and technical: some people are needed on the board
who have a knowledge of engineering, some with experience of
chemistry and research, some with an experience of commerce.
There needs to be at least some knowledge of most of the sorts of
businesses with which ICI is concerned, so, ideally, experience
is needed in everything from running an oil company to running a pharmaceutical business. Each of these businesses has
characteristics which are different from the others, and an
understanding of the marketplace, and the technical and other
problems involved, is desirable.

There must be, on the board, some people with a good
financial background, and in particular the finance director
must, of course, have an impeccable financial and accountancy
standing. Someone with experience and an understanding of
the different interactions between politics and economics in the
various countries and areas of the world is needed. In those
areas where ICI is particularly big, or has high ambitions, a
background of knowledge and acquaintance with the financial,

industrial and commercial leadership of the country is essential.
On this level, which we could call the level of broad experience
and knowledge, at least it is fairly clear whether the characteristics and experience required are there or not. Remember,
however, that we started by saying that we wanted to have a
small executive board of eight people at maximum, and probably about six or seven non-executive directors, so we are trying
to squeeze an enormous amount of world knowledge and
background within a small group of people.

This is one axis of our three-dimensional chess game. But the
other axis is perhaps even more important, and a great deal
more difficult to judge. The aim is, after all, to create an effective
team that can work together, collaborate, grow, develop, and
give a good example of the style which you are trying to project
to the company as a whole. One therefore has to look at the mix
of personalities, and try to form a judgement about the
individual chemistry between the people, and how you can
make the collective chemistry balance. First of all you must
make the relevant judgements about the ways in which people
will work in such a group, and this is not always easy, even
when you have known people over a long period of time. You
plainly need a balance of humour. Laughter is a great relaxer of
tension, and an aid to team building, and if you intend to run
your business in a moderately light-hearted manner it is
extremely difficult for one of those, fortunately few, beings who
have no sense of humour at all to, so to speak, 'join the club'.

You need a balance between the 'instant action' men, and the
'philosophers', between the extroverts and the introverts,
between those with strategic vision and those with tactical
ability, and you need, besides the essential requirements of
honesty and integrity from every one of them, people who, at
the least, can respect each other, and, hopefully, trust and like
each other. You need people, since you will often be travelling
together, whose wives get on well – or at least do not have a vast
antipathy to each other! You must have people you can trust to
represent the company, both by their behaviour and by their
natural character, in the way in which you hope to project the
company as a whole. Above everything you need difference,
because the creation of an effective board team is genuinely a
work of art. A work of art derives from the contribution of every
single part of the constituent form, supporting and contrasting

with the whole. You are really trying to create a team of people who are able to work together like a superb orchestra which, in terms of character, background and experience, can cover both the whole range of your business, and the whole constructive side of the human character.

If you have set yourself this aim you still have to bear in mind the third dimension of the chess game. You have to have people of different ages, different ambitions and different potential. I am lucky enough to have worked most of my life in a company where every member of the ICI main board had the innate ability to lead the company as chairman. A wise friend of mine on the board some years ago made this point to me, and the more I have thought about it the more true I believe it to be. It is a reflection on the wealth of talent that ICI has had that one can make such a claim, but I really believe that, in choosing our chairmen, we have been choosing more matters of style and experience than the straight capability and 'size' to take the job. This is a measure both of the richness of our company in terms of abilities, but also the wisdom with which individuals have been developed over the years.

The constraints placed upon one by the issue of ages of individuals one is trying to fit into the probable succession plans are surprising. Although the 'telephone book' system of working out the succession in large organizations has always been shown to be wrong, nevertheless one must work on the assumption that there will not be too many 'accidents', and that most people will continue to operate reasonably well up to their retirement age. By the 'telephone book' system, I mean the practice one has seen of people at the bottom of the organization going through the entire telephone book of the hierarchy above them, pencilling in ages, and working out, with a certain inevitability, that there is no way in which they can ever get the top job, or, if they did, arithmetically they could only hold it for a year at most. The sign of a well-run organization is that people are in position at the relevant ages, with the relevant experience and characteristics, and this takes a lot of planning because flexibility is essential at all stages.

One of the many characteristics which differentiates a life in industry with that of the services, or possibly civil service, is the unpredictability of people's performance when exposed to new levels of challenge. So often in my old service, the Navy, the future First Sea Lord was visible many many years before his appointment. As far as I can see, such is seldom the case in industry. People are sighted who appear to have extraordinary talent at an early age, and then either go off the boil, are over-promoted, or mishandled in some way, or suffer health or family problems which affect their first promise. The good news in industry is that it is never too late. It is never too late to be promoted to fill any particular job, and it is never too late to suddenly start moving, very fast indeed, up the line of advance-ment. I can think, for example, of the late J. C. Brown who was promoted on to the ICI main board when he was over fifty-seven and proved to be an absolutely outstanding director. He had an immense effect on the company and promoted more change in the short time that he was on the board than anybody I can remember in that period of ICI's history. I have thought deeply about the reasons for the differences, and I think they are really linked to the rate of change in the industrial scene. My friends and colleagues in the Navy would argue that they have suffered equally abrupt changes, both in role and in their tech-nology, but in industry it is the whole business that is either waxing or waning, and the whole world is in a continuous ferment. The man who appeared extraordinarily good at the age of thirty, dealing with the problems then, may simply not have the right mix of qualities needed to deal with the totally new sets of problems which are facing him at the age of forty or fifty. It is very seldom that one finds individuals who are both good 'bad weather sailors' and 'good weather sailors'. Some are superb at leading retrenchment, cleaning up, and setting businesses in new direc-tions, but it is a rare combination of man who is able both to carry out that distasteful, but necessary, task, and also to have the swashbuckling approach to drive triumphantly into the future.

Industry has no set tram-lines, and it is the easiest thing in the world to stretch down and move a young man into a position of high responsibility. Unfortunately it is also the easiest thing in the world, by so doing, to destroy his ultimate chances, or to promote him to such a level, as a sort of accelerated 'Peter' principle, that he is unable to perform adequately. Moreover, in this whole area of succession, one is giving messages to the organization as a whole which affect people's behaviour. It is highly desirable that positions on the board should only go to those who have a solid record of achievement behind them. Anything else gives the impression that the company is run on the basis of nepotism, and 'pleasing' the boss, rather than on the basis of solid achievement, which is the only way the company can survive. Furthermore, too much promotion of the overtly ambitious, those who do not care for their fellow men, those who have a reputation for selfish ruthlessness, or those who are known always to take a short-term view or hedge their risks, all give messages down the line which you probably do not want to convey. Large organizations are inveterate hierarchy watchers, and take their cue, to an extraordinary degree, from what they perceive as being the characteristics which are likely to lead to success. Every appointment is therefore scrutinized from below in quite a different way from how you may see it from above. You may be seeking to fill a particular gap of personality on your board; for example, if your board is unduly pessimistic you may be looking for an optimist. It is highly unlikely that it is read in that way down the line. There will be constant questions in people's minds as to why Mr X was promoted, and what 'the board' is about now.

One may feel, at the end of this formidable list of the things which are ideally looked for in the selection of one's board, that the task itself is impossible, especially bearing in mind that you start from a particular position, with particular people already developed or on the board. This is not actually true, and the converse, that one is starting with a totally green field, is equally incorrect. The good leader is not the man who merely selects the team of whiz kids, but rather the man who gets extraordinary results out of those people he already has, and you can be quite sure that the members of the board of any large organization have already achieved a great deal in order to hold their present positions.

The problem becomes much more one of how to cast the group that you have, and how to select the incomers that will inevitably be required. One of my colleagues is constantly pointing out to me that in all our planning of the board, and the board succession, the unexpected always happens. One of our colleagues is attracted to a major opportunity elsewhere, or becomes ill and is unable to carry the full weight, or is seconded to the government, or some other organization, to assist them.

The only certainty in running a board is the uncertainty of future events.

The whole problem of the balance of the board is really where the almost limitless choice that you have, when searching for a non-executive director, can be used to the best effect. With really careful thinking and planning you can fill in from outside, in any one of the three dimensions that I have mentioned, if you are clear about the characteristics that you are looking for. You can even, if you are lucky, fill in a sort of diagonal slice, which will cover all of the dimensions in one appointment, particularly if luck is on your side. Usually you will be seeking your executive colleagues from within your own company, and in the non-executive field you can go wherever you like, and seek whatever you will.

It has to be said, although it has seldom been our practice, that you are also fully free to select your executive directors from outside your own organization. I have always been somewhat loath to do this, because of the messages it gives within the company, and also because of the very high risk involved. Those within the company will inevitably look on an outside appointment as a criticism of all the people in that particular field who might have been promoted. They will not take into account the fact that you do not wish to move the young man of thirty-eight, who you think will make it later on, because of the age spread of those who are showing potential. They will merely assume that the whole of that field of activity in your company is not considered good enough. Even worse, they will then look to the man coming in from outside to perform outstandingly better than any of them could have dreamed of doing. Bearing in mind that the poor devil *is* coming from outside, and doesn't know the company, its values, those within it who are competent or incompetent, or the history of the various matters with which he is dealing, it is an unreasonable expectation, except in the very long term. All of these factors compound the risk. No matter how carefully you seek outside advice, and how carefully you interview a man, there is really no substitute for working with him. In comparing the executive you hire in from outside, and the man you know, you are almost always liable to short-change the individual in your own outfit, since you are painfully aware of his weaknesses and may not adequately appreciate his strengths, in relation to the outside market. In a large organization, recruitment at the top levels from outside should be looked upon as a sign of failure at having developed your own people, for, after all, you wish to encourage young people into the company in the sure belief that they can go the whole way up it, although I think that this may perhaps be a less potent motivator than it was in the past. Certainly, in my own experience, it is seldom that an individual believes that he would be capable of going to the top, but there is a difference between that, and the sure knowledge that you are unlikely to have the opportunity. Companies who habitually cut off their people at the management level, and invariably recruit from outside, take a quite severe risk of demotivating their own people, and may find it more difficult to attract the very high calibre of employees on which they will rely in the long haul.

The selection, setting up, manning and succession of the board are the beginning of the framework which the chairman must uniquely deal with, and I will discuss the other factors separately, although of course in real life the whole thing is a mixed-up ball of twine. Decisions in any of the other ways in which the board works will have an automatic impact on the balance, and also in the area of selection. Before we leave this subject, one further word, however, on development. It is very difficult to continue to develop men of one's own age, and there is, I think, a natural disinclination to try to do it in a very formal way. Nevertheless, if instead of describing the job as 'development' one described it as 'helping', it is clearly the responsibility of the chairman, and one which he should take on gladly and, as with most other things, should do thoughtfully.

The specific responsibilities and tasks which you give your colleagues all help to fill out gaps in experience which you may feel they lack. Working with certain people may also help to develop characteristics which you believe they have latently, but which have not been called upon. There is nothing more character-forming than being at the sharp end of real trouble, and there are individuals who have progressed through their lives without ever really working in an organization which has had its back to the wall. Helping such an organization survive, getting in amongst it and understanding the problems, trials and tribulations that it faces, is a most valuable way of helping to develop personal qualities which your colleagues almost certainly have, but may not have been called upon to show.

Advice of a process type is more difficult, but nevertheless has to be given, albeit tactfully. Always remember that it is no good giving advice unless it is actually received and acted upon. There is always a trade-off between the satisfaction of knowing that you have conveyed something bluntly, and the probable impact upon the recipient, which is likely to be a strong urge to tell you what to do with yourself, and an almost total rejection of the 'help' you have just given him. It is foolish to think that your colleagues on the board do not need help, just as foolish in fact as to think that you yourself no longer need it. Indeed, one's best friends, helpers and supporters, as chairman of a board, are those of your colleagues who will actually go to the trouble, and personal risk, of giving you the bad news about your own ways of reacting with them. It really is the most sincere compliment, and the greatest sign of friendship, for an individual to tell you if you are mishandling a situation or another individual. After all, he is taking considerable personal risk in order to help you to operate better. I have been lucky enough to work with two or three people over the years who have always seen this as a part both of their duty and their friendship for me, and I admire them beyond reason. I have been more grateful than I can say and only hope that I have always reacted in ways which have shown them how grateful I have been.

This whole area is one which is all too often neglected within boards of directors, both on the part of the chairman helping his colleagues, and, sadly, on the part of the board members helping the chairman. Nevertheless, a good board which is dedicated to making it happen will find ways of dealing with these delicate situations in such a way that everybody grows. That is actually what a board should be doing the whole time; and that is the real sign of the top job being done well.

11

Board Work

When I took over as chairman one of my first actions was to arrange for the executive directors and myself to spend a week away together in order to discuss how the board should lead the company, and how we should organize our work. Although, with the help of our own planner, I had prepared a vast analysis of how other companies operated, the differences in approach between them and the way that ICI managed its affairs, I had no predetermined solution. This evolved during the first three days of our deliberations, and it was fascinating to see how closely we agreed, both on the diagnosis of our ills and the cure. We started by reviewing what we saw as being the specific competitive advantages that our company had in comparison with others. Partly as a result of this study we came to the conclusion that some areas, which we had hitherto looked upon as weaknesses, could be turned to strengths. I have already mentioned that our very wide international and technological spread has both good and bad sides. It can constitute a source of complexity in organizational terms, but can also bring a competitive advantage in comparison with others. It is the antithesis of the concentration of business argument to look on such diverse technological inputs and geographical representation as strengths, and it may be that this explains why ICI was not quite as fast on its feet as some less diverse companies in the past. In tomorrow's more complicated and flexible world, however, I remain convinced that these will represent significant advantages, although perhaps not ones that we would seek to set up were we starting all over again.

Acceptance of these facts led us to conclude that our company would not only continue to be complex in organizational and directional terms, but was likely to become more so. From this concept of continuing complexity (and incidentally everything we have done since has tended to add to it), we reached the view that the company was too large and spread and diverse to be run by a single man, or a very small group. We also came to the view that the task of the board was to ensure that the company became more than the sum of its parts, not only in financial and personnel matters, but also in a technological and marketing sense. These beliefs, like all clearly thought-out decision trees, led quickly to a clear conclusion, and the rejection of the idea that our company could be run as a financial holding institution, even though we saw clearly the necessity to move towards that rather than the more detailed management style that we had been trying to pursue.

As a part of our preparations for these discussions we had studied the organization and operations of a number of other companies, both inside and outside the chemical industry, that we admired, and from whom we felt we could learn. We speedily found that none faced quite our problems. We were unique inasmuch as our technical basis derived from a common scientific background, although in some cases we had moved increasingly into analogous areas, but always from a basic chemical starting position. Our geography had grown from the history of our constituent companies, and the happy circumstance that we had always looked upon the entire world as our marketplace. Equally, the gaps or lack of balance in our world knowledge derived from our history. We were historically extremely strong in the Commonwealth countries, areas which, with their agricultural and resource bases, had been prolific users of the heavy chemicals on which our company had been founded.

Perhaps because of this, but also because of other factors in our history, we were under-represented in many of the industrialized and rapidly developing countries which, with their industrial and technological strengths, formed the bulk of our current and future customers. This meant in turn that we had to attempt to grow faster in America, and even more particularly in Japan and the new developing technological centres of the Far East. The organization of our businesses had, moreover, grown through history, adapting but never basically changing. The United Kingdom was organized into divisions, each with its own headquarters and overhead structure, each with its own traditions, and each as large as most United

Kingdom companies. The common background of each particular division had been a particular technological starting point, but as more and more technological developments occurred between the interstices of the technologies, so we found more overlapping and 'trespassing' on shared ground. Many of our divisions and business positions had derived from pressures, at various times in our history, to integrate, and so we had chains of manufacturing and technological strengths, which were divided by organizational boundaries.

It was apparent to us that it would be necessary to carry out many changes and much experimentation to evolve into an adaptable and responsive company which could alter its form in a chameleon-like way in order to grow with the emerging business opportunities which we saw moving so fast all around us. To add to the problems that we saw ahead, many of our businesses were developing on an international basis, and it was quite apparent that we needed to run them in that way. In some cases the world was rapidly restructuring into a smaller and smaller number of dominant customers who could specify, from one country, their demands all over the world. For example, even though Japanese companies were beginning to manufacture outside Japan, in South East Asia or the USA, they still specified the supplies and suppliers from Japan itself. The point of decision on matters affecting the quality of the product was seldom in the country of manufacture, be it the USA, Malaysia or the UK. These were vital control functions which the Japanese wished to manage themselves. In other cases the pace of development was so rapid and international, like the burgeoning demand for chemical services from the electronics industry, that the broadest perspective was vital if we were to be able to take our rightful place as world suppliers.

All of these factors led us clearly to the view that we needed to decentralize operating responsibilities while retaining, in the board, a centre that could reinforce the different divisions when they needed it – whether technically, commercially, financially or with people. We called our new organizational concept a strategic directing company. Because of the sheer size of the canvas and range of colours with which ICI operates we felt that a form of shared responsibility was essential. There was no way that two or three people could keep an adequate perspective on the myriad activities and countries in which we were involved and operating, and draw from them any worthwhile judgements. Moreover, since we foresaw that the board would be carrying out significant interventions in an organizational and directional sense, it was essential that we had the best balance between experience, contemporary judgement, and up-to-date perspective and intelligence of world trends, that we could muster.

For these reasons we evolved the concept of operating as an executive team, and that in turn dictated the maximum size of the group. This, together with my own prejudices, led to the view that we wanted a single level, with a chairman and between six and eight executive directors, depending on the balance of skills, age and contribution that we could assemble. It also meant that we committed ourselves to spending very large amounts of time together, so that each of us could learn from exposure to activities in each other's areas, and also have the opportunity to influence the thinking of the team. This reinforced the view that we wanted a very open, flexible and friendly organization, where we would have to accept that each of us was contributing in each other's fields almost continuously, and this meant trust, clarity and the perception of priorities. It also meant that we had to give up some of the rather pleasurable operational interventions which we had tended to allow ourselves in the past. No longer could we enjoy the delights of dabbling in the design of plants, or the organization of this or that subsidiary function. We had to keep our fingers out of the operational areas, to abjure the bicycle shed type of discussion and to concentrate on matters where we had an actual contribution to make.

Above everything we recognized that the company had to be a living and evolving organization, able to adapt far faster than in the past, and that the board had therefore to be evolving and adapting in the same ways. We wanted to avoid becoming stereotyped and being caught by our own self-established constraints. All of this thinking, which took only a short time to evolve, shaped the composition and organization of the board, its style and method of working, and its relationship with the operating units. It also provided a clear and coherent philosophy, which we were able to communicate both inside and outside the company, to explain what we were trying to do, and how we were trying to do it. This, in turn, helped to create an atmosphere where we were seen as being more responsive and flexible, and able to change direction more quickly than in the past. This, plus the feeling of responsibility being pushed more clearly down the line, I believe helped to induce more flexibility in an organization which had previously not been seen as particularly agile. ICI, in many people's minds, was rather similar to the elephant ballet in Walt Disney's *Fantasia*, rather than the nimbler, faster moving and responsive organization that we wished to create.

To a large extent people's beliefs actually affect what they are, and how they think and operate. A perception of ponderousness and slowness induces just that sort of behaviour. Equally, a perception that everything is being organized for speed, change and adaptability helps to release the energies in that direction, and develop a feeling down the line that 'nothing is immutable'. All of these are mutually reinforcing perceptions. They help people down the line to grow and also allow the patterns of board behaviour to develop. Sometimes this process can be painful, for we learn by our mistakes more than by our successes, and our successes are not always as evident to us at the time as they should be. But the important thing is that we are now very much more adaptable than we have been, and each year I have seen ways in which we have changed, as well as, of course, seeing ways in which we need to continue to change. But ICI's organization, composition and behaviour are all now evolving steadily and in some sort of harmony.

It would be idle to pretend that working as a group in this way does not have its disadvantages. Plainly, although we have shown the ability to move very fast on occasions, we do lack something in terms of speed, and we may add something in terms of caution. While I would like to see the former improved, I am not sure that I would necessarily want to see the latter removed. After all, as well as trying to move a company somewhere, one of the prime responsibilities of the board is to avoid making monumental mistakes. The industrial world is littered with examples of the really big mistake. Ford's Edsel car, Exxon's entry into electric motors and office machinery, Albright and Wilson's building of their phosphorus plant in

Newfoundland, or Burma Oil's foray into tanker operations, are all classic examples of large mistakes which had immense effects on their companies. The penalties of monumental mistakes now are extreme, greatly enhanced by the effects of low world inflation, and slow world growth in demand. In days gone by, major investment errors could be tolerated by large companies, and seldom emerged as starkly as they do now. I think, on balance, that while I would like the decisions to be taken fast, it is the quality of the decisions rather than the speed which matters most.

Many boards organize themselves on a functional basis, but I have always had the fear that such an organization tends to remove the individual responsibility and room for manoeuvre of the executives in charge of the actual businesses. Plainly, some functions are absolutely essential. It would be impossible for any board of directors to operate without a finance director, who deals with the complexities of the financing of the company, oversees the controller's function, and the preparation of the accounts. In ICI's case I have always believed that a chief scientist was needed on the board. It seemed to me that, when discussing any business opportunity, the three areas where it was necessary to have independent views were the financial impact of the proposal; the strength of the technological and scientific position in a competitive and absolute sense, and its relevance in terms of future scientific and technical developments; and thirdly a view of the adequacy of the personnel in the business to carry out the task that was being proposed. I still believe that those are the three essential functions for a business such as ours, and that this is the minimum functional cross-lacing to tie the fabric of the businesses together, for are the areas where it is possible to make more than the sum of the parts. It is very often in the areas of the people and the technology that it is possible to suggest changes in organizational or business structure which enable advantage to be taken of potential commercial opportunities. For example, early on in my time as chairman we discovered that we had no less than four different parts of the company with relevant skills and inputs into the electronics industry. It was plain that putting them together under a new organization gave us a much better chance of making an impact than working individually, and we speedily found, for instance, that for many effects you needed to modify both the dyestuffs and the film which was carrying them.

As times goes on there is an increasing and understandable wish to introduce other functional activities. Safety and environmental matters are a vital aspect of our activities. It is a clear part of the board's responsibility to ensure that rigorous safety standards are observed in the company. Centralization of this obligation can tend to weaken, to some degree, the feeling of responsibility of those actually operating the businesses, who are those with the power and the need to have the problem constantly at the forefront of their minds. You can have a common reporting system, and common values, without necessarily having a centralized department. Centralized staff departments will always seek control and thus may weaken the commitment of the operators to that function.

We then turned to the next area where we plainly needed a board overview, and it was easy to see that if the areas in which we believed we needed faster growth were the Americas and the Far East, then we needed members of the board who would take a particular responsibility for knowing those areas, keeping an eye on the multiplicity of our operations, and trying to encourage our growth and development in them. Paradoxically, the improvement in air travel which enables an executive to visit almost any part of the world for a few days at a time, without undue loss of working time, coupled with the improvements in communications, have not helped very greatly to remove the nationalistic nature of distant markets. As I pointed out earlier, there could hardly be more difference between American, British and Australian habits, activities and markets, even though we share an apparently common language. Perceptions from one country to another are almost always as different as the different sides of the reflections in a mirror, and in our day-to-day council it is vital to have individuals who can place themselves in this different perspective, and comment on our ideas and thinking from the other point of view.

It is surprising how often we 'get it wrong', how often actions which we expect to be viewed in one particular way, in another territory are seen or interpreted in ways that we had not even thought of in our discussions. This is possible even in a company that has a long history of operating in different countries, and where each of us prides ourselves on knowing the world, and having breadth of vision and perspective. We therefore wanted to have at least two territorial directors. In addition we had to have a reporting route for the executives in charge of our major subsidiary companies in Canada, India, Australia etc. and we needed some mechanism so that smaller, but very important, activities in countries like Malaysia, or Pakistan, or parts of Latin America, can relate to the board and be in touch with the board thinking.

Lastly, of course, we needed to keep in touch with the businesses. We had already decided that we wanted to have very much greater delegation of responsibility, and had debated at length how we should intervene with businesses. We knew that we could not be involved in any way in their day-to-day running, and we knew that the businesses themselves should be involved in setting any directions in which it was felt that they should develop. We had already realized, however, that there was a potential difference between what the business might want, and what we as a board might want. We therefore decided that we would have a very small number, initially three, of business directors, each responsible for a different group of our businesses, but all carrying out the task of defining what the corporation should reasonably expect from the businesses. In addition, each would be a channel of communication between the executive team and the business, and would be expected to know rather more of the business's problems, opportunities, capabilities, and the fitness of the people in it to achieve their goals, than his colleagues. Above everything, however, he was expected to be Abraham, and to be the first to offer the sacrifice of his business if he believed that it was in the corporate interest that such draconian steps were necessary.

In addition, we had defined to ourselves a series of growing interventionist steps which we would take if we thought a business was going seriously wrong. The last of the steps, plainly, was the removal of the chief executive concerned, but before that we saw a growing series of interventions, beginning to move increasingly into questions of the composition and leadership of the business. For instance, changing the commercial or finance director, or reinforcing the production or personnel functions. We would interfere more closely in the planning of the business and the setting of targets, we might even intervene in the actual way that the work was being executed, and so on. We saw our business directors as being the long-stops, who would be ready to intervene in this way. It was, in a way, a variation of the sort of 'president's rule' which applies in most federal set-ups, but, hopefully, a graduated series of interventions, which we would only embark on with the greatest reluctance and care. These needs, and their own skills, dictated to a large extent the internal organization of our executive team.

I had always wanted to have singularity of responsibility, and had not been too happy with the idea that we had had before, where each director should carry a territory, a function, and a business. In my experience these mixed portfolios meant that it was very easy for the director to neglect areas which were of less interest, or perhaps to fail to realize when trouble was looming up at the earlier stages – which is, after all, the time when it is easiest to take remedial action. I started with the ambition that each of us should have only one primary responsibility, and that one or two of us should carry a secondary one as well, but it never really worked out that way, because of the particular skills and experience of the team that we had. I have served on many other boards, who have not approached the problems in the same way at all. Typically, they do not start from where they would like to be, but from history, and where they are. They therefore seek to make marginal alterations, trying to remedy perceived immediate problems, instead of working their way through the problem in a logical, evolving way. As a result the board tends to fossilize in a particular time, usually quite some way in the past, and tends therefore to be less adaptable. It is probably too early to evaluate our system accurately, but all the subjective tests that have been applied seem to indicate that it is working better than the previous systems. Perhaps the greatest accolade has been that some of our ideas are now being copied by other major international companies.

It must be remembered that, while I am unrepentant about my enthusiasm for adaptation and change, directors' discharge of responsibilities benefits immensely from a period of stability. One's knowledge of a geographical area improves year on year, as does one's acquaintance with customers, competitors, and the political and environmental background in which one is operating. Boards and chief executives of subsidiary and other companies need to know the other members of the executive team who are helping them, and that sort of relationship can be badly disrupted by continuous change. You do, however, need to satisfy yourself that the music is right. Even with people who are chosen for their ability to work together, the 'vibes' can sometimes go heavily wrong, and such a situation can seldom be put right by counselling. It is no use telling someone, for example, to be more sensitive or to like someone else. You either do or you don't!

Some of the other boards that I have worked on have tended, as well as endeavouring to change by modest evolution the whole time, to resolve conflicts or problems of relationships by removal of the people below the board, rather than moving members of the board. This has always seemed to me to be a rather wasteful operation. After all, shifting the board responsibility directly affects the relationships between a much smaller number of people than moving a chief executive from a business. Any chief executive, whether good or bad, stamps his priorities and proclivities on his organization in a very personal way. Better by far to change the board portfolio than to expect thousands to adapt to new direct leadership. I have never understood clearly why some companies are able to work successfully with a type of organization which plainly fouls up others. It has something to do with variations in the actual companies' roles, ambitions and tasks, as well as the mix of people and the style and values of the business. Tailoring a board, its way of working and its relationship to the organization, and then making it really hum, is an art, not a science. There is no uniquely right way, and even the best running company needs continual adjustment and tuning if it is to accommodate to changes in its people and its ambitions. Some businesses do run well with executive directors operationally responsible for parts of the total show, while for others it is a catastrophe. I think it has something to do with the complexity of the company, and the ability of the chief executive to understand and administer the variety of businesses within the company in a pretty direct way. In those businesses where I have seen this operating it has seemed to me that it has very seldom 'added value'. It is extraordinarily difficult for the executive in charge of a business to stand back and take a totally open-minded view of that business. Who, in such a board, does recommend that Mr X's business be sold, or that Mr Y's business be placed in the role of cash cow, and has all its future expansionist and other ambitions relentlessly stamped upon? If you believe that the board has to bring something additional to the operation of the company, then you have to set it up and organize it in such a way that it can do so. If it is set up with mutually contradictory internal divisions, it is very unlikely that it will perform the added value role which you are seeking.

There was, at one time, a great enthusiasm for what is known as matrix organization. A matrix organization is an attempt to codify the inevitable conflicts between running a business internationally, and simultaneously managing it on a national dimension. For example, it is important, not only fiscally, that many decisions are taken in Germany or Japan for all of ICI's businesses there, while at the same time, for instance, the pharmaceuticals business in both those countries needs to respond to an international pharmaceuticals leadership for many aspects of its business. To add to the complexity, the finance director of the whole company – or the research director, or the main board member responsible for safety and the environment, and other functional directors – will all seek, correctly, to bring influence to bear. Here you have a description of the problem that matrix organization sought to solve by prescription. Moreover, it sought to resolve these problems at a level above the operating one, where the real solutions and knowledge lie. The hapless chief executive of a business that operated internationally might find himself having to satisfy one or more business directors, depending on what his internal links were, two or three international directors, and four, or maybe five, functional directors. Even if the board was perfectly organized, and all the directors had shared expectations from the business, such a complex organization, which sought to replicate, in a structured way, problems which can only really be resolved in an informal way, posed immense problems. I have found very few examples in the past where complicated matrix organization actually helped to make things work better. It tended to lead to confusion and a massive replication of the braking system, while doing relatively little to help the chief executive. After all, the company will only succeed if its businesses succeed, and the task of the board is plainly to create the best conditions for the executive to operate. For this, above everything, clarity of expectation, and the ability to deliver reinforcing help plus unambiguous advice, are the conditions which are most helpful.

Once the board organization is set up it is necessary for the chairman to spend time thinking about the programme of work of the board. Many of these points have been touched upon elsewhere in this book, but this is a reflection of the fact that planning of board work is often so poor, or barely carried out at all. The work of a board does indeed have a life of its own, which can either take the board over, or from which the board can struggle free. Because of its legal responsibilities, ultimately a board decision is required on most major activities of the company. A decision will certainly be required on all financing measures, on acquisitions or disposals of businesses, and probably on major items of investment. Interestingly, unless you set it up that way, very few boards retain any control whatsoever over commercial decisions, and most boards of directors do not require to hear the details of very large contracts for purchases or sales. This is particularly relevant since, in many cases, companies have been brought to the edge of collapse through mistakes in purchasing policy, or by making very large contracts for sales with bad pricing or escalation provisions.

Equally notable is the fact that most boards of directors have no provision at all to review the general strategies and directions in which businesses are going, and, apart from intervention in individual decisions of investment, play only a small role in strategic direction. In addition, even more surprisingly, while the appointment of people is a clear board responsibility, the number of companies who actually review at board level, in any helpful way, the availability of personnel for the top jobs, and the quality of the recruitment and staffing of the company, is sadly small. After all, the appointment of executives responsible for running your individual businesses is one of the key management tools the board can wield, and only they should appoint the individuals to those jobs. While it is right that the out-going man should make his recommendations to the board, it is very unlikely that he will suggest someone who will correct his own weaknesses, of which he may be blissfully unaware. Knowledge and understanding of both the individual and the task is required. Even those companies that do make such a review, tend to rely on a quantitative analysis, which shows that you have, for example, adequate cover for the top thirty jobs, were the worst to happen to the individuals holding them at present. Management development plans, the quality and rate of recruitment, the adequacy of management back-up, particularly in the highly specialist functional fields, and the actual characteristics of the individuals that the board may ultimately be required to choose between for the very top appointments, are seldom discussed.

One of the key areas is the avoidance of too much duplication. If you set up an executive committee, as most boards do, it is almost impossible to avoid some repetition of matters at the board itself, and this can, if you are not careful, reduce the effect of your non-executive directors to near impotence. It is all too easy to have subjects introduced at your formal board meeting which are merely replicating discussions which you have already had at some length, a short time before, in the executive committee. Under such circumstances there is very little real likelihood of a change of decision. It seems to me to be important that it should be made very clear whether items arising in board agendas are introduced so that opinions can be formed, so that warnings about decisions which may be taken in the future can be heard, whether they are in effect just a notification, or whether the discussion can lead to real decisions. Such clarity helps to focus the discussion, as well as enabling balance to be created. The balance of meetings between these various sorts of items has an important bearing on how satisfying the board meetings are, and also on the degree of enthusiasm and support you can expect from your board members.

High-powered people do not like wasting their time, and need to feel and know that their advice is both wanted, and on occasion acted upon. High-powered people are not so foolish as to believe that their views on everything are of equal importance, or indeed that they can express opinions without understanding a great deal about the background. They are usually patient and tolerant of briefings, presentations, or the seeking of preliminary advice, provided that they have the satisfaction of knowing that ultimately they will have affected things. It is helpful in this respect to tell them when they have influenced things, and this is a part of the lubrication of board work, which in turn enables you to ensure that the board continuously improves its performance. Nothing is more frustrating than spending a year of one's time working on a board, and, at the end of it, sitting down and racking one's brains to think whether one has had any effect whatsoever. Equally it is often the case that a really decisive intervention, which changes the whole board's course on one major item, may be of far greater worth than the more easily recorded satisfactions of having seen large numbers of small items modified as a result of an individual's contribution. The chairman of the board needs to be watching, and all the time keeping a mental tally of which of his board members are actually contributing in these ways, and how. But he has to have the wisdom and the patience to recognize that it is well worthwhile carrying the man whose interventions are few but decisive.

When we designed our method of board working we were particularly anxious to avoid the trap of setting up a whole string of subcommittees to handle particular parts of our collective responsibility. Thus, in quick order, we disposed of the finance committee, the personnel committee, the capital programmes committee and so on. We have quite often set up a working group to tackle a particular task. The delight of that approach is that the group itself is self-extinguishing once the task is done. The removal of subcommittees meant that we had to be much more ruthless and thoughtful about the setting of our board agendas. We had to prevent overloading, and to ensure that we spent our time on the most important subjects, rather than being taken over by a self-created monster which fed on itself. There was one exception to our genocide of the committees, and that was the salaries committee. It is totally iniquitous to have the executive members of the board setting their own salaries, and nothing has irritated me more than the comments of people in the media to the effect that I had awarded myself a particular pay rise, or salary. Had any chief executive done so he would have certainly merited the opprobrium that would be heaped upon him, but practically all companies nowadays have the salaries of the chairman and the executive directors set by a salaries committee of the non-executive directors. Here again, it is important that the committee should be a real one, and should work. I can certainly testify to the reality of the discussions and interventions made by ICI's salaries committee, who take an extremely strong grip and express their views very forcefully about how the board reward structure should be set up.

The whole subject of rewards for top people is almost material for a book in its own right, and like everything else, patterns are changing. There are still very large disparities between the rewards paid for executives in different countries, and these are becoming increasingly difficult to sustain, with executive skills becoming more and more transferable between countries. Great publicity is given to the American executives who have been hired at much more substantial salaries than are usual in the United Kingdom, to work in large British companies. Very little publicity is ever given to the reverse situation, where British-born (and in many cases -trained) executives have risen to the top of large American corporations, and commanded the glittering salaries that go with them. The ways in which rewards are paid to the top people in a company depend very much on prevailing public opinion in that country. The American system is much more tolerant of large salaries, provided that these are linked to performance. Moreover, the American system is specifically designed to allow accumulation of capital, and tends to disdain the sort of 'perks' that are such an unwelcome feature of British executive rewards. The all-pervasive 'company car' in Britain, and in some parts of Europe, is a relatively little used incentive in the USA.

Recently there have been marked shifts in British executive reward systems. First of all, more and more British companies are seeking to link a substantial proportion of the executive's pay, up to a third, to the performance of the company, measured in a whole variety of ways. Secondly, there is a growing distaste for giving large terminal payments to those who have been dismissed for perceived inadequacy of performance. It is important, under these circumstances, that the

salaries committee should have a very good understanding both
of international trends in these matters, but more particularly of
the socially acceptable reward systems in the prime country of
operation. In ICI's case, therefore, the salaries and rewards of
our top people in America are settled, after consultation, with a
valuable group of American businessmen who can put them
into an American perspective. In the United Kingdom the top
salaries, and the salaries of the board members, are set by the
salaries committee, which involves all the non-executive directors, of whom slightly more than half are United Kingdom
based, and have a good knowledge of United Kingdom trends
from their own business backgrounds.

The interaction between the chairman and his salaries committee is a delicate one. The chairman, after all, has the ultimate
responsibility for motivating and managing his board, and
therefore the salaries committee must take his views into
account when making their decisions. Equally well, the salaries
committee must not, under any circumstances, become a rubber
stamp for the chairman, since they will have to stand up at the
Annual General Meeting, and elsewhere, and take responsibility for their own decisions. I remember some years ago, when
I was the non-executive director of another company, being
taken to task by a shareholder for the salaries of the executive
directors, which had been set by the salaries committee, of
which I was chairman. I had no hesitation in explaining the
rationale behind the decisions of the salaries committee and
defending, I believe to the satisfaction of the questioner, the
decisions we had taken.

It is almost impossible for the chairman of a company to
defend his own salary. That is for others to do. Ultimately it is
for the shareholders, who have plenty of ways of getting rid of
the chairman if they feel that he is not worth the money, or is not
performing properly. For all these reasons I am a strong sup-
porter of the concept of performance-linked payment, provided
that the linkage is a real one, and that salaries can be shown to
go down as well as up. During the first two years of my
chairmanship the ICI directors received no pay increase whatsoever, because of the poor performance of the company. It is a
sad commentary on the world in which we live that when
eventually we got a substantial increase in pay, no mention was

made in the press of the frozen award which we had accepted quite willingly, but that fact does not vitiate the strength of the argument.

One area of concern which top management tends to neglect is that of the environment in which discussions are held. I have already indicated elsewhere in this book my belief that this can have a very substantial effect on the type and quality of the discussion. There are now consultants who will help with these matters, and there are growing fashions for particular forms of boardrooms to enable graphical and other presentations to be made. Many old-fashioned boardrooms were set up in such a way as to deliberately reinforce the authority of the chairman, and to enable 'discipline' to be maintained, rather than to encourage openness and frankness of discussion. The chairman had a chair which was both higher and larger than all the others. The boardroom table was designed in such a way that there were very substantial distances between the individual board members and discussion across the table was inhibited. The acoustics were sometimes bad, and the heating and ventilating systems were often poor. The more the formalities of boards can be loosened up the better, and it is worth experimenting, and varying the layout until you find the one which works best for your particular team. Nothing is worse than having a meeting with only half the board present, and sitting with empty spaces between you, the vast echoing gaps pointing out even more strongly the absence of your colleagues. There is a growing interest in having boardrooms which do not have a single board table, but flexible individual seating, with comfortable chairs, and either lap tables or small tables which can be arranged in different ways to suit the occasion. There is an almost limitless amount of gadgetry that can be produced for visual displays. The important thing in all of these areas is that the boardroom layout should have been thought out carefully. It should be one of the tools used by the chairman of the board to create the discussion environment which he wishes to set up. Again, a small amount of thought is infinitely more valuable than the expenditure of very large amounts of money. It is worth remembering that, although the consultants can give you a very wide range of options, they are mostly interested in selling their wares, and can complicate the whole issue!

We have found that many of our meetings are better held outside our main office, and away from our normal working environment altogether. ICI's executive team meets two or three times a year, in a conference centre outside London, which it takes over completely for two days. The essential thing here is to be in a pleasant environment with no local distractions. Here it is possible for a host of subjects to be opened up in an informal way, which would be difficult in the office, where there is constant distraction from telephones, messages, secretaries, etc. Trial and error has shown that the best pattern for these meetings consists of two working days, and one night spent away. The night is essential, both because the board are able to relax together, but also because much of the discussion and thinking evolves over drinks in the bar, or meals, or walks in the grounds. The quality of these meetings is of a different order, even from those that are held in the informally set-up boardroom in the main office. I have worked in a number of other companies who involve the non-executive directors in such strategy meetings, on an annual basis, and I am bound to say that as a non-executive director I have always liked this. It gives one the opportunity to see one's executive colleagues operating in a quite different way and enables you to have a much better idea of their capabilities. In a more relaxed atmosphere, with plenty of time, it is possible to think more deeply about problems than is possible in a board meeting, with a timed agenda, and clear priorities of business. Almost all decisions benefit immeasurably from having some of the time pressures taken off them.

It is quite surprising that, despite the Parkinsonian belief that work expands to fill the time available, most problems under discussion have a specific time-life of their own, after which recycling tends to take place. Despite this the chairman should not be concerned that opening up unfettered time horizons for a problem will automatically mean that the time is used in this way. Rather the reverse, provided that you are alert to stop regeneration of the problem. It is surprising how often what you think will be a very long discussion runs out of steam with a clear consensus and agreement having been reached quite quickly. This is very often the case after an evening spent tussling with an apparently insoluble problem. In the morning it suddenly seems clear.

Some boards use external counsellors and consultants to help them in these discussions. ICI has, for the last fifteen years at least, had the services of one absolutely excellent American consultant, who has helped the board processes very greatly. He is not by any means an expert in ICI's business, nor would he set out to be, but he is an expert at helping the board to help itself, and to bring to the surface niggling problems. Very often he is able to sort out process difficulties, or to suggest ways in which discussion problems or relationships can be dealt with. He has worked for ICI for so long and knows everyone so well, and is so well liked by everyone, that it is really like having an old friend at work. He has, on occasions, sat in on full meetings, but has more often helped members individually, or by assisting with 'off campus' discussions, where he has been of particular value. Of course ICI also uses consultants who will report to the whole board on the specific tasks that they have been asked to carry out, in just the same way as the auditors would be asked to report to the whole board, but these are the exception rather than the rule. By and large, consultants are asked to give advice down the line, the executives make up their own minds on the executive course that they wish to follow and then report to their colleagues, quoting the relevant parts of the consultants' report.

There is one other area of board work to which I wish to refer. This is the whole area of contacts with the external world. As a group ICI entertains quite a number of different constituencies. A feature of British senior work is that a great deal of it is done on a social basis, but there are a number of people that it is valuable for executives, as a group, to meet. ICI's most important customers, its competitors at board level, politicians of all types from all the countries it operates in, major bankers, and senior civil servants in territories ICI operates in, are all the sort of shared interest which help to inform and enlighten decision making and discussions. Great care is taken to operate apolitically. It is important to ensure that if you meet members of the government in power, you also meet their opposite numbers in the opposition, not only in the United Kingdom, but also in the other countries. ICI goes to great trouble to try to ensure that the company does not take any particular political stance. Hopefully one's company will endure over many changes of government in many countries, and today's opposition party is tomorrow's government.

It is essential that you are able to operate with whatever government is democratically chosen in your own country, and this process is helped immeasurably by keeping contacts, providing information and facts to politicians of any persuasion with whom you may be dealing. In undemocratic countries, or ones with centralized governmental systems, contacts and understanding with those in power are even more important, since their range of interventions in business matters is invariably greater than in democratic ones. In addition, it is important to ensure that the local members of parliament in the areas in which you operate are kept fully appraised of your thinking, and have access to your executives as well as to the main board. These relationships should be prized and it is difficult to overstress their value. Very frequently, through these links, it is possible to pick things up much earlier than you would otherwise have done, or to scotch misunderstandings before they have become insoluble. Relationships are built up, not when you are in the storm, but rather patiently and over a long period of time, when neither side is in trouble. In order to maintain this continuity over a long period of time, it is valuable to involve all members of the board in these contacts. I am constantly surprised when I look at the record sheets to see when I first met senior members of the government, or the opposition. It was invariably many years before they or I were in our present positions, and that can only be helpful.

The areas that I have sought to cover here are the ones which enable the board to actually function. The functioning of the board is of course critical to the organization as a whole, and while I have dealt very largely with ICI, as a large organization, the same broad principles can apply to any business of any size, anywhere. The attention to the identification of the task, the selection and organization of the people to do it, the organization of the actual work that the people have to do, and the attempt to ensure that as much relevant information as possible is presented to them in an easily assimilable and usable way, are the key steps to 'making it happen', not only for the board, but for the whole business.

12

The 'U' Factor

So far in this book I have written entirely on the basis of personal experience, and the ideas and theories that have accumulated during my years working in a large business. I have felt reasonably secure in the views that I have expressed, because almost all of them have been tried and tested, and have been shown to be successful against the harshest criterion of all, which is business success. In this chapter I want to talk on a more personal basis, about the problems of managing one's own time, and of retaining as large an amount of one's personal freedom as one can. I am very conscious that this is an area where I have been much less successful, at least against my own standards of success. I know the nostra that I have tried to follow, and I know the tricks that I have used to enable me to cover ever more ground, but I am bound to admit that in terms of producing the balance of life which I would personally see as being the ideal, I have been relatively unsuccessful so far.

It has to be admitted that operating in the business scene has an all-pervasive fascination, and, because of the sheer variety of the work and the opportunities for making changes and improving things, it is extremely difficult to control the degree of one's commitment to it. Indeed, I believe that if one has the opportunity to run a large business, and affect the lives and futures of very large numbers of people – shareholders, employees, suppliers and customers – they are entitled to expect your total personal commitment; nevertheless, these jobs are ephemeral. They last for only a limited period of one's life, and, when the time comes to move on to do other things, you still have to live with yourself, and hopefully with your family, if they have managed to survive the trials and tribulations that business life places on them. Balance is vital, and it is not a question on which you can get much help or advice. The demands on each person, and their individual priorities, are so different that it really is a problem that you have to resolve for yourself. This involves ruthless self-criticism, intellectual honesty of the highest degree about one's own motives, and a degree of introspection which most of us find hard to carry out.

There cannot be anybody who has held a senior position who is not plagued with continued self-doubt. The more confident the external appearance, the more likely the individual is to torment himself privately with questions as to whether the achievement is enough, the commitment is enough, the certainty is enough, or the risk is too great or too small. As with almost everything else in business it is indeed the balance that one has to try to achieve, for the total avoidance of risk is the highest risk of all, while, as another example, overcommitment makes it impossible to be objective, and produce the breadth of input that is required. There are individuals who are blessed with this natural sense of balance, and may be able to manage their lives in an ideal way. I imagine I meet them almost all the time in my opposite numbers, but when one talks to them privately, and they let their hair down, one finds that they have the same problems and doubts that one has oneself.

I have often said that the prime characteristic that I have detected in top leaders is mental and physical toughness. There is no doubt that these jobs are immensely demanding of time, concentration, sheer grinding brain power, and the ability to live an intrinsically unhealthy existence with some sort of control. The hours are, of necessity, very long, and one's body is continuously exposed to cruel punishment, not of the sort that toughens the muscles and develops strength, but rather of the sort that just places demands, without producing the increased ability to cope with them. Over the years I have only met one person who appeared totally impervious to jet lag. A life where you are never out of an aeroplane for more than a few days at a time is not a healthy one. It throws one's biological mechanisms into continual turmoil. Even if you are a man of the strongest possible character, and able to resist good food and drink, you are still almost certainly faced with the problems of entertaining at least twice a day, and now, with the fashion for working breakfasts, possibly three times a day. Most of your life is spent indoors, and you start early, and finish late. Physical exercise has to be sought as a matter of deliberation. It does not, so to speak, come packaged as a part of the job. When you get home at weekends, you find that your clock and your family's clocks are out of kilter. You have spent your whole week wining and dining, and dashing from here to there. They have been looking forward to the weekend as an opportunity to go out, to entertain, and generally to live it up a little. All in all, if one sought to design a life style which was destructive of the individual, the way that business has structured itself would seem to be almost ideal!

As well as this there are also the added hazards which go with any top job. I have referred many times to the dangers of sycophancy, and my fears of the effect of power. It is almost impossible to avoid contact with one, or more likely both, of these hazards to one's own ability to see oneself and one's motives clearly. No matter how much you make it clear that you like the bad news, rather than the good, the world would be a strange place if there was no one who wanted to tell you when things had gone well. Equally, there are still a surprising number of salesmen, competitors, or others with whom one has to do business, who believe that the application of flattery is a good way to establish a relationship. Personally I find it embarrassing, and an almost total switch-off. Nevertheless, I have to recognize that some businessmen appear to have a greater tolerance than I of this particularly corrosive form of social contact. Moreover, is one ever absolutely sure that one is being honest with oneself? While you may be embarrassed, does the embarrassment perhaps conceal a degree of personal pleasure, which one cannot face up to admitting, even to oneself?

Eventually you rely on your ideals, and the picture in your mind of the sort of person you would like to be, and would like to remain. I think it is necessary to have this idealistic portrait to which you aspire, tucked away where you can check up to see how far, like Dorian Gray, you are altering. It is possible, although very difficult indeed, to hang on to quite a lot of yourself, if you recognize what is happening in time. It is quite hard to become a nicer or better person under these circumstances, or at least that has been my experience so far.

I suppose the most essential part of this struggle is the management of one's time, and here there are a certain number of key things that can be done. I have always believed that when I am at work I should work as hard and as effectively as I can, all the time that I am there, but that equally, when I am not working, there should be a clear line between the two experiences. In order to cover the sheer amounts of work, of contact, reading, writing and so on, it really is necessary to use every moment of enforced working time to the best effect. There are some obvious gimmicks which I suppose practically everybody uses, but at least it may be of value to mention some of them in case they help others in the same position. I ensure that wherever I am I can dictate notes and letters, etc. People are surprised, and frequently appear disapproving, when they see me using a pocket dictating machine to answer correspondence in trains, in airport lounges, in cars, or in aeroplanes. However, such a habit ensures that you can produce notes of a meeting while it is still fresh in your mind, and also saves time which could be spent doing other things. My secretary has learnt to decipher my mumbles from every sort of background noise known to man. Although she had excellent shorthand I'm afraid I have been responsible for that particular skill withering away. I simply found that neither she nor I could afford the luxury of sitting down together while I decided what I wanted to say. I have a quantity of portable dictating machines, and am never without one. It is essential equipment in my briefcase, my overnight bag, my car, etc. and I am also never without a large supply of tapes and spare batteries, for nothing is more certain but that, just when you have some vital meeting note to make, the machine will run out of power, or you come to the end of the tape. Similarly, I have reading files constantly being filled up. I consciously put aside or bring forward reading matter for air trips or train journeys or long car trips.

I am perhaps fortunate that I am able to read, dictate and even write after a fashion in most forms of modern transport, but I know that there are some who find themselves affected by cars and cannot read in them. If you are in such a situation it is perhaps worth seeing whether any of the modern travel sickness cures can enable you to gain that extra time, or alternatively whether you can organize yourself so that you use your car time for dictating or telephoning. Since time management is the key, and the saving of time is absolutely vital, it follows that you should not be mean with the gadgetry. Even if your car telephone only enables you to save an hour or two a year, or make an urgent contact without breaking some other engagement, it is worth ensuring that you have one. I actually bought the house in which I and my family are now living on the car telephone, and have made many other deals or arrangements by the same medium. The point is that these things enable you to use your time more effectively, and therefore to work more efficiently.

Similarly, although you will inevitably have to hold a large number of meetings in your office, I feel that it is preferable to drop in on other people's offices in your headquarters building. If you hold a top job this helps to demonstrate that you are approachable and not remote, and it also gains you two other advantages as well. If meetings are held in your office, it is necessary to develop the skill of tactfully indicating that the meeting should be coming to a close. It is a great deal easier for you to leave someone else's office, than to persuade them to leave yours, and if it is a matter of meeting one person for a private discussion, then this is almost always the most time and cost effective way. If you call in on them you are more likely to be in command of the time that you spend there, and this can be achieved with less possibility of affront. It is surprising how much you can learn from sitting in someone else's office, seeing the state of their desk, hearing the number of telephone calls that interrupt your discussion, and so forth. These can all give you a different perspective on the working habits, and effectiveness, of the individual. If it is a matter of a very large meeting then plainly it has to be held either in your own office, or in a meeting room. In this case, large meetings held in your own office are more easily ended with a tactful interruption by your secretary on the telephone, than would be possible in a meeting room.

Moreover, although this is an area where I have had more difficulty in coming to grips with myself, the use of private aeroplanes is a valuable business tool. One of my wise predecessors pointed out to me that it was essential to do everything possible to reduce wear and tear on the top management, and I know of at least one other very successful company who run their own helicopter service, and insist on their top management using it. My own rule has always been slightly different. I am so conscious of the cost of private aircraft that I tend to use them only if such use enables me to do something which I could not otherwise achieve. There is, however, one exception to this broad rule, and that is that on a Friday evening I will take whatever means of getting home quickly appears to be the most effective, although not, of course, without any thought of the cost. I believe that if I have given every moment of the rest of the week as efficiently and effectively as I can to prosecuting my business, I should reduce the 'dead time' involved in getting home at the weekend as much as possible. Quite often the use of a private plane is the only way to get home on a Friday night, as opposed to a Saturday morning. The psychological effect of spending even a short part of the Friday night in one's own bed and waking up in one's own home is quite surprising. I am convinced that the beneficial effect of a full weekend at home is quite disproportionately greater than a broken weekend. Even the prospect of my leaving home late on a Sunday night somehow spoils the whole of Sunday, at least in our family. In many parts of the world the use of private planes is looked upon as a natural tool of the executive and in many parts of America it is almost impossible to call on other companies without using one. In countries such as India it is quite impossible to visit outlying plants without running your own plane, but in this country, perhaps because the distances are so much smaller, it is still looked upon as an extravagance and a bit of personal 'hype'.

It is important in these matters that you should conform to some degree to the general social expectation, although the attitude of one's people is sometimes surprising. When I took over as chairman of ICI, I spent much personal time worrying about whether or not to replace the chairman's Rolls-Royce. Tradition, from the setting up of the company, had dictated that each incoming chairman had a new Rolls-Royce bought for him, which was replaced at the end of his tenure of office. ICI was in a poor way at the time, and we were reducing our manpower very sharply. We on the board had already endeavoured to set an example, returning some of our pay, and also freezing our ongoing salary awards. I had practically made up my mind that the Rolls-Royce should be dispensed with, as another symbol of all being in it together, when I was called up by my friend David Plastow, the chairman of Rolls-Royce. He said that he hoped that I would be replacing the Rolls, since he felt it would be bad for his business if ICI changed its pattern. With the downturn in business many companies were holding off from ordering Rolls' cars, and there was a danger that the demand would deteriorate greatly if the car lost its position as a visible symbol of success. He felt that if ICI was to change its tradition that the chairman was driven in a Rolls-Royce, a tradition which had existed since the founding of the company, a message would be given which would inevitably harm Rolls-Royce's total business. On balance, and after further reflection, I decided that we should replace the car, but I am bound to say that I had a guilty feeling about it, particularly as I have never been very moved by these external trappings of power. However, I decided to go ahead, and a new Rolls-Royce was duly procured. Sometime later I was talking to some of my shop stewards, and mentioned that this was a problem that had worried me. To my surprise they said that they were glad that I had decided to buy it, as they did not want to have the feeling that they belonged to a company that was in such a poor way that it couldn't afford a Rolls-Royce for its chairman! It was not a viewpoint that I had either expected or taken into account, but it merely shows that one needs to be sensitive to the differences between what is seen as extravagance, and what is seen as being necessary, either for prestige purposes, or for social comparative purposes in the country in which you are operating.

While on this subject of cost effectiveness, a word about entertaining. It is certainly the custom in the United Kingdom, perhaps to a greater degree than in many other countries, for an enormous amount of business to be done over meals. I personally find this a good use of time, working on the principle that I have to be at work during my lunch hour, and very often in the evening as well, and I therefore prefer to use the time to some good business effect, rather than just as an interlude in the day. I start on the basis that every lunch hour is committed to the business, and my lunches are booked ahead in a ruthless way. I always carry with me, in my mind, the next available 'free' lunch date that I have, and this is usually some three or four months ahead. As far as ICI is concerned, a certain number of days are set aside when all the executive directors of the company who are available are able to eat together in an informal way. On these occasions a buffet is provided, so that people can serve themselves, and then relax and have an open discussion on whatever might be bugging them at the time. These days were always blocked out in my diary. All other days were, however, 'up for grabs'. When it comes to the evenings, I have for many years been prepared to dedicate four evenings of the week to business engagements, if necessary, and certainly over recent years it has always proved to be both desirable and necessary.

ICI tends to entertain in its own establishments, again on the basis that it saves time, and allows the maximum amount of effort and time to be put into the business in hand. Standards of entertaining depend very much more on thought, care and taste, than on the expenditure of money. I am always fascinated to see how pleased businessmen are to be served ordinary, but very good quality food, rather than the exotica which tend to be offered in restaurants. I know one or two companies that are past masters at carrying out entertaining in a memorable, pleasurable, and entirely cost-effective way. Perhaps the greatest of all, in this respect, are Marks and Spencer, as I suppose one would expect them to be. The meals at Marks and Spencer are never elaborate, but the quality, simplicity and thought are absolutely first class, and it is this sort of standard to which we have always aspired. One of the many things which businessmen do *not* require is more calories. Some time ago I asked our company doctor to keep an eye on our menus, and to try to ensure that we reduced the, so to speak, 'obligatory' calorie intake with which we were faced. Moreover, most guests do not want lashings of cream, or butter, or other highly fattening goodies. Bangers and mash still tends to be the favourite meal served to our directors although since the calorie counted regime has come in, we see it very much less frequently than we used to! When entertaining, messages are given not only by the standard and type of food, but also by the standard and type of service. Again, I was lucky enough many years back to recruit for ICI an absolutely top-flight butler, who, as well as being a superb professional in his own field, I am proud to consider as a personal friend. Even if ICI was prepared to drop its standards, which hopefully it would not, I know full well that he would never countenance any reduction in the quality of the service he provides. He recognizes that he represents ICI, and that he gives a whole series of messages to others about the company, its people, the sort of business it runs, and its behaviour, and expectations of behaviour.

The impressions that people outside the company form of it, and the messages that you give internally, are all affected very greatly by the ways in which your duties, entertaining and reception are carried out. The way in which the telephone is answered has already been pointed out by Robert Townsend in his excellent book as being one of the first introductions that people get to your company. I wonder how often chairmen visit their telephone exchanges, or actually thank those on the switchboard for the way in which they respond for the company. It really is an essential port of call, at least once a year, because, just like everybody else in your business, the telephone exchange like to feel that they are working for people who care, and it means a lot to them to know that a quick response or pleasant manner is valued. Nothing is worse than calling up and being left waiting for a long period, while the telephonist vainly searches for the individual you wish to speak to, without telling you whether you are still connected or not. Even when the telephone connection is made, the way in which your secretary, or secretaries, deal with queries is a projection of yourself and your values. I have been lucky to have secretaries who, besides being extremely nice people, have been possessed of an excellent sense of humour (probably necessary to work with me!). Particularly for people a long way down the line, the chairman's secretary can be a very forbidding person, and if you want to pursue an open door policy you are not going to get very far if the secretary carries her – perhaps necessary – task of protection to extremes, and in a dictatorial or tactless way.

These are precious assistances to you in your top job, and the support that you get from really first-class people is an absolute essential if your time is to be managed economically. With regard to secretaries, it is a case of penny-wise and pound-foolish. In the first place it is vitally important that you have enough secretarial back-up. Even if you have enough back-up for normal purposes, it is very useful to have an emergency response system, so that you can draft in more help in a hurry, if you are hit by a crisis. I have always made it a rule that I try to answer, so far as putting a letter on tape is concerned, every letter that is addressed to me personally, and I try to ensure that the answer is dictated the same day that I see the letter, always assuming that I am in England and in the office. One speedily finds the sort of norm of letters that one can expect to get out every day, but from time to time some unexpected event – or even worse, an expected one for which you have not made adequate allowance – puts these calculations out.

I was guilty of having totally failed to appreciate the sort of response that I would get when I was asked to give the Dimbleby lecture in 1986. On my previous television appearances there had been an increase in letters to me, but one which we had been able to cope with by our usual method of drafting in one additional secretary from elsewhere in the organization. Dimbleby was a different case altogether, and as the letters began pouring in, my secretaries and I looked at each other in dismay. Fortunately, we had on one previous occasion been so overwhelmed by incoming mail that we had asked one or two of the retired staff to come back and help us out for a short period, and this is what we did on this occasion. I am afraid that the letters were not answered as quickly as the norm that we set ourselves, but they *were* answered, and they were answered in what I hope was regarded as a reasonable period of time. But if we had been functioning properly we would have made provision for this influx in advance, and been a little more sensible about the likely result of a lecture of this type.

My four secretaries at ICI operated on an open office principle, so that any one of them knew pretty well what was going on, and could stand in for the others. We shared two large offices, and each of them was aware of what the others were doing, although we had 'lead operators' for different sorts of activity. For example, I had a personal secretary who normally dealt with most of my personal mail, and also with most of my correspondence with other board members. What is important is that you have plenty of back-up, and project the sort of responsiveness which one hopes one's company is going to give its customers as a general rule.

In this whole question of time-economy comes the use of the

chauffeur-driven car. Time spent trying to park and leave one's own car is all dead, non-working time. Although it is just about possible to telephone and drive at the same time (a practice which is in any event illegal), it is plainly impossible to read or write and drive simultaneously, or at least not for long! Time spent in the car is valuable. It gives one a last opportunity to read the notes and briefings before going to a meeting. It enables one very frequently to reach other people on the phone, particularly if one is calling overseas. It is uninterrupted, and therefore one can read and annotate, or read and dictate one's replies. All of these uses of time are ones which would be precluded if one was driving oneself. The use of a chauffeur is not, under these circumstances, a prestige matter, it is actually a means of saving your own time. In addition to these points there is also the quite vital one of being able to find one's way! Not infrequently if we are working to a very tight time schedule (as we often are) my driver, when visiting somewhere he has not been to before, will make a trial run to find out the layout, the approach, and the best parking and so on. All of these are good reasons for being chauffeur-driven, and I have no doubt that the back-up staff that are employed increase one's productivity by a great deal more than the cost involved.

Having said all of that, I do like, as often as possible, to answer the telephone myself, and my secretaries and I try to work out whatever is the most convenient division of labour between us. There are times when they are so busy that it is helpful for me to take my own phone calls, and times when it is easier for me to do a handwritten letter of thanks rather than to ask them. In addition I make a practice of carrying around in my pocket a card pad, headed with my name, address and telephone number. On many occasions I can write a very brief note, during a meeting, or a cocktail party, or a meal, and the card can be photocopied and sent off immediately without having to be retyped. There is, of course, a snag about this system: it depends upon having legible handwriting. Just as senior jobs cause deterioration of all sorts of other faculties, I am bound to say that my handwriting has not improved, and has gone from being poor to dreadful over the past years.

While dealing with this whole problem of economizing on time, there are two other areas which are very helpful. The first is the ability to read fast. I have never actually done a rapid-reading course, since I am able to scan very quickly, but if I did not have that ability I am sure that such a course would be time well invested. There is a logical basis for teaching rapid reading, for experiments have shown that one's reading speed is limited by the time it takes one's eyes to move, and therefore if you can teach yourself to scan, without moving the eyes, you can increase your reading rate. I have to admit, though, that fast reading and retention do not always go hand in hand. Rather as learning a language in a very short time fails to imprint with the same solidity as learning a language slowly, so it appears to me that documents that are very quickly scanned have only a limited 'shelf life', compared to those that one has really pored over. Nevertheless, rapid comprehension of the contents of documents is absolutely critical if one is to handle the large amounts of paperwork involved in top jobs, and anything which can help this process must be a good investment.

The other area where I believe one can learn a good deal is in the whole area of public speaking. I do not think that public speakers are born. I believe that it is an acquired skill, as most things in life are, and there are a number of ways in which one can help oneself. Although in the Navy I had been taught to do a certain amount of public speaking, and had overcome some of my initial timidity and shyness, I was lucky enough to be given a two-day public speaking course shortly after I joined ICI, and I consider it to be one of the best investments ever made. There are now a number of specialists who teach public speaking, and there are some simple rules which help the whole process. I have a particular aversion to reading speeches, and an even greater aversion to having speeches written for me. In my view, if you are asked to speak to any group of people on any occasion, it is not the views of an anonymous script writer that they wish to hear, but yours. I believe it to be rude at minimum, and condescending to boot, to accept an invitation to speak and then stand up and mouth somebody else's concoction. Equally, acceptance of an invitation means acceptance of the obligation to think carefully about the theme you wish to follow. One of the difficulties about public speaking is that there is a great shortage of people who are prepared to do it. When I initially began getting large numbers of requests for public speeches I was flattered, and attributed to myself oratorical powers which I plainly do not possess. It only took a short while to realize that it was not my speaking ability that was the attraction, it was the paucity of anybody else who was prepared to speak at all, and in this, as in many areas, the one-eyed man rules in the kingdom of the blind.

I believe that speeches which are delivered from notes are almost always better than those which are prepared and read out. There are a certain number of occasions in which it is inevitable, because of the dangers of making a slip, or for subsequent publication, that a speech has to be written, but to my mind it always lacks both the immediacy of a speech delivered from notes, and the ability to adapt and improvise. I find that speeches date very quickly. I always try to prepare the broad outlines no earlier than a fortnight before giving the speech. Anything earlier than that tends, in some funny way, to portray a lack of immediacy, and ideally I do my first draft notes about a week before, and my last revision a day before. One of the blessings of public speaking is that people very seldom want long speeches. Experience has taught me that the ideal after-dinner or -lunch speech is a minimum of eight and a maximum of fifteen minutes, and woe betide anyone who goes longer than that. After a good meal people very seldom want to have a long or serious diatribe. Equally well, however, if they want a comedian there are a number of excellent ones who will give after-dinner speeches, and one assumes that you are asked because they actually want to hear your views on something. For a long time now my practice in these matters has been to limit after-lunch, or -dinner, speeches to two, or at most three serious points, made fairly simply and directly, and fill in the remainder of the time with such badinage as I can muster. Unfortunately I am not one of those blessed people who are good raconteurs, and I can almost never remember jokes. I therefore have to rely on the mood and the occasion for the derivation of humour, and, while this is a risky business, it at least gives the impression of immediacy, and bridge building with one's audience.

One of the penalties of any top job is that you will do an immense amount of public speaking. Here, besides the benefits in time-saving in running from notes, there are some other advantages as well. I have a personal statistical data bank which I use as background for speeches. Nine times out of ten I am able to obtain the relevant numbers, or examples, from this relatively modest statistical basis. It is surprising how often the annual report is able to produce most of the factual stuff which is required. But, in addition, one needs a certain amount of relevant and up-to-date data on external trends and events. It is in the projection of figures, in ways which are easily envisaged by others, that the skill lies. It is almost impossible for anybody to envisage a million of anything, and large numbers have to be put into some sort of proportion by their relationship with everyday matters in order to make them understandable, assimilable, and measurable to the ordinary mind. I find that I can prepare speeches almost anywhere, but unlike most other things which I can do on tape, a speech outline has to be written down on two or three sheets of paper. The notes for an after-dinner speech really have to be capable of being written on both sides of an A4 page, if you are to keep within your self-imposed time limit. Once I have written my notes out, I normally have the key points that I wish to make transferred on to cards which I revise again the day before giving the speech, and finally, not infrequently, after I have gone to the occasion itself.

It is surprising how often one realizes how totally wrong one's perception of what is required at an occasion may be. I remember one particularly poignant example where I had been invited to speak to the management club at one of our Scottish factories. I had been told with great solemnity and seriousness that it was the tradition for the chairman of the company to speak to this august body, and that he was expected to produce some thoughts which would enlighten the group. I expressed surprise and concern at this idea, since I felt I knew my Scots. Since the dinner was the social event of the year, I couldn't help thinking that an august and serious speech wouldn't quite fit the mood of the moment. However, I was assured by everyone that that had been the previous practice, and I looked at the files to see the speeches that one or two of my predecessors had given. On the night in question I was saved by meeting, at pre-dinner drinks, an old friend of mine who was already reaching the glassy-eyed and knee-buckling stage before the dinner began! He looked at me, and said, 'Well, John, I hope to ---- that you are not going to produce the same dreary old drivel that your predecessors have done! Nobody wants to hear a serious talk at a party like this!' Needless to say, my meal was spent concocting a very different speech to that which I had brought with me, and I had the pleasure of tearing up my speech notes in front of them all, and accusing them of misrepresentation before I even began! It is on occasions like this that the ability to change tack in mid-stream is invaluable, for once you 'lose' your audience you can never get them back.

This way of producing speeches is economical, both for yourself and, even more so, for your staff. Every speech writer requires his speech to be checked, and will in any case be working in the abstract, because he will not know either his audience, or the reception that his speech gets. Better by far to take your life in your hands in the way that I have described, as well as being more economical in terms of time. To work in this way some training does help; a little training and a great deal of practice, and I would unhesitatingly recommend anybody who has to do much public speaking, to ignore their *amour-propre*, and go for a short professional course.

No amount of 'tricks of the trade' will avoid the need to set some sort of priority when allocating one's time. No matter how carefully and cleverly every moment of the day is utilized, and no matter how ingeniously staff, gadgetry and the most modern devices are used to improve one's productivity, there will never be enough time to do everything that is asked of you. This is where you must set clear guidelines as to how your time is to be spent, and it is well worthwhile discussing the basis of these time allocations with your staff, and reviewing them from time to time. Some priorities are immutable. In my own case, in ICI, anything which had to do with customers, or customer relationships, took absolute priority over anything else. Any of our people in the world who wished me to appear to talk to customers, or to help them with a customer opportunity, or problem, always got an automatic priority. Priorities can only have effect after you have set your fixed dates, and the fixed time that you are allocating, for example, to the operation of the board, and the organized meetings, strategy discussions, and informal free time that you spend with your colleagues.

After the relatively simple problem of deciding one's first

priorities you must then establish some sort of pecking order, and how you are going to allocate your time between internal and external matters, between showing the flag and troubleshooting, and so on. I have always had a disinclination to do too much flag showing. It is all too easy to persuade oneself that the job of being the head of a large organization is helped by ensuring that everyone in the company has seen you, or that you regularly visit all your works, or countries, or establishments. To take a real judgement on this, you must spend some time trying to assess the actual value of such visits, and what effect they have on the ultimate performance of your team, and business competitiveness. Plainly, like many things in life, if you do none at all it will have an enormously bad effect. Equally, to be able to say that you have visited every establishment and agent in the world, is unlikely, in itself, to have boosted your company's performance.

My own internal rules in these matters were drawn up over a fairly long period of time. I rationed myself in the case of visits which did not have a specific background purpose. In the United Kingdom I normally made about four a year, and in those I gave priority to where I was invited by my shop floor, rather than by management. Do not, however, assume from this that I only made four visits to UK operations a year. Under normal circumstances I only visited, either in the UK or overseas, if there was a specific task which I believed needed my attention. If, for example, an operating unit was going off the boil, or there had been local pressures on our management, or we were operating in an area which was having very large local problems, or we had just put in new leadership, or had industrial relations problems; to my mind these were all good reasons to pay a local visit. Sometimes, overseas, a difficult local situation either with competitors, government, or customers, may well warrant a special visit. Changes of leadership are almost always worth following up. By all means give your people six or eight months to settle in, but then there is great value in paying a local visit and 'taking the temperature'.

Any experienced industrialist can get the feel of an organization, a factory, or a manager's 'grip' and leadership abilities with his subordinates very quickly indeed. There is no manual or book on how to do it – it is more a question of having seen large numbers of operations, and having a 'sixth sense'. There are a myriad tiny giveaways which show you whether there is mutuality of trust and a good, common understanding of the objectives or not. I remember paying two visits to the same factory, outside the United Kingdom, spaced some ten years apart. The contrasts could not have been more stark. On the first trip round none of the work people looked at me, or smiled, but kept their eyes on their work. I was not introduced to the people who were actually working there, in any of the various parts of the factory that I went to. I insisted, as I always do, on making myself known to them, shaking their hands and speaking to them. After all, visiting a control room or an operating floor is almost like visiting a man in his home, and you would certainly not walk into someone's house without making yourself known to them, and passing the time of day. On the first occasion, while the factory gave the impression of being superficially clean, if you looked round corners you could see where the debris had been put. The managers were officious, there was little laughter and the overall atmosphere was one of tension. The second visit, with a new management team, could not have been a greater contrast. Everybody wanted to meet and talk to me, people came out of workshops to see me, and there was a real feeling that if I had not visited every nook and cranny of the factory, I had somehow failed. The managers not only introduced me to their people, but knew all about them, and spoke of them with pride, recounting incidents in their private lives, or things they had done in the factory. It goes without saying that on the first occasion the factory was performing badly, and on the second it was extremely successful.

When making visits for specific purposes it is as well, both immediately after the visit and at some time in the future, to try to make an assessment of the results of one's intervention. It may be equally important that one's own view of the situation has been changed, as to have made some intervention which has led to a different way of doing things on the ground. As a broad generalization, unless you can look back afterwards and see some local change, or change of perception on your own part, you have been wasting both your own and everyone else's time.

Visits by top people, even in the most unstuffy companies,

are enormously expensive and time-consuming. They are invariably organized some time in advance, and everybody goes to a lot of extra trouble to ensure that they make the best possible impression. Sometimes this particular effect can be put to very good use. When an executive tells you that he is going to do something within the next six months, and you fix the date then and there to visit him at the end of that period, it puts real pressure on for performance. On the other hand, the bland information that you will be visiting such and such a country, uninvited, and on certain dates three or four months ahead, is far more likely to cause reallocation of effort, and disruption, than it is to act as a stimulus to particular achievement. My own rules on visits, either in the United Kingdom or overseas, have always been the same. I allowed myself the luxury of stating what my personal objective was, but apart from that, my time was at the disposal of the managers concerned, including the right, albeit sparingly taken up, to say that it would be far more convenient if one visited at another time, or even 'Please don't come'! The test really should be that the manager, and the people you are visiting, feel that they have had the opportunity to show you all the things that they want to show off, and that they have been able to use your presence for whatever local purposes are needed.

Nine times out of ten you will be overcommitted and overbooked this way, and of course everybody believes that senior managers are inexhaustible, and don't need sleep or relaxation. One chief executive of another large company, whom I admire very greatly, told me recently that he had solved the problem by insisting on having every other night as a 'quiet night'. He claims that this enables him to operate better, and he feels that the added quality of his input more than outweighs any disappointments which may occur locally. I have never found it easy to take such an attitude myself. I have always felt that people locally should be able to look back and know that you had knocked yourself out for them, and should feel your interest and enthusiasm as an almost tangible thing. While a 'quiet night', and early to bed, would undoubtedly be a great personal boon, I feel that people on the ground are not likely to look at it that way, when they see you perhaps once every one or two years. It is worth bearing in mind also, that the example that you set can very easily be taken as an indication of the pace and commitment you expect from them.

A particular problem in time management occurs when you are invited to external events, conferences and the like. The more prestigious they are the more they require careful consideration. The argument that your absence will be noted, and taken adversely, always seems an implausible one to me. Even if true, which from personal experience I doubt, I find it impossible to believe that the memory lingers on for long. It is a tempting 'cop-out' to think that one must turn up at such and such because one's absence will be noted. If it doesn't fall within your own priorities then I doubt that it does much harm turning down even the most prestigious external invitation. I have never had any sign that my failure to accept an invitation for a charity event being hosted by a member of the Royal Family, or at the Mansion House, has caused any offence, as long as I have had good internal reasons. It has always been my practice to write and explain what prior engagements have made it impossible for me to accept, and this has always seemed to me to be accepted as a perfectly natural sense of priorities. My own allocations between prestige and responsibility have always been to consider the numbers of people involved, as the overriding consideration. A commitment to talk to the ICI conference of safety officers, or to carry out an external speaking engagement which was judged to be of value to ICI, simply had to take priority over even the most flattering and prestigious personal invitation, if only because you are letting down a large number of people, and giving a clear message as to where they rate in your own thinking.

In this respect, external speaking engagements are a particular problem, because once written in they are virtually impossible to alter or cancel. Some sort of clarity about your criteria for acceptance or rejection of speaking engagements is necessary, although the priorities will vary from time to time. At the time of writing this I have been particularly concerned about the position of science teaching in our schools, and therefore I have moved my priorities for external speaking somewhat, to give some additional claims to platforms which will enable me to express, to influential audiences, my concerns in this area. It could be that the problems of European integration, or international trade, or the exchange rate policy, may be items which deserve particular platforms, and it is important to be clear in one's own mind what the messages are that one is trying to get across, and to select the appropriate platforms from those that come your way.

In all these questions of time management an absolute necessity is to try to block out the time that you would like to keep for yourself and your family. I have touched on the necessity of guarding the weekends to the degree that that is possible, but there are large areas of the world where it is impracticable to make a visit without either flying out or in, and uncomfortably often both, during the weekend. It is an almost total waste of time visiting Australia for one day, for example. The travelling time, and wear and tear involved, is so great that a four to five day visit is essential, in order to get any sort of balance between the wear and tear of travel, and the effectiveness of one's contribution at the other end. No matter how hard you try, many weekends will be broken into, and this is almost inevitable. It is certain that, without a really major effort on your own part, far more weekends will be broken into than would otherwise be the case. Blank out your holidays, and start by trying to protect as many weekends as you possibly can. The actual time that you can devote to your family is only one aspect of the broader balance that you need, in order to pace yourself to be able to operate at high effectiveness.

Here again, people differ enormously. I have never known whether to envy, or feel sorry for those people who appear to have no other interests than their work, and are able to pursue their working interests twenty hours per day, three hundred and sixty-five days per year. It has to be a matter of metabolism, and personal predilection. Personally, I find it very difficult to keep going for a year at a time, without fairly frequent breaks. My early years in the Navy featured quite regular leave periods, which, unless one was operating overseas, came round some three times a year. I also need a better balance than just work interest, and I seek this both in the deliberate choice of my hobbies and interests, as well as, or perhaps even more particularly, in my choice of reading matter. I am lucky that as a boy I was a voracious reader, and I still seldom read fewer than two novels a week. I choose my reading matter deliberately to contrast with my work. I have confessed elsewhere to being a constant reader of books on my craft of management, but I do not look on those as being relaxing reading. I need a generous dose of imaginative escapism every week, and books have always enabled me to switch off from work and, so to speak, to recharge my batteries.

Similarly, many of my hobbies and interests do the same. It is impossible to sail and to think of business, and I find the same happy effect occurs when driving my pony, or donkey and trap. The balance of contact with nature is, for me, immensely important. Possibly because of my years as a sailor I have an absolute hunger for the harmony that is created in life by a closeness to nature, and natural things. One of the features of this century, and the application of the human mind to very large business ventures, is a growing remoteness from the sheer power and wonder of our natural habitat. Man-made conditions and events pale into insignificance compared to the natural ones, but with our growing belief in science, and our presumed ability to manage our own environment, we often forget this. We forget that even the largest, most modern man-made vessel can be sunk by the power of the sea, and we forget that nature's disasters, such as drought, pestilence and so on, exceed, by an enormous quotient, the worst that man has, so far, been able to do to himself. If you want to see real power at work you should see a volcano erupting, or sail through a typhoon, or be present at an earthquake. I cannot pretend that my forays into nature are of that scale, but the wonder, and the sense of power, and the balance and proportion that is created by watching nature in a micro, or macro, way have the same effect.

These sorts of things happen to be the ways in which I have sought to preserve my own balance, and my own view and sense of proportion, but each has to find his own way, and for some it will be music, or poetry, or drama. What is important for any manager, anywhere, is that he should seek consciously both to understand his own needs, and to make sure that he orders his professional life by such external contacts, interests and stimuli. For everything in business is to do with balance, and the creation of the right balance of forces. Unless you start by doing this for yourself it is difficult to see how you can have such an effect on other people.

13

And So to Tomorrow

Anyone reading this book will have realized by now that there are two aspects of business that obsess me: one is people, the other is change. Without change nothing is possible. Not to change is a sure sign of imminent extinction. Remember the dinosaurs! Whether change is comfortable or not, it is inevitable. The forces of change are many. Much industrial and commercial change is brought on by the actions of others, and indeed one of the keys to success is to be leading the pace of change, and therefore forcing others to react, rather than the reverse. But there are underlying forces for change which we have to recognize and react to. Around the world immense effort is being put into extending the frontiers of human knowledge. There has been more fundamental discovery in this century than in all the preceding ones, and barely a day goes by without significant scientific advance being achieved. The process of science is, in itself, an accelerating one. A discovery in one field enables doors to be unlocked in others which have, hitherto, appeared to be impassable. We are not within miles of utilizing the science that is already available to us, both in a material and industrial sense, but more particularly in a human adaptive and social sense. The rate of utilization of scientific discovery is limited much more by our human abilities to adapt than it is by the technical processes of discovery and application. Time and again we find, in ICI, that inventions, or discoveries we have made, and regarded as interesting technical developments, require the stimulation of a perceived need before they are developed and exploited, so often in ways quite different from the original perception. Polythene was invented as a result of fundamental research into behaviour of chemical reactions at very high pressures. At first it was thought that its use would be as a very superior electrical insulant. Indeed, without its invention it is possible that radar would not have been developed, and without radar the war might well have followed a completely different course. At that time no one thought that an entire new industry had been born, which would produce products which society would incorporate into its day-to-day life and come to depend upon, such as household products, cold water piping, packaging, and so on.

Today we see an outstanding example of this delay in applying technology in the whole field of information technology and computers. Here, the advances in technology are at a rate far beyond our ability to apply it, or to adjust to it. It is perfectly possible, today, to run much of our business from home. Meetings can be organized by tele-conference instead of travelling, it is possible to communicate instantly by electronic mail, to avoid filing paper altogether, to shop from home, and even read our newspapers on the screen, without collecting them. But we don't. We adapt slowly and take up the advantages at our own pace. The pace of change is, however, hotting up at a terrifying rate. Ten years ago we set up our first sales office in Korea, because we recognized the stirrings of the emergence of an industrial power. Today there can be very few homes anywhere which do not contain a product made in that country. Contrast that rate of change, and the challenge to industrialists to recognize the opportunity and seize it quickly, with the pace of the Industrial Revolution in Britain, looked on in its day as an unbelievable rate of adaptation. Perhaps the biggest changes of all are in people's knowledge, education, and expectations, which pose far greater opportunities and obligations on leadership than at any time in history.

Eventually large business enterprises consist, in an enduring sense, only of people and their collective values, and one of the fascinating features of business is that these values are transferable, and transmittable. If you look at a company like ICI it consists of a large amount of physical assets and a marvellous selection of ironmongery. Because of the inexorability of technical progress, the day that one puts up the most modern plant in the world it is already becoming out of date. The whole concept of business is to preserve one's assets, which means replacing them, and continuously updating them. This process in itself means that your newest plant is obsolescent as soon as it has been built. It would be difficult, therefore, to claim that the company consists of its ironmongery. Equally, it would be even more difficult to claim that the company consists of its financial assets. One only has to look at recent history to see how quickly even large sums of money can be lost, or disappear. Shareholders always have the ultimate choice of voting with their feet. Large organizations have very large fixed costs, and the profit is the relatively small difference between very large numbers. Heavy losses cannot be sustained by even the largest of companies for a long period. Moreover, the actual value of the money in the company can be changed almost overnight by variations in the exchange rate, or interest rates, or a dozen other things that cannot possibly be controlled. The one enduring feature of any company, or enterprise, is the people, and the skills that they have, and even these skills have to be continuously regenerated and brought up to date. Individuals must be constantly stimulated if they are to continue to contribute, and the leadership must be perpetually renewed.

It is only relatively recently, since the publication of books like *In Search of Excellence*, that attention has really been focused on the values and spirit that can be built up in a company. These values are usually traceable to individuals much further back in the history of the company, and, if they are of the right intrinsic worth, they have been preserved, built upon, and transmitted through generations of people. The great belief in the primacy of people over technology in ICI derives from its founders, and is directly traceable to them. The very first speech, made at the very first meeting almost immediately after the foundation of the company, between the chairman of the company of that day and the representatives of his work force, is a speech that could have been made by any chairman of ICI, and is as relevant today as it was in the 1920s. The values and examples that the leadership sets affect, in turn, the values of young people who are just joining the company, and, if they are of the right stuff, the relevant ones will be handed on in turn, to another generation for the future. It is curious that this spirit, which has been recognized in the military for generations, should only recently have been appreciated in the world of business and commerce. Organizations such as the Royal Navy, the Brigade of Guards and so on, cherish their traditions. Although on the face of it there is no resemblance between the Navy of Nelson's day, and today's highly technical service, the values are jealously preserved, and the traditions recognized as being of fundamental importance to the continuance of the service and its effectiveness. Every military leader seeks to reinforce this tradition, to modernize it, but to enforce its continuance, while few industrial leaders can even describe the particular characteristics of their company which they regard in this way.

Perhaps because victories in the business world are more difficult to perceive, and the effects of leadership in industry and commerce may only become apparent many years later, nothing like the same attempt has been made to identify these strengths in our business life. Values and beliefs cannot be created out of thin air. Unless they are real, and permeate everything that is done, they will not have any effect. It is no use constantly mouthing platitudes about safety, if you are not prepared to put your money where your mouth is, if you do not exact the highest possible standards, and unhesitatingly place safety before profit. Enduring values in companies, which spread the whole way down the line, are reinforced by business success, and become almost articles of faith for their companies. Belief in people, and technological leadership, are absolutely second nature to ICI, but these are not recent inventions, nor have they been produced as a result of a couple of days brainstorming in a country hotel. They are the basis on which the company has always operated, they are the basis on which it has always dealt with its people, and on which it deals with the young men and women of today. If these values are to be preserved, they must be perceived as being relevant to the needs and aspirations of succeeding generations. If they cease to be relevant they must either be abandoned, or adapted to be applicable to the future.

Increasingly, companies will only survive if they meet the needs of the individuals who serve in them; not just the question of payment, important as this may be, but people's true inner needs, which they may even be reluctant to express to themselves. People want jobs which have continual interest, and enable them to grow personally. It goes without saying that they want adequate rewards, but in my experience people are less greedy, and far less motivated by reward, than capitalist theory would suggest. It is certain that every individual not only expects, but should be entitled to, a reward which recognizes his contribution. The needs of one's people are also wider than just the pay-packet. They wish to feel that they are doing a worthwhile job, which makes some contribution to society. Certainly, when talking to young people today they seem to be much more concerned about the variety and interest of the job, than they are about the career prospects, in straight promotional terms.

We in industry have the opportunity to have interesting and broadening careers: to help people to grow, and at the same time to enhance their capabilities and expectations; to help to produce many of the devices and conditions which will enable tomorrow's world to be better than yesterday's, and to enjoy the task of their creation. There is understandable concern, widely held, about the effects of materialism on individuals. Organizations like the Club of Rome have drawn a picture of the rape of the planet for the pursuit of sheer profit. Many of today's young people reject the idea of materialism, and profess to believe that a return to the simple life would be a better way ahead. I would be the last person to mock those brave individuals who follow the appeals of alternative technology, and attempts at self-sufficiency. I happen to believe, to some degree, in both of these concepts. But there is very little understanding of the freeing effect of technology, and even less of the advantages that technology can give us, as individuals, and as societies. There is now a range of choices and opportunities that our forefathers did not have.

Very few women recognize the enormous changes that have occurred in their lives due to the development of the small electric motor, indeed I don't suppose too many of them give it even a first thought, let alone a second! Even in the 1930s, washing the family's clothes was a full day's job, and ironing, before the invention of easy-care fabrics and tumble driers, was another. Cleaning the house, even though vacuum cleaners and other devices were just beginning to be introduced, was a backbreaking job. It was extraordinarily difficult for women to free themselves from the tyranny of housekeeping. Yet today's inventions, washing machines, driers, detergents, easy-care fabrics and finishes, dishwashers, kitchen devices, and so on have liberated time for women to use in other ways and to their own choice, rather than by necessity. This is perhaps a less obvious example of the effect of technological advance on social change. More obvious ones lie in the whole field of health, life expectancy and birth control. We tend to take for granted the possession of pure water, and yet a hundred years ago most water for human consumption had to be boiled. We would find it very difficult to imagine a world without antiseptics and, even less so, without anaesthetics, or modern pharmaceuticals, which, in a very short period of time, have eradicated diseases which had the most terrible effects on individuals' lives. People today have almost forgotten the horrors of poliomyelitis, or that scarlet fever was a most serious disease. Tuberculosis sanatoria have almost ceased to exist, and all of these things are due to industrial processes which have both invented, and brought to public use, these medical developments which have enabled our life expectancy to increase from about thirty-five to its present high level of over seventy years. These industrial processes include water purification, mechanically and chemically, sanitation and sanitary systems, methods of preserving and distributing food, enabling better balanced diets, and so on. The increase in life expectancy has been helped by better knowledge and understanding, but it has been enabled by industry and its processes.

More controversial are the effects of modern transport and communications on our lives. As a young man I spent some time in Bermuda, in the days when that island still forbade the use of motor cars. I returned after the war to find that the island, which I had thought of as a vast world, was in reality only some twenty-five miles long, and could be covered easily in an hour or so. When I first went there the only means of communication were horse and trap, bicycle, and the railway. A journey from the naval dockyard at one end of the island to the other, was a full day's trek; in fact you could not get there and back, as I recollect, in twenty-four hours. In that particular case, it seems to me, the advent of the internal combustion engine has not enhanced the quality of life there, but that is, of course, the reflection of an occasional visitor. I have little doubt that for those who make their lives there the change has been of immense value. Certainly, I notice very few people who choose not to have a motor car, or not to be on the telephone, or even not to own a television set. Perhaps, in these areas of communications, we see an outstanding example of technology as a potentially beneficial enabling device, but where the use to which we have put it may be more open to debate.

Industry and technology are the enablers. They enable us to have choices, but ultimately the choices, for good or bad, have to be made by us. Industry, however, also employs large numbers of people, and has the opportunity to influence them, and their views. To that extent we have the unique opportunity of affecting our own future, if we only have the wisdom, and breadth of imagination, to do so. Marks and Spencers' celebrated determination to source their goods from within the United Kingdom was a matter of enlightened self-interest since, if they were able to buy their products in the United Kingdom, they created employment, which in turn enabled their customers to have more money to spend in their shops, and so on. Much of the impact of future technology is first seen in industry, and it is here that we have the opportunity to create an awareness of the potentials of such technology, and to affect people's reactions to them. We need to recognize that all of these factors, together with many others, such as the changes in the educational system, communications and the media, and world travel, have made massive changes in the values, expectations, and motivations of young people, compared to those which we had when we started our industrial careers. When you do not have your basic material needs catered for, there is no room for any consideration other than how to provide the money for shelter, heat, food etc. Once there is adequate, even if unexciting, provision for these basic needs, and some sort of provision for medical care and education, choices can then be made.

The world has changed immeasurably in my lifetime, and I look back to before the war, to conditions which seem almost as though they existed on another planet. At that time, as now, the overwhelming concern of even the best educated person was to find a job and a career, but we were prepared to work for pittances in order to have prospects for the future, and few of us believed that we could manage on our own. The most important thing was to have a clear career path, and we looked for a degree

of security and paternalism which is often viewed with suspicion today. After the war, with the concept of full employment, a career in itself became less important, because most of
us believed that we would be capable of supporting our families
in any one of a variety of ways. There seemed no limit to the
opportunities, and there was a far greater urge to achieve
material self-sufficiency. Young people today find it difficult to
believe that my wife and I did not own a car until I was aged
thirty, and that it was only after leaving the Navy that I had
enough money put together for the down payment on a house.
Our goals appeared relatively easy, and we never had any
doubt about our ability to achieve them. I remember my wife
and I debating, when I left the Navy with no skills, how we
would survive, and I remember my own confidence that
whatever happened we would never starve. There appeared to
be limitless opportunities for work provided only that one
didn't mind what one did. Very different I fear from today.

Perhaps because our goals were relatively simple, and our
aims were more materialistic, we accepted unhesitatingly the
need to conform to the organization that we had joined. The
Navy was, in fact, a hard task master in this respect. From the
day that I joined, at the age of twelve, I could only leave that
career with the agreement of the Board of the Admiralty. I found
out from personal experience that this was not easy to obtain,
and even when I was released, it was only because of exceptional personal grounds. Interestingly enough, a year later the
Navy were trying to bribe people out of the gate, with 'golden
bowler' payoffs, but in my time, despite what seemed to me to
be an unanswerable case for release, it was a matter of touch and
go whether I would be allowed to resign my commission.
Similarly, leave and holidays were a privilege in the Navy, not a
right or a contractual commitment. Equally, in ICI, I accepted
unhesitatingly that I would have to go wherever the company
wished to send me. I expressed the hope that they would listen
to preferences, but it was made quite clear that if they wanted
me to work in Timbuctoo it was their right to ask me to do so,
and my only recourse would be to leave my new career if I didn't
like it. We accepted that; just as in the Navy the service
considered they were entitled to my whole working life, so in
ICI I was employed on a twenty-four-hour-a-day basis, and, if

my company demanded it, I worked the hours that it took to do the task. None of these conditions were resented, they were accepted without question if one wanted to be employed by a decent organization with a hope of good future prospects. It would be difficult to find acceptance of such views by young people today although they will, and do of their own volition, work just as hard and with every bit as much commitment and enthusiasm as we did. The difference is that they are willing to give, but do not believe that they are obliged to sign their rights away. In many respects this is a better way, but it shows a difference of perception and expectation.

I believe increasingly that in the future the organization will have to adapt to the needs of the individual, rather than expecting the individual to adapt to the needs of the organization. This is not necessarily as anarchic as it sounds. Adaptation to the individual will release energies, creativity and imagination of a different order from that generated by the outfit which expects conformity to somebody else's wisdom. It does mean a radical change of thinking, and a much greater attempt to understand both the generality of expectation and the degrees of flexibility which individuals may require as a condition of their service. These conflicts between the needs of the individual, and the needs of the organization, are appearing at present most markedly in the armed forces, where, by definition, one cannot fight a war on a nine-to-five basis, and requirements and expectations for primacy of control of an individual's life are much more strongly marked than in the fields of industry and commerce. Since commercial success depends, and will continue to depend, on attracting the very best people and motivating them, failure to read the trends will lead to inability to attract and switch on the best people, and, in time, that will inevitably lead to the decline of one's business.

There are immense differences both between the starting points of today's young graduates, and those of my own generation, and between their expectations and ours. In reality these changes are no greater than our forefathers had to cope with as we grew up, but my adolescence was a sort of lost period, during the war. One day I was a boy at the Naval Academy at Dartmouth, and the next, at the age of seventeen, I was a young officer at war, in charge of men older than myself.

What that experience did teach me was the immense capability of ordinary people when expected to perform in extraordinary ways. The captain of my submarine in the Far East was aged twenty-four. I had been sunk twice before the age of eighteen. At the age of twenty I was a veteran. This experience of growing up fast had a fundamental effect on my beliefs and understanding, and one of the greatest mistakes we make is of taking too little risk with individuals. One of the legendary figures in ICI, Sir Ewart Smith, had a motto, which was that one should 'promote ruthlessly', by which he meant that one should not look on age as any encumbrance, and should push a man as fast as one could, to the highest level of which he was capable. A far cry from today's constant calls that Mr X or Mr Y requires more experience before he is 'ready'.

Our young people today have a number of advantages over us. They start with more material possessions, and more material freedom than we did. They are also more self-aware, and more determined to manage their own development than we were. This does not mean that they are not prepared to accept help and guidance, but that they see their own development as individuals as being their own personal responsibility. They are very much more international in outlook. It is quite difficult to find a young person over the age of twenty who has not visited overseas, spent holidays overseas, and had friends of various nationalities and colours. This is totally different from our own upbringing, where, in the 1930s, the possessor of a foreign 'pen pal' was an object of envy and curiosity. Young people today are plainly much less repressed than we were, and are also, I think, much less collectivist in their approach to life. They recognize individuality, are more tolerant of individual difference, and they have a fear of regimentation. They are more outspoken, and much more intolerant of double standards. They are quick to perceive the difference between what is said and what is done, and they do not forgive easily. They are less competitive on an individual basis, more tolerant, and more willing to carry those less able than themselves. They despise the individual who succeeds at others' cost. They are much less frightened of change, because they start with more security. They are, to an astonishing degree, computer-literate, and literate in a quite different way from the older generations.

I see a real gap between people in my own organization over the age of about thirty-five, and those under. The over-thirty-five-year-olds tend to use computers as a sort of calculator. We formulate a sum in our own minds, and then ask the computer to solve it for us. Young people today interact with their computers, so that they form almost a different 'leg' to their intelligence, and they are able to communicate with each other through computers in a way which their elders find extremely difficult. Perhaps the biggest change of all between young people today and those of my generation is the relatively recent emergence of women as professional managers in technical areas in their own right, not only in the UK and the USA, but all over the world. The most astonishing phenomenon of the early 1980s has been this almost total change. Quite suddenly much larger numbers of young women have chosen to follow scientific and engineering careers, and this enormous new reservoir of talent, together with very different expectations from employers, is going to make exciting, and inevitable, changes in the ways in which we organize and think about work. It is almost as though a magic wand has been waved over millions of sleeping beauties, for in countries as diverse as India and Japan, the USA and Latin America, we are seeing the emergence of a new, and very welcome, field of female talent. Highly trained, highly motivated, and very involved in their work.

The emergence of more women at senior positions in management will, I believe, be of immense help to industry and commerce. I am bound to say that young ladies in ICI tend to react somewhat badly when I try and point out that I believe that men and women bring different approaches to thinking, and have different strengths and weaknesses. They feel that such remarks are patronizing, whereas I actually intend the reverse. Perhaps the people of the East understand the relative difference between female and male approaches to things better than we. I fervently believe that, as in my family we usually make better decisions when both sexes are involved, so the same applies to industry. Women seem to me to have better intuitive capabilities and a deeper, inbuilt, sense of fundamental responsibility. They are prepared to stick with details longer than men, and to ensure that things are actually done right. They also have a different perception of other people's reactions

and, by and large, are more sensitive to them. The best decisions, and the best results, will come where men and women
work together as a team, respecting their differences of view,
and contributing equally from their own experience and
approach to the formation of the policies which they will then
try to carry out.

The degree of success in moving in these directions varies
quite markedly from country to country, but the trend and
direction is the same for all of us, and I believe this to be a change
of the greatest possible importance and excitement for the
future. It is, however, a trend which brings with it its own
necessity to adapt. Most women still wish to have families, and
to bring them up themselves. This necessitates far more consideration than just the giving of maternity leave, or enabling a
good woman manager to return to work at some later stage,
after having seen her children through their first, formative,
years. All families are different, with different requirements.
Children have accidents and illnesses, and they have crises in
their lives, all of which require the attention of their parents. We
are already beginning to see the emergence of families where
the responsibility of bringing up the children is shared equally
between the man and the woman. We have also seen occasions
where men ask for the maternity leave, so that their wives can
pursue their own careers with less interruption. We have also
seen many cases where men have refused promotions, or the
possibility of moving, because to do so would disrupt their
wives' careers. All of these call for degrees of understanding far
greater than anything which the personnel policies of yesterday
can apply. Merely offering somebody their job back at the same
level has proved difficult enough for most of us, without the
additional complexities that the caravan will have moved on,
and returning at the same level is, in reality, to have missed
one's place in the queue. Women managers, whether it is true or
not, believe, almost without exception, that they have to be
demonstrably very much better than their male counterparts to
succeed. I have always doubted the actual validity of this
viewpoint, perhaps because, personally, I have been so anxious
to see more women in the higher reaches of my company that I
have tended to discriminate the other way round. I have said
publicly that, given a choice between a man and a woman

manager of absolutely equal abilities (a most unlikely scenario I may say!), I would always choose to promote the woman, because there are so few of them, and I believe we need to correct the balance. Be that as it may, what people believe is a fact in itself, and if women managers are convinced that they have not only to try harder, but also to be able to demonstrate superiority over their male competitors, the perception has to be accepted as real. Cynics would argue that such a feeling can only be good for the company, since it increases the competitiveness amongst managers. This may be true, but I don't actually believe that industry is, or should be, a straight competitive rat race. Practically everything that we attempt has to be done by working together in groups, or as teams. Competition here can actually reduce efficiency rather than increase it, particularly if it is ill-directed competition.

The effect of increasing numbers of women managers on our approaches to career planning and personnel administration is an obvious force for change, but the less obvious ones, which I have outlined earlier, are equally cogent. Just as I believe that the task of the large company is to try to achieve the benefits of both the large and small organization, so I believe that the race will go to the organization that is most able to harness human endeavour by making flexible demands upon their employees. As so often in life, such an approach will pass the onus for response to the employee. My guess is that people will be very surprised to see how accommodating individuals will be to the companies that set out to achieve the reverse.

Tomorrow's leadership style has to comprehend all of these changes and to react to them. We have to devise ways of receiving the benefits of the small organization, while still retaining the ability to put the concentrated power and resource of the large one to play. The paradox is that while individuals' needs are moving towards small, quickly responsive, adaptable and flexible organizations, the sheer scale of many of today's developments requires the deployment of large resources. The costs of development are getting larger and larger. Today it costs perhaps a hundred million pounds to launch a new pharmaceutical product. This can only be recouped by selling the product world wide, and by having the sort of competitive advantage and leading success that will enable substantial profits to be made. But what of, let us say, the year two thousand, when such development costs may well be approaching half a billion pounds for each new product? Even though the human need may well be to work as individuals, such developments can only be made by organizations possessing enormous financial resource, the capability to concentrate massive human effort, together with heavy capital investment in research facilities and the ability to cope with the sheer financing problems of launching such an item.

At the same time human needs are for more choice, more freedom, and more self-determination. These three needs are not as unattainable as may at first appear because, as so often in the past, technological advance is coming to our assistance. It saddens me that when people look at the impact of information technology they think so frequently in terms of organizing business in the ways that we have in the past. The enormous powers that are now within our grasp are used merely, so to speak, to mechanize what we have done rather imperfectly before. I see the advent of information technology in a rather different way. The whole nature of selling, and the relationship between the customer and the supplier, will be changed by information technology. Those who see this as a business opportunity are already developing the close links with their customers which will be essential for the most efficient operations in the future. We have already got all the knowledge and information available to operate a system where an industrial purchaser will order automatically, through his computer system, from an industrial supplier. The computers at the supplier's end will order up the raw materials, program the production, make out the invoices and the records, almost certainly ensure automatic payment of the raw materials supplier, while collecting from the customer. The products will be produced in automatic factories where the only human hands seen will be those of an occasional maintenance man. The only human interaction that is necessary occurs when the product is labelled, tested and automatically delivered, on its pallet, to the lorry that will drive it away. Indeed, at some time in the future even that process may not require human intervention. One has to look ahead in these ways because what is needed is a totally different relationship between the customer and the supplier.

They will have to work together to achieve the enormous savings and the greater efficiencies that will come from such systems, and this means increasingly that the customer/supplier relationship will become more and more like a partnership, which, in good commerce, it already is.

But this is only a small example of the ways in which we fail to see the real opportunities that lie ahead through the imaginative use of information technology. Vast amounts of human effort have been made in large organizations to coordinate and optimize, so to speak, at the centre of the wheel. The only way we knew how to achieve effective optimization was to get all the information in from the perimeter of the wheel; then, very much later, and without an adequate knowledge of the circumstances that we were dealing with, seek to optimize things centrally and pass the necessary instructions to those on the edges. Information technology has transformed this organizational concept. Given clarity of purpose it is perfectly possible for all those at the rim of the wheel to self-optimize, and to align themselves. The advantages of this must be immediately apparent to anyone who has worked in the centre of a large organization. The reality of life is that they are the only people who can optimize, and so much of past management theory has been to try to find ways in which they can be encouraged to do so. In even the largest organization it is now perfectly possible for the man in Ecuador, let us say, to see the whole world picture through the use of relatively inexpensive computer systems, and to see how his contribution is relating, and the opportunities that may lie there for him.

As I have repeatedly said in this book, people are self-motivated. They do their best work when they have come to believe, through their own processes, that what they are going to do is worthwhile. The free man is always better than the slave. These marvellous opportunities increasingly give us the chance to be our own free men. Even more than that, they give us the chance, and the opportunity, to work in our own time, and at our own pace. Already the majority of sales people in ICI work from their homes. There are some complaints about the continual invasion of the equipment that the company provides on the space available in their homes, and many of my friends have seen their garages filled up, and even an encroachment on the dining room or spare room, and so on. But the advantages of being able to decide, on your own accord, when you are going to work, and how; the advantages of being able instantly to access all the information about the customers you may be dealing with; the advantages of being able to leave messages without having to actually contact the individual directly on the telephone, and to clear your own messages when you get in at the end of the day, are obvious. All of these give freedoms which, in my view, more than compensate for the slight feeling that one is becoming the servant of the machine, instead of the master.

These examples, of themselves, show some of the ways in which imaginative thinking about the use of computers in business will transform the ways in which things are done, and some of the first steps which would enable us to achieve our objective. But all of this needs coherent and urgent images of how the individual will gain from such a system, and also how his, or her, input will enable the whole to become greater than the sum of the parts. These sort of networks will demand greater consistency of values, greater tolerance and under-standing of each other, and will call more and more on the ability to relate to people perhaps half a world away, and working in quite different cultures, whom one may never meet in person. You will be bound by the values, by the information that is available to you, and by the feeling of mutual reinforce-ment which you will give each other, and this in turn will lead to an enhancement of the feeling of belonging to the same team; so important for most of us. It will be your network against the other. You will not only gain satisfaction from this, but will be enabling your colleagues and unseen friends to gain as well. Such a picture places totally new demands on leadership. A vision is needed, and the ability to transmit and transfer that vision of what the company will be. The leader's task will be to try to work out the business objectives, by the processes of iteration that I have exemplified earlier, and then to transfer the ownership to the network as a whole. Even more importantly than that, the leader's task will be, as it always has been, to tie in and relate the human needs of the people in the network to the competitive imperatives of the business.

I think that that is an exciting picture of tomorrow's world. I think that business leadership is in itself an honourable, testing, imaginative and creative job. It is not just about the creation of wealth, it is about the creation of a better world for tomorrow and the building and growing of people. It seems to me that the sort of opportunities that I have been talking about will make tomorrow even more exciting and challenging. Above everything they will call for more creativity, and just straight humanity, because business is, and always has been, about people. Management is about people, and manufacturing is about harnessing, motivating and leading people. It always has been, and I hope it always will be.

Index

Aberdeen, 185
acrylic, 41
Aden, 75
Admiralty, 4, 200, 253
Allied, 20
Albright and Wilson
  (phosphorous plant in
  Canada), 209
ammonia, production of by ICI,
  22
annual general meetings, 152,
  220
Armstrong Whitworth and Co., 9
Aromatics (multi-stage plant
  construction), 90
Auckland, 185
Australia, 212, 244

Bahadur, Maharajah of, 10
BAT, 20
Badische, 11
Bayer, 11
Beatrice Group, 43, 140
Beechams, 148, 180
Berlin, 11
Bermuda, 251
BICC, 148
Blake Grid (management
  technique), 146
Bleachers Association, 9
'boiler plate', 162, 189
board of directors, composition
  of, 210
boardroom design, 221
Bolckow Vaughan, 9
British Institute of Management,
  146

British companies, directors'
  responsibilities in, 26
British Leyland, 114
British motorcycle industry, 14
British Shipbuilders, 114
Brown, J. C., 200
BSA Motor Cycles, 14
Burma Oil, 30, 210

Calico Printers' Association, 9
Cambridge University, 3
Canada, subsidiary companies in,
  212
Carrington Viyella, 173
Central Agricultural Control, 12
China, 39
'Chinese Copy', 88
Ciba Geigy, 11, 158
Clausewitz, Karl von, 24
Clarke, Tom, 61
Club of Rome, 250
Coates, J. & P., 9
Colombo, 75
compact disc, 42
computer systems, 34, 259
Confederation of European
  Chemical Industries, 81
Condor, Captain Eric, 4
Conoco, 23
Coverdale System, 77
Coverdale, Ralph, 77
Crimplene, 27
Critical Path Schedule (planning
  technique), 81
Cuckney, Sir John, 195

Dalgetty, 194

Dartmouth, 3
Desert Island Discs, 69
Dimbleby lecture, 234
Donne, David, 194
Dow, 11
Dupont, 11, 23

E Boat, 5
EEC, 81
Ecuador, 185
Electricity Generating Board, 168
Emmerson, Donald, 131
Empire Foy (troop ship), 74
Exxon, 209

Far East, 39, 74, 206
Ford (Edsel's car), 209
France, 10

Geneen, Harold, 193
Germany, 1–5, 9–12, 76, 122
Glaxo, 148
Gomia, India, 120
Grace, W. R., 20
Grand Metropolitan, 148, 166,
  169
Grinstead, Sir Stanley, 148
Guinness, 148, 189

Hanson Trust, 20, 167
Hall, Sir Arnold, 43
Herzberg's Theory, 68–9
HMS *Amethyst*, 74
HMS *Royal Rupert*, 4
Hoechst, 11
Honda, 14
Hoover, 101

Iacocca, Lee, 26, 193
IBM, 1
ICI: Agricultural division, 22;
  American competitors, 23;
  American consultant, 223;
  Ardeer (explosives), 121;
  aromatics production, 90;
  availability of chairman to
  staff, 65; AGM feedback, 151,
152; boardroom and board
meetings, 112; chairman of, 6;
chairman's personal butler,
232; choosing staff for
international postings, 124;
Dyestuffs division, 85, 137;
development on international
basis, 207; English customs,
121; fertilizers, production of,
22; Fibres division, 38, 82, 85,
101; Gomia, India (explosives
factory), 121; Heavy Organic
Chemicals division, 131, 137,
139; inventions, 246; India
(industrial relations at factory),
127; interest in new materials,
83; international competition,
11; international postings, 123;
investment in heavy chemicals
and 'effect' chemicals, 153; late
entry into seed business, 158;
lead from board, 205;
managers, transfer of, 7;
Millbank, 111; Mond division,
131; non-executive directors,
172, 178; oil strategy, 30; one
billion pound profit target, 102;
organization in UK, 206;
Petrochemicals, 85, 86, 90, 153;
Polythene, invention of, 37;
private board discussions, 148;
profit-sharing scheme, 98; raw
material to end product, 141;
responsibilities of
redundancies, 110; salaries,
221–2; special work bonuses,
69; strategy meetings 'off
campus', 189; Terylene,
production and development
of, 27; training of overseas staff
in Britain, 122; Wilton site, 77,
133
Imperial Group, 20
India, 10, 39, 121, 212
industrial relations, 133
Industrial Revolution, 247
Industrial Society Industry Year,
  74

International Business School, Peking, 117
Institute of Directors, 146
In Search of Excellence (Peters and Waterman), 248

Japan, 11, 14, 17, 23, 75–6, 94, 122, 124, 207
Jarrett, Alex, 167
Jenkins, Brian, 77
Jones, Reg, 106

Kentucky Fried Chicken, 23
Korea, 94
Korean War, 74

laughter, as tension relaxer, 198
Lego bricks, 78
London Docks, 104

Macdonald, Howard, 174, 175
Malaya, 75
Malpas, Bob, 19
Manchester Business School, 139
Mansion House, 243
Marks and Spencer, 232, 252
matrix organization, 215
McDonalds, 23
merulite (packaging material), 32
Mexico, 13
microchip, 39
Middle East, low-cost raw materials from, 35
milk pasteurization control, 12
Montgomery of Alamein, 1st Viscount, 24

Nalco (USA), 43
Naphtha, 61
New York, 11
nitrogen, 37
Nylon, 41, 137, 140

Oates, Captain, 101
open door policy, 233
Organic chemicals, 29

Paley, William, 193

Pakistan, 212
Paraxylene plant, 75
Parkinson's Law, 222
Peking, 117
perks, 219
Plastow, David, 231
Plomley, Roy, 70
Polythene, 36, 246
Polyester fibre, 41, 49, 82
Port Said, 75
public speaking, 237, 239

radar, 36, 247
radio isotope testing, 34
Reed International, 148, 154, 167, 168, 174, 175
robots, Japanese and British, 8
Rolls-Royce, 45, 106, 230-1
Rotterdam, 104
Royal Family, 243
Royal Navy, 2, 4, 248, 254
Ryder, Lord, 147, 167

secretaries, 233
Singer Sewing Machine Company, 20, 101
share option schemes, 70
Shell, 23, 158
shop stewards, 73
Smith, Sir Ewart, 255
Soviet Union, 2, 10
Switzerland, 11
synthetic fibres and aromatics, 90
synthetic materials, 41

Tactel, 27
Taylor, Arthur, 138
'telephone book' (system of succession), 199
Telfer, Dr Rab, 139
terephthalic acid, 138, 139
Terylene, 27
T-groups, 135
Thorn EMI, 106, 148, 180
Tokyo, 11
Townsend, Robert, 233
Triumph Motorcycles, 14

Unilever, 23
Union Carbide, 36
USA, 9, 11, 13, 77, 121, 125, 138,
    161, 195, 206, 219

Vinyl production, 22

Welch, Jack, 106
Wheeler, David, 5
Wilhelmshaven, 2, 4, 5
Wilton site, 73
Wright, Roland, 132